I1026577

Where To Go
When The

Bank Says
NO!

11/14/13
To Paul —
Hopefully this book
will plug many of the
leaks of your client's
businesses

Best —
Steve Replin

Where To Go When The

Bank Says NO!

Steve Replin, CPA, MBA, JD

with Victoria Rosendahl

©Copyright 2012 by Steve Replin. All rights reserved.

No part of this book may be reproduced in any manner, whether written, electronic, recording, or photocopying, without written permission of the publisher or author. The exception would be in the case of brief quotations embodied in the critical articles or reviews and pages where permission is specifically granted by the publisher or author.

Although every precaution has been taken to verify the accuracy of the information contained herein, the author and publisher assume no responsibility for any errors or omissions. No liability is assumed for damages that may result from the use of information contained within.

Books may be purchased by contacting the publisher and author at:

Barber's Chair Press, LLC.
P.O. Box 6572
Denver, Colorado 80206
email: sreplin8@yahoo.com
www.hardmoneybooks.com

Cover Design: NZ Graphics
Interior Design: WESType Publishing Services, Inc.
Publisher: Barber's Chair Press, LLC.
Editors: See *Acknowledgments*

Library of Congress Catalog Number: 2011910707
ISBN: 978-0-9840685-2-4

1. Finance. 2. Business. 3. Lending. 4. Hard Money. 5. Entrepreneurs.
6. Business Startups. 7. Real Estate.

Printed in the United States of America

This book is dedicated to the memory of my entrepreneurial father, Morris Replin, who infused me with a love of business and all of its incredible flavors and opportunities.
He started or bought many business opportunities throughout his life. His ideas were brilliant but even the best ideas without the necessary fuel to succeed go nowhere.

I learned many valuable lessons watching him succeed and fail with his many endeavors.

The school of his hard knocks was an outstanding teacher both for him and for me. I decided at an early age to learn as much as I could from him, to be a student of business and of what works, what doesn't and why.

How many of you have met self-made successful business people in your lives? Isn't there something magical in their focus, their attention to reality, their drive and their passion? Hearing and living these stories with my father my entire life is the energy that inspires me to become the best at what I do as well.

I am hopeful that you take inspiration from the material that follows. Learn from the mistakes of others. But mostly I want you to know that you can succeed! Where there is a will, there is a way! Let hard money be the path to your success.

Contents

Acknowledgments

It takes a village to raise a child so they say. But you don't have to go looking for a village to write and publish a book. The village comes to you in ways that you can't even envision before you start with a project of this magnitude. And yet, it seems so easy. You just sit down and write. What could be hard about that? And the finished manuscript comes out the other end. Right? Not in the real world as I know it!

Well, I'm here to tell you that it's hard, it's lonely, it's frustrating, and it's time consuming. But in the entire process, there have been certain wonderful and believing people who have encouraged me to continue when I was ready to throw in the towel. I can't express my thanks enough for the privilege of working with them through this seemingly eternal process.

Let's start with **Victoria Rosendahl** who helped me put my experiences and insights into words. She is the ultimate wordsmith ... thanks Vic ... you're wonderful for sticking with me and this project!

And, then there was **Diane Hartman** who was one of the editors of this book, and lucky for her, had no idea what alternative finance was about before she started. What a lesson it must have been. Thanks for your good work, Diane!

And, to **David Yeager**, believer, business strategist and book editor who feels just like I do, that this book is a "mitzvah" to vulnerable borrowers!

Where would I be without my wonderful and loveable "slave driver", **Judith Briles**. All I can say is Judith, Oye Vay—we finally made it! Thanks for your continual encouragement, friendship, mentoring and whip snapping. I'm sure that I've avoided many a wrong turn because of you. You're the best!

Jennifer Gibbs, another of my editors added her two cents in whether I wanted it or not. Clear points and good explanations ... thanks Jennifer. You are too cool!

John Maling, was about as helpful as an editor and a friend could be. You do great work, John. Thanks for your wisdom, humor and skills!

And to **Courtney Messenbaugh**, my ace marketing guru. She hasn't started to work her magic, but I know that it's coming and will be "the bomb!"

And, **Ronnie Moore**, what can I say but thanks and thanks again!! Your help, your opinions, and your friendship in the layout of the book were invaluable. I would recommend you to anyone, anywhere without hesitation!

Michelle Darné, it's you who organized my dreams and aspirations for this project. Your participation will ensure that *Where to Go When the Bank Says No!* helps the maximum number of people. Thanks, Michelle!!!

Nick Zelinger, my cover designer, did great work in bringing the feeling and impact of my message to the book. Thanks, Nick.

And lastly, I thank my wife, **Bunny,** and my fun loving and honest to a fault, African Grey parrot, **Schmoozer,** both of whom were my loudest and worst critics but who always said what was on their minds honestly.

There are also those who stand beside a writer thinking that he is some kind of nut to do all of this work just for a book. However, in their own way they were all there with me throughout the whole experience with their full support and sincere encouragement. Thanks to you all more that you'll ever know!

Jim Arkebauer
Dave Block
Sandy Buckstein
Chester Cedars
Andy Clary
Lisa Elstun
Rock Essary
Mary Essary
Giles Fox
Jim Fullerton
Susie Hayes
John Pontius
Warren Goldberg
Bruce Goldstein
Kathy Green (dec.)
Karla Horowitz
Barbara Huff
Jenna Oliver
Russell Owens
Stuart Pack
Robin Pack
Jeff Fryer
Bernie Belandres
Rick Steel
David Ratner
Laurie Rhoades
Kerry Mayer
Annie Schlax
Phil Smith
Eric Sundsvold (dec.)
Steve Tannenbaum
Wanda Wages
Mad Max Young
John Backland

Preface

My real love over the years has always been entrepreneurialism and an understanding of the ingredients of what it takes to successfully build something out of nothing. People who come from humble beginnings and make something work by the sweat of their brow and their creativity and an unwillingness to throw in the towel get my highest admiration.

As I began to have experience at providing financing to a wide variety of business people in need of capital, what I was doing was almost totally unknown. The only image that was commonly held was that I must have been what was then known as a "loan shark." And, nothing could have been farther from the truth. Imagine the embarrassment of my family when others asked what I do for a living. Back then, no one could adequately describe this business activity of what I now call "alternative finance."

Now that hard money is not as stigmatized, it is finally becoming somewhat respectable. A name you might remember, Michael Milken, was one of the first and most visible alternative lenders out there in corporate America. His desire to provide financing to even the most credit and cash flow challenged businesses in the country made him a hero to certain groups of entrepreneurs who could get money in no other way. His creative structuring of financing packages was innovative and very forward thinking. Not that he was an angel, of course. But he made handsome profits by providing these creative funding plans.

Over the last number of decades, the economy has changed dramatically. Banks have merged, been taken over, and/or closed in large numbers. The rapid adoption of the Sarbanes-Oxley legislation has literally killed the ability of hundreds of thousands of small businesses in this country to start and grow because the proprietors can't get funding *anywhere*.

You might ask how our government could continually be so short sighted. Small business is the backbone of any economy by providing jobs—the magic elixir that results in growth. Without access to its life blood, capital, what future does small business have? Is it any wonder that jobs are going overseas? Why can't our politicians seem to get it right? Small business needs capital to grow!

Hard money is one of the few resources that produces this funding to entrepreneurs and business people needing money which can't be secured anywhere else.

You are about to learn some things that few others know; and, it will put you in the driver's seat when competing with others for deals that need fast decisions and equally fast closings.

You can't take hard money borrowing classes in school; you can't apprentice with any hard money lenders; there are no industry associations, no degree programs and, no jobs in the business. The only way to learn it is to do it. Let's hear it for the school of hard knocks.

I have had the sadness of seeing many, many deserving people get taken advantage of during this rush to find the opportunity capital for their dream business. This book is my way to give back to those in need of money. I feel compelled to share my experience and understanding of how the hard money business can help and, equally, how it can hurt prospective borrowers. People who are at very vulnerable times in their lives are regularly taken advantage of by unscrupulous participants in this business known as "hard money."

Along the way, I've made money and lost money, all in the name of learning lessons. I am pleased and excited to be able to share these lessons, so that you can use them to your benefit.

I look forward to hearing stories of your success ... and stories of your challenges. Please feel comfortable and be encouraged to contact me with comments, suggestions and stories at the following:

Barber's Chair Press, LLC.
P.O. Box 6572
Denver, Colorado 80206
email: sreplin8@yahoo.com

I would certainly welcome the opportunity to help you grow your business as I have done with literally thousands of people throughout my three decades of hard money lending experience.

Please feel free to join our mailing list by sending us your name, address, email address, and any comments that you care to share to my email address identified above. I will keep you in touch with all of the latest materials that I am publishing. I will also have special information from time to time, only for my readers, that will help you better understand and access good hard money lenders. And, I'm excited to know that you are going to be much smarter about hard money at the end of *Where to Go When the Bank Says No!* than you are now. Good reading! Enjoy.

Best regards,

Steve Replin

Prologue

Money.... It's a blessing and a curse; and it is certainly something you need in order to survive. It's been called the root of all evil, a false God, the Almighty Buck. There are those who couldn't care less about it; and, there are others who live and breathe the dollar. Money buys status and status symbols, luxury and fame, a roof over your head and necessities. And, most often, you must spend money to make money.

But, what if you needed money fast—*I mean yesterday*—but your credit is only so-so? Or, perhaps you're an independent contractor who can only prove an income stream with annual 1099 statements. Or, the bank has already tied you up nice and neat with your existing debt obligation. And until you repay the loan that you now owe them, they won't make you any other loans. By that time, the opportunity you have to invest will be long gone. What would you do if you found yourself in a similar situation?

The answer: You would be hard pressed to find a fast and effective answer to this situation. That is until you picked up this book. I am going to teach you about a place to go for the funds that you need. And, once you find out how easy it is to access fast money, you will ask yourself how you ever could have been in business without using this resource.

Known in the business world as "hard money," once you understand its *ins* and *outs*, you can and will turn those nightmares into big opportunities. Hard money lending is about to be your life-changing event. Think about it: no banks, no credit scores, no income verifications, just cash. And, it's not just cash, it's about cash whenever you need it. Does it get any better?

> **Steve Sez:**
> Hard money can and
> will change your life....
> Imagine money
> yesterday without
> a bank!

We all know someone—perhaps it was even ourselves—who needed money fast, went to a bank only to have the loan officer turn you down flat. What's even worse is to go to your bank and have them say, "Yes," when they really mean "No" ... and not find out until a week before the closing. Think of how much time, money, and aggravation this causes, especially when a terrific opportunity to invest and make some really good money has fallen into your lap.

That opportunity might be a chance to buy some property at below market value to remodel and resell; or perhaps it's a new business. Have you always wanted to open a bookstore or an exotic pet store? And, do you have your location all picked out? Well then, what are you waiting for? Here's the chance to pursue your dreams. But, wait.... Banks take anywhere from 30 to 120 days to approve and close most loans. Will that perfect little storefront still be available? Will the seller be willing to wait? These are the risks you take when you go to a bank for your funding.

It's a sad, sad state of affairs when the only people who can get money from a bank are the ones who truly don't need it.

What is "hard" money anyway? You may be saying, "Hard money as opposed to what soft money?" Well, yeah. As you read my book, I'll talk a lot about hard money, hard money lenders, the opportunities it provides and what you should do to make the most of this opportunity. At the outset, it is sufficient to say that, generically speaking, *hard money is anything you borrow from someone other than a bank or lending institution.*

> **Steve Sez:**
> Here is the *BIG
> BENEFIT*: Having your
> money *today* allows you
> to take advantage of big
> opportunities that
> others can't match.

I know what you're thinking: Whoa, hard money sounds like the kind of thing that's going to get my kneecaps broken. Not so; old mafia movies have given the wrong impression about borrowing from individuals rather than institutions. You can thank gangster movies and TV crime shows like *The Sopranos* for that. Do unscrupulous loan sharks named Guido still exist? Sure they do; but, they clearly aren't who I'm talking about when I refer to authentic hard money lenders.

There is one critical difference that separates legitimate hard money lenders from "Joey the Kneebreaker"; with a true hard money lender you get a legal and lawful loan documented with promissory notes, lawyers, loan commitments and title insurance policies. Joey will give you a brown sack with cash today, expecting two sacks of cash by Friday. Joey, being the great guy that he is, doesn't care about notes, mortgages, loan commitments or title insurance. His collateral is,... well,... his collateral is YOU and your near-term health. Don't forget your shin guards if you deal with guys like him!

When you borrow from a real hard money lender, you get a loan and the kind of partner you want—one who will be there to help you with funding whenever you need it. And this money source is ready to help over and over again when the need arises.

> **Steve Sez:**
> The right hard money lender can and will become your best *"partner!"*

How I Got Started as a Hard Money Lender

Allow me to introduce myself: My name is Steve Replin, president of Regatta Capital, Ltd., in Denver, Colorado. I was in the hard money lending business for 30 years and during that time I've trained many hard money lenders, educated many, many borrowers, and reviewed more than 250,000 loan requests. Let me tell you a short story of how my hard money lending career began.

An Actual Experience

How I Met Frank Harrison.

Many years ago, I had just started working in a Denver law firm as an associate tax lawyer. A client I'll call Frank

Harrison (not his real name, of course) came into the office seeking legal work for his startup business. Since I was one of the younger associates in the firm at that time, I was the lucky person who got to work with Frank.

At the end of the project, I asked him about the plans for his future business. Frank told me how excited he was about his new endeavor. He told me how he had quit his 20 year job in order to put the pieces together for his dream business. He was ready to go forth and build his Great American success story.

After he'd put the finishing touches on all of the details surrounding his business start-up, Frank went to the bank he'd dealt with for years. He just knew the bank would be as excited as he was about his vision and his future.

Boy oh boy, was he completely and totally wrong about that one!

Frank was told by his banker, kindly and apologetically, that he'd done it all backward. Imagine that. By leaving his job first to assemble the pieces of his incredible business, not untypical of many entrepreneurs, without a job, he had just cut off his only predictable source of income.

And then Frank told me that he couldn't understand how the bank could say no; after all, he owned his home free and clear of mortgages. But the bank demanded two sources of repayment. Without his salary, he had no such resource, which resulted in a loan denial from his longtime banker.

I was shocked to hear that his bank had rejected their long-time customer. And, a loan turndown with a valuable piece of collateral that has no mortgages attached to it and a great business idea to boot? I really felt badly for Frank. He had been wronged, thought I. It wasn't fair that he couldn't get a loan.

After stewing about Frank's situation, I went to the partners of my firm to ask if I could make Frank a loan to help him start his business. And that is when my career as a hard money lender began; and, totally by accident.

After Frank had signed all of the loan documents and had received his check, he got up, walked over to my side of the closing table and gave me a big hug. "Steve," he said, "If it weren't for you how would I have ever been able to start the business of my dreams? I know that I really messed up my planning. I imagined that my long time banker, my friend so I thought, would make it all possible and when he said no, I was literally without anywhere to go. Without your help, I would have never been able to undertake my business. With your loan, just you watch what I can do!"

I came away from Frank's loan feeling great. I knew that I had helped someone follow his dreams, and at the same time, wondering how many other people find themselves in a similar predicament. I could help them out, I would earn a good return on my money, and it would become a complete win-win situation for everyone. How does it get better than that?

I started calling loan brokers listed in our local paper to let them know that I would be happy to offer commercial loans to others to whom their bank had said "no." Most of those to whom I spoke didn't know what I was talking about. They were too busy originating vanilla residential and commercial mortgages. But I kept calling and finally started getting a few referrals. And, from there and now 30 years later, I built one of the largest national "private banks" anywhere. I guess that I should have called my company "The National Bank of Frank" just to give credit to the person who actually opened my eyes to a large problem in the business world about which I had never heard. From there, each of my clients who loved fast money passed my name around.

Thirty years later, my business has been responsible for
assisting hundreds and hundreds of borrowers with business
capital. I actually call it "opportunity financing" that they
could not have gotten anywhere else.

In every type of economy, hard money lending is the ideal solution
for fast and easy money for seasoned businessmen and women in
need of capital to start and to grow their businesses.

Over the years, I've learned that only a very lucky few are familiar
with the concept of hard money lending and the unlimited opportunities it can bring. I often spend more time educating my clients
on the variety of creative financing options available to them than I
do on their actual loan applications. My biggest concern is that every
day, literally tens of thousands of qualified borrowers are missing
out on potential opportunities simply because they have been turned
down by banks and have no idea where to go from there.

It certainly doesn't have to be that way! Hard money lending is
available to almost every borrower out there with a need for funds.
Too many people take rejection from a bank as a sign that they are
unworthy or financially stupid. It's just not right.

The idea for this book came after doing a series of seminars with
real estate and business start-up professionals. People would come
up to me after my seminars looking like they had just discovered
the pot of gold at the end of the rainbow. The most typical comment
that I got was, "Oh my gosh, I wish I had known about you last
week when I had a situation in which my friend needed money in
two days." Few really know much about hard money lending, but
everyone is continually excited about the opportunities that hard
money lending makes available to them.

I want *Where to Go When the Bank Says No!* to empower you!
I want to help *you* find your own personal success and financial
security with the help of this amazingly unknown resource. So sit
back, get comfortable, and get ready to learn something that can
and will change your life. Fasten your seatbelt! Let's go and have
some fun.

SECTION ONE

Banks, Institutional Lenders & Hard Money Lenders

Similarities, Differences & YOU

CHAPTER 1

Banking Today ... and Yesterday

Fasten your seatbelts:
Here is where your new financial life starts.
—Steve Replin

Where do you go when the bank says no? It's a question lots of people have asked themselves at one time or another, and because of the economic meltdown, banks are no longer the answer to many questions. Historically, however, banks have become the most well-known and popular place from which to get the loan that you need.

Years ago, banks were truly relationship-based lenders and loans were much easier to get. Your loan officer became your friend because he had known your family since you were a toddler. Banks approved your loan requests because you were good old Bob and Phillip Jones' son and grandson, and he had known them both and their business for over four decades. Your loan officer had made loans to the business over the years that had always been paid responsibly. Where was the risk?

Located in neighborhoods or central downtown business districts, these banks were locally owned and staff turnover was remarkably low. The loan officer you'd known since he'd started his career 40 years ago would be there for you throughout your business career.

If your bank officer ever retired, the bank would make sure that his replacement was someone equally concerned about local businesses—*and your business in particular*. It was a time when your word was your bond; when a handshake sealed the deal. No lawyers. No stacks of papers to sign. Those were the days of trust, relationship, and small business. Boy, have times ever changed!

Before we glance at the history of lending for a better understanding of where we are now, let's go back a bit further and take a look at how the whole idea of money came about.

"Money" as we know it today didn't begin as currency that is common worldwide (see 1. in Bibliography). The concept of paying for a good or service arose somewhere between 9000 and 6000 B.C. when livestock and grain were used to buy things; something of value was given in exchange for another thing of value. But, back then, there was no standard value for goods and services. In fact, pricing goods and services could be quite arbitrary—I might think my six prize cattle were the best thing that ever mooed but you may disagree. There was no uniformity to value.

The concept of banking traces its roots to Mesopotamia between 3000 and 2000 B.C. when temples were used to store grain and other items used in trade. In fact, Babylon—the birthplace of banking and finance—had a financial system quite similar to ours today. In his book, *Financing Civilization*, William Goetzmann states that the fundamental principles and financial tools discovered by ancient Babylonians remain at the root of all investment contracts today (see 2. in Bibliography).

The History of Lending

Let's take a brief look at how banks came to be what they are. Now, don't go running off down the block or sit there with your hands over your ears, screaming to drown out the noise of history; we're not going to get that complicated here.

Modern banking began in 17th century Florence, Italy. During the Renaissance, the Medici's—a great banking family—loaned both the government and individual's money for urban development projects and international trade. Goldsmiths began the more widespread practice of holding the gold deposits brought to them. Finding that they always had more gold on deposit than was demanded by their depositors, the goldsmiths realized they could safely lend some of their reserves and charge interest on the loans they made.

The concept of the fractional reserve bank began with the Medici family. The term "fractional reserve" means that banks would keep only a portion of their assets in reserve, using the rest for loans at a particular interest rate. This concept is responsible for the growth of money in a modern economy and makes the financing of all types of personal and commercial development possible.

The first commercial bank in America—the Bank of North America— was chartered on January 7, 1782, in Philadelphia, just five years after we declared independence from England. The brainchild of Robert Morris, this bank lent money to the government, held deposits, and made loans to private individuals. The bank issued currency or bank notes in exchange for gold. It successfully provided a stable currency but ran into political trouble when the Pennsylvania legislature out-lawed private banks and its charter was not renewed.

In the 1840s, the United States economy grew rapidly and the idea of free banking began. The government issued bank charters to any group able to meet the requirements; many individuals and groups instantly qualified for one of these charters. The number of banks grew quickly, each issuing its own bank note or currency. As the system grew larger and more complicated, the government began the treasury banking system in an attempt to regulate and control banking. Many Americans are surprised to learn that it was not until the end of the Civil War in 1865 that a uniform U.S. currency was finally established. Banking continued to grow and became more important to the stability of our economy.

When the economy faltered and then failed in the 1930s, a number of laws and regulations aimed at stabilizing and regulating the bank-ing industry were passed by congress. Most important was the founding of the Federal Deposit Insurance Corporation (FDIC) in

1934. Created out of the financial chaos of the Great Depression, the FDIC is a federally-backed corporation that provides stability and assurance to the public that bank deposits are safe regardless of what happens to the banking system and any individual banks.

Initially, the FDIC insured deposits in banks up to $100,000; that limit has now been raised to $250,000. In addition to insuring deposits, the FDIC also steps in when an institution fails and administers the sale or liquidation of the failed bank.

How Interest-ing!

The concept of interest came about in a novel way. The first evidence of interest being charged on money loaned is found in the records of an ancient city in what is now southern Iraq. Around 3200 B.C., Uruk was the largest settlement in southern Mesopotamia, if not the world. Travelers and traders throughout the region flocked to Uruk to conduct business. The careful records of such commerce formed the basis for the development of written contracts, financial records, and cattle (see 3. in Bibliography).

In the Sumerian and Greek languages, the word "interest" was the same as the word "calf." Here's why: let's say I lent Omar a herd of cattle for a year. During that period of time, I would expect more cattle to be born. The understanding we would have would be that the surplus cattle would be shared between Omar and me.

Too much like those word problems in junior high math? Well, at least I didn't ask you to tell me when the cattle would get to Chicago on Amtrak arriving from Middleburg, Virginia, if the train was going 36 miles per hour.

The notion of regulating rates of interest developed in 1800 B.C. when Hammurabi placed a ceiling on maximum interest rates of $33\frac{1}{3}$ percent for in-kind exchanges of grain and 20 percent on silver and other commodities. The penalty for charging more than the allowable rate was cancellation of the debt. An interest rate that was too high was considered usurious—you were being "used" to make more money than the lender was entitled to. This word and concept still exist today and can be found in all state's usury laws.

The development of commercial banking started in order to facilitate trade or "commerce" between businesses, cities and countries (see 4. in Bibliography). When a bank loans money, it's considered commercial banking. If the bank is the agent that joins those with money to those who need it, it's called investment banking or merchant banking.

Money lenders, money changers, and merchants have gotten a bad rap over the years. If you'd been a consumer in ancient Rome you would have had two options: buy goods from a local merchant or hit the high seas to search for places to buy those goods directly. The second option, of course, involves a year or two of your time and the risk you'd have had when traveling to strange lands. Some form of interest had to be charged to finance trade. It was considered fair for the amount of time and risk involved to bring goods and services to the consumer.

Back then, interest related directly to risk. If there was the slightest chance that any part of the money loaned could be lost, the lender or investor would want some incentive in order to place their money in jeopardy. This remains the main reason why interest is charged and a return on investment is expected. Moreover, interest still deals with expectations of future (and current) rates of inflation.

Risk is the same today as it was in Hammurabi's time. And, it's the same risk that banks and other lenders both use to evaluate the amount of interest to be charged on a loan.

CHAPTER 2

Banks and Hard Money Lenders

*Any informed borrower is simply less vulnerable
to fraud and abuse.*
—Alan Greenspan

Even if you've never applied for a loan at a bank, this book will give you insight into how the world of lending works and, more importantly, its impact on you. Haven't you wondered why banks do what they do, to your detriment? Even a seasoned pro might learn something.

In this chapter, you'll take your first look at a relatively unknown source of funding called *hard money lending*, what it is, how it differs from the lending policies and practices of most commercial banks and why it may be just the ticket for you in this period of strained economic opportunities.

As you will read and soon understand, hard money lenders have the ability to make loans that wouldn't even make it through the front door of a bank. And talk about an incredible asset? You will not believe how quickly a good hard money lender can close a loan. (Would you believe that sometimes loans can be made within two or three days of application.)

Let's start with the most obvious question: What exactly is "hard money lending"? As I've mentioned in the Introduction, hard money lending is funding that comes from a private lender—an individual or organization other than a bank. A hard money loan typically moves very quickly from consideration to closing, and is for a short-term capital need.

Steve Sez:
Banks do not provide hard money loans; hard money loans are made by individuals and small companies.

"Hard" in this instance applies to the collateral—or specific property—used to secure the loan. Collateral can be in the form of real estate, personal property such as shares of stock, artwork, an antique silver collection, even intellectual property.

"Soft," in contrast to "Hard," means *you*. No, I'm not saying you're not a strong and capable person. "Soft" simply means that the evaluation of your loan request is focused on you. Your credit, your income, your employment, as well as your other financial history are all on the line when you apply for a "soft" loan. These and other factors will determine whether or not you get a loan from a bank.

Steve Sez:
There are easier ways to find the money that your business needs to grow than from a bank. You are about to discover what few people have heard about and fewer understand. Stay tuned for an incredible education on an exciting new topic.

Hard money loans are all about what I call "yesterday" money. It's money that you need in a hurry. In reality, yesterday isn't usually soon enough. As we'll discuss shortly, banks can take as long as 30 to 60 days to review, approve (or disapprove) and fund a loan request. That's no help to you when you truly need your money yesterday.

Hard money loans often can be funded within days of an application. Imagine the power you'll have when you can access significant amounts of cash within days or weeks! If this doesn't empower you and give you a major competitive advantage in the marketplace as a purchaser of real estate and other assets, then you haven't lived yet.

When you work with a hard money lender, you will be able to close a transaction within a few weeks or shorter, which puts you on a level playing field with people far wealthier than yourself. Imagine being equal to the wealthiest people in your community in your ability to secure fast capital.

There are as many reasons for needing money fast as there are bagel varieties in Manhattan—from having a chance to buy distressed property inexpensively, to getting a great deal on a piece of land, to buying inventory from a bankrupt company, even to bringing a loan current after falling behind on some payments due to an unexpected business loss, illness or accident. These are times when the help of a good hard money lender can save the day for you.

Hard money lending is sometimes referred to as bridge lending and the reason is simple: It helps you create a strong, financial bridge from where you are now to where you want or need to be *very soon*. It permits you to obtain a bridge loan today and then it gives you some time to refinance later when you can do so in an orderly and thoughtful way.

> **Steve Sez:**
> **Hard money loans are all about buying time. They are a "bridge" from money now to longer term funding.**

Banks and Other Financial Institutions

This is not a book about bank bashing. In fact, you'll probably end up with a bank loan in order to repay your short-term hard money loan. What a hard money loan does is give you some exciting business or investment options within very tight time frames.

Bank Loans

Bank loans come in a variety of flavors. There are four Basic Types of Bank Loans:

- Mortgage loans,

- Vehicle loans,

- Personal loans, and

- Commercial and Business loans.

Mortgage Loans

A mortgage loan is a secured loan using real estate as the primary collateral. This means that you've promised to give the bank your house, land, investment property and maybe even your bank accounts—but not the family dog or your mother-in-law—if you fail to repay the loan.

Failing to make your monthly payments on time or to repay the entire loan when it's due is called a *default*. If you default, the bank has the right to foreclose on your real estate. After foreclosure, the bank will then own your collateral in the hopes of selling the real estate in order to recover all of the money it lent you.

The reason that they are called mortgage loans is that the document that operates to grant the bank a secured interest in your property is called a mortgage (deed of trust in some states, but it basically means the same thing).

Vehicle Loans

A vehicle loan from a bank which uses cars, trucks, motorcycles, RV's or any other type of vehicle as collateral is also referred to as a secured loan. It's secured because the bank is often holding the title to the vehicle and is listed as the lien holder.

Remember in the movie "Repo Man," when you didn't make the payments on your car, the bank hired someone to come and repossess your car by literally driving it away from your house or business and putting it in their holding lot before they sell it? Well, that's what will happen if you don't pay your vehicle loan.

Because the loan involves property that moves as its collateral, it's less secure for the bank as compared with real estate that doesn't go anywhere. The bank has a lien recorded on the title of the vehicle with the state Department of Motor Vehicles—but they don't have possession or direct knowledge of the whereabouts or condition of their collateral at any particular time. Banks often like vehicle loans because they are a way of developing customer loyalty and can lead to a customer opening a checking or savings account. It's a service that banks provide to existing customers who also need some assistance in purchasing a vehicle. It's just good PR for the bank all the way around.

Unsecured Personal Loans

This type of loan is just what it says ... unsecured; there is no collateral whatsoever. These loans are made for any number of reasons. The bank makes unsecured loans primarily to their existing customers because the customer has, historically, kept good deposit balances with the bank, doesn't bounce checks written on his account at the bank, and has excellent credit, income, and employment.

Personal loans are, by nature, short term. These loans are exceedingly difficult to come by because they are completely unsecured as the name suggests, and are very risky for the bank.

Hopefully, the bank has selected its unsecured borrowers carefully because if they are wrong about any borrower, all the bank has to go after if the loan goes bad is the individual who signed the loan.

Commercial & Business Loans

These loans are meant to help business people with their needs for short-term funding in order to purchase inventory, pay bills, and buy equipment or any of hundreds of other reasons. Commercial and business loans can be either secured or unsecured.

Steve Sez:
Don't even give an unsecured loan from a bank any serious thought until you truly don't need the money; and then and only then might the bank give you a second look. Otherwise, they don't exist in the real world today.

Some lucky businesses have unsecured lines of credit or basic unsecured loans that can be drawn upon for seasonal operating needs or for anything else that the business needs. For example, Madeline Dow is a florist with three greenhouses. She needs to buy bulbs, soil and other supplies now in order to have a viable inventory next Spring. Each year, she draws on the unsecured line of credit that she obtained from her bank. Next March, as she begins to sell plants, she'll use the sales proceeds to repay her line of credit to the bank. So the balance goes up and comes down many times throughout a year. This is how a line of credit is supposed to operate.

Other business and commercial loans and lines of credit are secured by accounts receivable, inventory, business assets, or personal assets of the business or its owners. Business loans are, however, very difficult to obtain from a bank in all but a great economy.

Loans made to most businesses, however, are usually just set up with a level monthly payment of principal and interest that retires the loan over a period of time.

The most important aspect of any business or commercial bank loan is that the bank will evaluate its decision to either approve your loan request or not, based upon your financial statements, your recent income amounts, and your recent credit scores. This is going to be the outcome regardless of the collateral being pledged to the bank. The decision to loan money to a business for any reason is almost universally based upon credit, cash flow, other debt and income ratios. The collateral will be secondary to this evaluation. Without proving your ability to regularly make the payments on the loan, you probably won't get the loan that you need from a bank.

Steve Sez:
Bank loans are very difficult to obtain unless you are wealthy, have great cash flow, and truly don't even really need the loan. If you don't meet all of a banks requirements for a loan, you are just wasting your time to even apply.

Bank loans have many requirements with which to comply; not so with hard money loans. As loans go, there are more differences than similarities between banks and hard money lenders.

Similarities between Bank and Hard Money Loans

Banks and hard money lenders are also the same in many respects. The following is not an exhaustive listing but merely a representative list:

- Both loan money at set rates of interest.

- Both loans are legally made and fall within all applicable laws.

- You must apply for both loans.

- You will sign legal documents with both loans (e.g. promissory notes), agreeing to repay the loan at a set amount per month with a specific maturity date.

- You will participate in an event called a closing.

- If you fail to repay your loan, there will be a consequence typically called foreclosure to recoup the money lent to you.

- Both loans utilize collateral.

Both lenders focus on the collateral for the loans, but each does it a little differently. The bank will treat the collateral as secondary to the loan decision. The hard money lender puts the collateral in first place in importance, with a scant look at the borrower himself. That's about it for similarities. What follows is about distinctions and differences between a bank and a hard money lender.

Steve Sez:
No matter what banks say, their loans are based upon YOU, your financial statements, your cash flow and your credit.

Fourteen Differences between Bank and Hard Money Lenders

The differences—this book's real reason for being—are a hard money lender's life blood (and represent your biggest benefits). The following is but a *partial* list of differences between a hard money lender and your banker that we'll explore more in depth as we go along.

1. **Collateral:** With a bank it's all about you; with a hard money lender, it's all about collateral.

2. **Short-Term:** Hard money loans are all short term. Some banks also have this short-term product, but they are still banks, and, underneath it all, their short-term loans have all of the same requirements as their other loan products.

3. **Loan Documents:** The loan documents for a hard money loan closing are creative and structured to reflect the agreement of you and your hard money lender. Bank loan documents come in only one flavor; the flavor of corporate approval.

4. **Regulations:** Banks are highly regulated by both state and federal laws; hard money lenders are not!

5. **Ratios:** Banks live for ratios; not so with hard money lenders.

6. **Creativity:** Banks are locked into a few distinct loan types. Hard money lenders can be very creative in their loan structures.

7. **Lender Specialization:** Banks rarely specialize in loan types (which is both good and bad news). Hard money lenders do specialize in specific types of loans, so if you search, you will find those that suit your precise needs.

8. **Relationships:** With most banks, you'll be lucky to deal with the same person from the start to the payoff of your loan. Hard money lenders are in it for the long haul.

9. **Application Documents:** The documents required for a bank loan can single-handedly destroy forests. Hard money loans have fewer paper strings attached.

10. **Business Plans:** Banks often require detailed business plans if you're starting a new venture. Hard money lenders will only need to know the basics about the business and your future plans.

11. **Formal Appraisals:** Banks will always wait for a formal appraisal before making a loan decision. Not so with most hard money lenders.

12. **Flexibility:** For bank qualification, you must fit into specific income and credit models. A hard money lender will work hard to be as creative and flexible as your project requires without focusing on income and credit for qualification.

13. **Terms:** Borrowers are locked into bank requirements when it comes to negotiating the terms of their note. Borrowers have much more room for flexible payment terms with a hard money lender.

14. **Closing Costs:** Banks rarely negotiate lender's fees. Most banks have a schedule of fees and costs and individual loan officers often do not have the authority to alter these established "prices." You can negotiate with a hard money lender over closing costs in many cases.

Chapter Summary

If you are like most people today, you do not have access to capital as quickly as is necessary to take full advantage of opportunities that are here today and gone tomorrow. A hard money loan can often provide you with immediate access to the financing necessary to take full advantage of short-term opportunities.

1. Commercial and business bank loans often require significant time to evaluate and approve or disapprove. Even disapproval can take substantial time at a bank.

2. Hard money loans are all about *yesterday* money—funds you need in a hurry.

3. Hard money lending is also referred to as "bridge lending": it helps you create a strong financial bridge to get from where you are today to where you need to be in the near future.

4. There are 14 notable differences between hard money and commercial or bank loans; they are discussed in-depth throughout this book.

Let's start looking at the differences between these types of loans.

CHAPTER 3

Three Major Differences Between Bank Loans and Hard Money Loans

You are surrounded by simple, obvious solutions that can dramatically increase your income, power, influence and success. The problem is, you just don't see them.
—Jay Abraham

This chapter begins our discussion of the nature and structure of hard money loans and the people that make them. Notice that I said people. Although your bank might advertise itself as people friendly, it is by nature, an institution. Like most institutions, it survives by following a set of guidelines that are inflexible and focused on fitting within the federal and state guidelines in order to stay in business.

Not so with a hard money lender, as you will begin to understand in this chapter. Hard money lenders really are more interested in saying yes whenever possible. If they don't make loans, they don't make money. Banks at least have the interest and fees that they earn on checking and savings accounts to fall back on as one of their significant sources of revenue.

Traditionally—and that means because your Mom, Dad or Aunt Eva did it this way—most people head to a bank when they need money. Isn't that who you would think of first if you needed money right now? It might be to get a loan for a car, a house, for personal reasons or business purposes. We don't just go to any bank, either; most of us return to the bank we've dealt with over the years for all of our financial needs.

If you live in a small or medium sized town, the bankers and tellers all know you. They, like you, have been with the same bank for decades. You might even be on a first name basis with the president and officers of the bank. After all, they go to your church, eat at the same restaurants as you, belong to the same civic organizations and so on.

In an earlier time, these local banks could and would make you and your father and probably your grandfather a loan just because they had a good feel for your family's integrity. Many times, all you had to do was to walk into the bank, express your need for some money, and walk out with the funds in your account.

My grandfather borrowed money for his business from his local bank in Denver with nothing but a smile and a need. His loan officer, with whom he had been doing business for decades would prepare the documents days after the loan was made, and my grandfather would stop by to sign for the loan as he could (i.e., at his convenience). But he always repaid his loans in a timely fashion. His banker loved him and knew that he was a man of his word and because of this, they would keep him happy first, and get the banks paperwork in order later. But, gone are the good old days—forever!

Let's start to review how hard money loans work. You'll gain insights in the following chapters that will give you the upper hand when you need money quickly. You'll learn what might make hard money the right choice for you:

Hard Money Difference #1: Collateral

Banks focus on you and your ability to make the payments; hard money lenders focus only on collateral when they talk to borrowers.

The first basic difference between banks and hard money lenders is how banks make their loan decisions. Banks want to know about *you*; they are judging you and your past, present and future when making the decision to approve or reject your loan application. It's a decidedly *subjective* process. Banks will look at things like your credit score, your financial ratios, your assets and liabilities, and your bank statements and average balances before deciding to loan you money or not.

You may be thinking, "Well, yeah; of course they are looking at me. After all, this is the bank I've been dealing with for a good part of my life. Why shouldn't they focus on me?" Do you remember my grandfather's experiences with his bank? The focus on him was about his integrity and his history. Today, the review process is about you as a financial machine complete with the entire numerical measurement tools that are now available to banks. Because most banks are now national, they don't have the same type of personal relationships with their customers anymore.

With a hard money loan, the process is far more streamlined because it's objective. Of course, a hard money lender will look at your application, but he won't convene a loan committee to examine why you were a day late on a credit card payment—in January, 1973. In fact, if you have ever filled out an application for any type of a loan at a bank, you will instantly notice that a hard money application will surprise you with its simplicity. In most circumstances, hard money lenders don't even require application forms.

Collateral and How It Helps

You'll recall that collateral is the thing that you offer to the lender as his security in exchange for the money that he is loaning you. It's what gives you the incentive to repay the loan in order to avoid losing your property. I use the term "property" in a more generic sense here because collateral can be anything from real estate to a stamp collection, or any of literally thousands of other categories of "property."

The first reason why real estate is such an attractive form of collateral to most hard money lenders is that it can usually be valued quite

Steve Sez:
The fear of losing your collateral is what makes you want to repay your loan ... and therefore, it is what makes hard money lenders willing to loan you the money that you want and need.

easily. Independent appraisals (not often used by hard money lenders) or a site visit by someone with experience will usually provide a good sense of the real estate's condition and value. Real estate has historically held its value far better than most non-real estate forms of collateral.

The second reason that real estate is the most commonly used form of collateral is that it is what most people have. How simple is that?

Instead of digging through dusty boxes of old documents for prior years' tax returns, prior years' financial statements, and prior years' bank statements, you'll only need information about the details of your property. And, this is information that you either know or can get easily.

Although I'll talk about using a personal residence as collateral in the real estate section, it's important to briefly mention it now. When you get ready to apply for a hard money loan, you may be thinking about using a residence as collateral. Historically, hard money loans—despite what you use for collateral—were considered to be commercial in nature. Anything that constitutes an investment is the focus of hard money. Very rarely were these types of loans necessary in the world of owner-occupied residential real estate because there was, and is currently, an extensive mortgage system in place for these types of loans.

Unlike residential lending, the world of business and commercial lending has always been and will always continue to be very fragmented. Every loan is quite different from every other loan in the commercial world.

Steve Sez:
Real Estate Collateral is King in the eyes of a hard money lender!

The need for speed and creativity is nearly always present in business and commercial lending because of the pace of business in general. It is these needs that have given rise to hard money lending.

Hard money is far less prevalent in residential situations because of the layer upon layer of federal and state regulation built into all residential loans. Residential lending is regulated by interest rate limitations (known as usury laws), licensing laws (often for both residential mortgage brokers and lenders), disclosure laws, rescission laws, and other extensive documentation requirements. The level of regulation is so high, and the availability of owner-occupied funding is so prevalent from mortgage companies that are set up to insure compliance with these laws that hard money lenders don't even attempt to compete.

There are, however, circumstances in which the need for fast money is compelling and the borrower's only item of collateral is his residence. In many states, as long as the purpose of the loan is commercial in nature (for example, you may want to open up an ice cream store, buy a franchise, or buy an apartment building), a hard money lender will allow you to utilize your home as the primary collateral for the loan.

Why Hard Money Lending Is Such an Attractive Alternative to Banks

Why would you ever look to a hard money lender to secure the financing for your new commercial venture? After comparing the value added to a transaction against the extra cost, the answer to that question is easy: why not?

When you have a genuine need for money, why even go to a conventional lender like a bank with its complex application and approval process with no assurances that you'll ever receive the funding? Why not first go to a lender who will be more flexible, significantly faster and more certain (or not) of granting your request for money?

The reasons *not* to use a hard money lender typically come down to one: *cost*. I firmly believe that the true value of a hard money loan must be measured in more than just dollars of extra costs. The real expense of using a conventional bank can be far greater than it appears.

Let's say that David Thompson, a serial entrepreneur, has an opportunity to buy an asset like a parcel of real estate, a business opportunity, or more inventory for his business at a significant discount if he can close quickly. What do you think the real cost will be if he has to wait 30 to 45 days to get a response from his bank to his loan request? From past experience, he knows all too well that these types of opportunities will likely not wait for bank approval. Think about David's position: If the opportunity will result in significant profits to him, what is his true cost if he doesn't get the money that he needs to take advantage of his opportunity?

> **Steve Sez:**
> The extra cost of using hard money must be balanced against the extra advantage, benefits and profits that getting the money will yield over foregoing opportunities.

If the investment opportunity goes away because it couldn't wait for the approval of the bank, what was the true "cost" of the money? This is often referred to as the "opportunity cost" of an investment. Arguably, you can "cost" yourself a great deal more in lost profits than you would pay in the extra interest expense of a hard money loan. Think about the profits that you have foregone because you didn't have access to fast money? How sad is that for you? Here is the opportunity for you to take advantage of your contacts, your business connections and your "once in a lifetime" opportunities by just making one change in how you go forward to finance your activities.

I've known for these last 30 years about the significant benefits of hard money loans and I have always wanted to spread the word. I have seen people literally come away from a closing table making millions of dollars in profits because they had access to fast capital. To them, the small extra cost was an insignificant part of the profits equation.

I'm often frustrated when I see people in need of closing funds for exceptional opportunities but who have never even heard about hard money. The concept of hard money financing has existed for centuries. But we all—and I do mean *all*—have been conditioned to go to a bank or other lending institution first (mortgage company, savings and loan, credit union) when we need money.

There is an army of people out there to help you. However, it's not easy to access these people for the most part. Now you are becoming one of those fortunate people with significant knowledge about how to borrow money fast.

Hard money lenders are a quiet, reserved group. Who even knows about hard money lenders? How can you find out who and where they can be found? How can you become educated about hard money and how to best approach a hard money lender? How do you separate the good lenders from the bad lenders? There are so many questions about which almost everyone knows nothing. Soon, you will know these answers and many, many more.

Hard Money Difference #2: Short-Term (Bridge) Lending

Short-term (bridge) lending is the Hard Money lender's specialty. Hard money loans are short term bridge or "gap" loans; some banks offer what they refer to as bridge loans to some customers, but underneath it all, banks are still highly regulated and must follow federal and state lending guidelines to which true hard money lenders are not subject.

A hard money loan is a bridge loan. It bridges the gap between your need for money today and a more permanent conventional solution—possibly from a mortgage company. Hard money loans are typically short-term, ranging from six months to two years in length. Most hard money lenders prefer to make loans that are on the shorter side of this range. Hard money loans are not meant to be long-term financing. It is not how they are structured.

Yes, many banks do make short-term loans and they may even call their loans bridge loans. But you must still jump through the

Steve Sez:
Think of a hard money loan as a short term bridge to a more traditional long term loan.

bank's qualification hoops in order to receive any loan approval. Even though your bank knows that you may wish to borrow the money for a relatively short span of time, the application and approval process can still take 30 to 60 days, as most do with your bank.

When the general economy is weak, banks are hesitant to make new loans. Offering short-term loans in the midst of a weak economy will be among the first lending service to be cut by most banks. But, that will only be after they have made the process of obtaining a bridge loan from them increasingly complex, time consuming and expensive because they are afraid of the current economy.

Steve Sez:
Extending a short term bank loan can be like qualifying for a new loan with the same documents and process. Extending a hard money loan is typically no more than a fast review of your payment history and of the collateral's current value. Which sounds easier and more efficient to you?

A bank's process for extending a bridge loan looks nearly identical to the process of getting the loan in the first place. Before granting the extension, banks will update all of the information that they initially acquired about you and your property when you first secured the loan. If the loan has been outstanding for a year or more, many banks will require you to go through the entire qualification process anew; and when you reach the loan committee, it may not go in your favor! It's like you are a new customer.

A hard money lender's idea about the extension of his loan is quite different: If your payments on the original loan have been made in a timely fashion, and the lender has a way to reassure himself that your collateral's value has not declined since the original loan was closed, then there is no reason *not* to approve the extension. So, the decision can usually be made quickly. Loan extension documents can be prepared in a matter of days and the closing can be done shortly thereafter.

Difference # 3: Loan Documents

As I mentioned above, if you elect to accept a bank bridge loan, the bank may strongly suggest that you use that bank for your permanent loan as well. If you do, you could effectively cut off your ability to find the kind of permanent financing you really want with more flexible terms and a lower interest rate.

With a hard money loan, though, you have adequate time to locate the best permanent loan at the lowest overall cost to you. And unlike the bank, your hard money lender doesn't care who you choose as your permanent lender. The most important thing to your hard money lender is that you ultimately pay the loan off in a timely fashion. Pretty simple, don't you think?

No, hard money lenders aren't loan sharks. They won't send Bruiser down to your house or business every Friday asking for more money. A hard money loan gets repaid just like you've repaid all of your other loans—by making regular payments each month. There are documents like promissory notes, a mortgage and property insurance to be signed. These are exactly the same documents you'd sign if you'd taken a loan from any conventional commercial lender.

But to make sure you don't fall into the hands of lenders who are not completely ethical, you need to pay close attention to what you will read in this book.

Steve Sez:
Hard money lenders are *not* loan sharks! They are like all other business people attempting to make reasonable profits from their lending activities.

Chapter Summary

1. Unquestionably, banks and other commercial lenders play a crucial role in American business. But, it is not in your best interest to sign away your ability to take advantage of potentially rewarding opportunities just so you can do business with your neighborhood banker. Banks' approval processes are slow and cumbersome; waiting for your bank to approve a bridge loan can ultimately cost you more than the loan's value when measured in terms of lost opportunity. Banks look at their borrower's financial and credit history, and his means of repayment when deciding whether or not to extend a loan.

2. Banks can make what they call "bridge loans," but they don't make them fast enough to matter.

3. Securing a loan extension from a bank is often exactly like applying for a new loan—they can ask for an entirely new set of application documents.

4. Don't let a bank talk you into placing your long-term loans with them in exchange for a bridge loan; the trade-off is probably not there!

5. Hard money lenders are not "knee-breakers"; they are just as professional as the banker down the street.

Next Chapter Preview

In the next chapter we'll examine "ratios" and how banks can use them to disqualify you, and we'll also discuss how state and federal banking regulations give rise to my book. With these banking regulations, nothing can happen quickly.

CHAPTER 4

Know Your "Ratios"
(See ... Your Teacher Said That This Stuff Would Be Important Some Day ... Like TODAY!)

If you think nobody cares if you're alive,
try missing a couple of car payments.
—Earl Wilson

As is true for most things in life, if there isn't a genuine need for something, it wouldn't exist. The concept of hard money exists because of the need for a viable alternative to a bank. Banks are regulated, and hence they must operate in accordance with some-one else's idea of prudence and safety. As the result, banks focus on making sure that everything that they do fully complies with all of the rules and regulations of federal and state agencies. You can expect a bank to spend more time focusing on complying with rules and regulations than on helping you achieve your financial goals in a timely fashion. In this chapter, we'll take a look at the differences between hard money lenders and banks in how each handles your loan request.

Rules and Regulations:
Financial Boundaries That Can't Easily Be Crossed

Ask any child what he wants to be when he grows up and you'll hear a rainbow of colorful answers: astronaut, president, movie star, athlete, writer, pilot, doctor, and teacher; the sky's the limit when you're a kid. What you likely won't hear, however, is that he looks forward to existing from paycheck to paycheck and taking a series of dead-end jobs just to pay the bills. What changes from child-hood to adulthood? What holds us back and keeps us from pursuing our dreams, achieving our goals, and reaching our full potential?

If you said access to money as one of the top reasons, you're completely right.

Steve Sez:
You don't have to be at the mercy of the bank. Take Action Now to Reach Your Goals! You can get the money that you need to pursue your dreams.

Hard Money Difference #4: Regulations

Banks are highly regulated by state and federal banking authorities; hard money lenders are not. Why is it so hard to get a loan from a bank or other mortgage lender? It is because they have a virtual army of state and federal banking and lending regulators watching over them. Mistakes are painful for bankers in many ways.

There are several types of financial institutions: commercial banks, mutual savings banks, savings and loan associations, life insurance companies, private pension funds, public pension funds, foundations, venture capital pools, mortgage companies (mortgage bankers or brokers), real estate investment trusts (REITs), mutual funds, credit unions, mortgage pools, and so on.

Steve Sez:
Federal banking regulations require that banks have complete documentation in a file before a loan can be approved and funded; the process takes considerable time, costs *you* money and effort, and results in many turn-downs.

The charters that guide the authority of these institutions to accept and either lend or invest their funds can also define them as private, govern-mental, or quasi-governmental. For the sake of our discussion, we'll refer to any institutional lender as a bank.

Due to strict government regulations, the bank loan approval process can be very time-consuming and require reams of documentation. Quite often, the application process and subsequent evaluation results in many application denials. If there are any problems with credit, income, verification of income or employment, or validating other sources of income, most banks won't even get to the value of the applicant's particular collateral.

It's enough of a challenge for most people to maintain one good stable source of income over time; having ready-access to more than one such source is nearly impossible. Yet, without being able to clearly demonstrate and verify to the bank that you have a variety of strategies in place for keeping the payments current as well as repaying a loan, you will likely be out of luck. You will undoubtedly be turned down. And, it's all because of a something you learned in elementary school: *ratios*.

> **Steve Sez:**
> Just as we saw with poor Frank's business earlier, all loans approved by a bank must have multiple sources of repayment.

Let us return briefly to your years in the fifth grade. If you were lucky enough to get a fifth grade teacher who could explain math to you, then you are going to breeze through this discussion. If, on the other hand, you were not paying attention the day that Miss Johnson explained ratios to you, do not fear. You'll understand their impact even if you still can't compute one after this chapter. A ratio is really nothing more than a proportion or a percentage of something. For example, this simple proportion is used by bank loan officers when looking at your debt and income.

Debt-to-Income Ratios

One of the big calculations for a bank or mortgage company (but not so for a hard money lender) is the debt-to-income ratio. A debt-to-income ratio measures your monthly payments versus how much you earn each month. See how easy this is? Aren't you sorry that you weren't paying attention in class that day?

Why is this so important to banks? In their opinion (and,more importantly, that of the regulators), it's a mathematical way to weed out those whom they consider to be bad risks. It identifies people who have too many monthly payments in proportion to the amount of their income. Computing this proportion (ratio) helps keep the banking system safe from people who become too heavily in debt.

This ratio has also taken on additional significance recently as the worldwide banking system has been strained by long standing liberal bank lending policies. The pendulum has now swung back to the other extreme, and regulators have taken away almost all of the discretion that banks have in this area. The analysis of debt-to-income ratios is now carefully scrutinized by bank regulators as a measure of the risk to the bank's portfolio.

What does this mean for many borrowers? Here is an example: Gregg Deveroux has the opportunity to purchase a new property at an incredible discount if he can close quickly. But, Gregg has already used all three of his other properties as collateral for other loans; he has, therefore, severely limited if not completely eliminated his ability to borrow more money from any bank, regardless of the strength of the deal he is putting together now. The analysis of his excess cash flow over his monthly obligations becomes quite lopsided when he owes money on multiple mortgages. His "ratios" quickly become unacceptable to a bank.

It's not only Gregg's other mortgages that impact the amount he can borrow from the bank. The bank's loan committee's computation takes into consideration all of his debt including credit cards, lines of credit, non-bank indebtedness, unsecured obligations and all other debts that require monthly cash flow to keep his loan payments current; they *all* factor into the ratio analysis.

Steve Sez:
Every aspect of your financial life impacts your ratios; it's critical that you take the time to understand how they work and plan accordingly.

Hard Money Difference #5: Ratios

Although banks require acceptable ratios as a rigid requirement for loan approval, the approval of a hard money loan application isn't determined exclusively by ratios.

Besides the debt-to-income ratio we mentioned, banks look at some of the following ratios when judging your loan application. Listed are sixteen Important Ratios used by Banks (often to your detriment):

- Current Ratio;

- Current Liabilities to Net Working Capital Ratio;

- Total Liabilities to Net Worth Ratio;

- Fixed Assets to Net Worth Ratio;

- Accounts Receivables Average Collection Period;

- Inventory Turnover Ratio;

- Sales-to-Inventory Ratio;

- Quick Ratio of Current Assets to Current Liabilities;

- Assets-to-Sales Ratio;

- Sales-to-Net-Working-Capital Ratio;

- Accounts-Payable-to-Sales Ratio;

- Return on Sales Ratio;

- Return on Assets;

- Return on Net Worth Percentage;

- Loan-to-Value Ratio;

- ... And many, many more.

How many of these ratios deal directly with the value of your collateral? Strange, isn't it, and most particularly because real estate is the ultimate and most common collateral for a loan? Most of these ratios are determined by your income and expense, and by the various aspects of your business data each of which can change in a very short period of time. These ratios can quickly fluctuate in ways you can't understand, and over which you have little control. The bank's evaluation focuses primarily on your cash flow, your credit rating, your ratios, more of your ratios, and even more of your ratios as well as on your personal and corporate financial statements, projections, multiple sources of cash flow and repayment, and lastly, on the value of your collateral.

Hard money lenders, on the other hand, focus on your collateral first. It is that component of your financial profile that serves as the primary safety factor for the loan.

Remember, if speed is critical, a hard money lender can look at a piece of property in a day, make a decision the next day and schedule a closing shortly thereafter. Can you see your banker giving you an answer on your loan in weeks or even over a month let alone within a few days from the date of your application? How can you ever take advantage of opportunities with your bank's timing and review schedule?

Have you ever had this experience? You've applied for a loan—it might be a mortgage loan, a car loan, or a loan for a business venture—only to be told that your ratios don't fit their requirements? But, you make all your credit card payments on time; you just received a huge raise at work; you own some wonderful income-producing rental properties. How can you *not* fit the model?

You've been the victim of ratio discrimination!

The best example of ratio discrimination is found in a mortgage loan situation. In the real world of bank procedures, there are more figures that go into ratio computations than I've described here. But, let's run through an easy and common situation:

Numerical Example

Historically, most residential mortgage lenders have allowed a maximum of 28 percent of your gross income to be allocated to your housing expenses (mortgage payments, taxes, insurance, and maintenance). A total of 36 percent of your gross income has been the limit for joint housing and consumer installment debt. The recent limit for all payments regardless of source is approximately 48 percent of your gross monthly income. This percentage fluctuates over time as regulations change and the economy grows.

Let's say your gross income is $50,000 per year. In order to comply with the 28 percent of gross income requirement described above, out of your $50,000 you can spend $14,000 per year or about $1,166 per month on your rent or your mortgage payment. If you're combining housing expenses and consumer installment debt, you can spend $18,000 per year or about $1,500 per month (which is 36 percent of your gross income).

You've done the arithmetic and see that you'd fit into the ratios. But you're still denied the loan. Why?

It isn't always that you'd made your installment payments on time—and that you're likely to continue doing so—it has to do with a combination of the types of accounts you have. For example, credit cards are treated differently from lines of credit, which are treated differently from unsecured commercial revolving indebtedness similar to credit cards. Often, business indebtedness is counted differently than consumer and residential debt.

Ah, the smoking gun!

I'll bet that this never crossed your mind: You can be penalized for the type of installment account you have. Credit card payments and any other mortgage payments you pay each month—like for investment or rental properties—can seriously impact the bank's

Steve Sez:
I'm afraid to tell you that the ratios that banks use to approve or disapprove your loan request are, sadly, here to stay! If anything, banks are even more regulated and aggressive today than they were just 10 or 20 years ago.

opinion of your ability to service its debt with the required margin of safety. How about secured and unsecured commercial lines of credit, equipment purchase loans, leases, and so on? All have a very different impact on your ratios.

Lets take a look at revolving debt as an example. If you have revolving debt—like credit cards you pay month-to-month—traditional lenders will look at three things:

• How recently the account was opened,

• How much of the limit has been used, and

• What has been your payment history since you opened the account (including whether you pay your balance off each month or carry balances over from month to month)

A traditional lender will also look at the number of installment accounts you have as well as how much you owe and the payments on each. To the banker, $10,000 in installment debt isn't nearly as bad over two or three credit cards as it is on one card—especially with that one card being at the credit limit.

Steve Sez:
Make sure you know how your bank calculates their debt to income ratios in advance; it will make your borrowing life significantly easier!

If you have one card with a $15,000 limit, and you have a $12,000 balance on it for a year (even if your payments are completely current), this is a definite negative for a bank, and for your credit rating as well. These ratios and installment debts are then weighed against other risk predictors like credit scores.

Some lenders also look at how a borrower has created his/her monetary security blanket. This kind of review is more focused on your reserves rather than your income. That means the banker wants to know what reserves of cash you've built up that you can rely upon if your business gets slow for a time. The banker also wants to know about your liquidity as another measure of the safety of the loan. These reserves can be found in 401(k) plans, stocks, cash value in a life insurance policy, or just good old plain cash in a savings or checking account.

I'll tell you a little secret that I heard from someone who does what they call "credit repair." He told me that if you buy that couch of your dreams from a furniture store that advertises "no interest and no payments for a year," this type of transaction has a significantly negative impact on your credit score. Who can only guess how a bank treats this transaction in their ratio analysis?

Loan-to-Value Ratios (1)

The loan-to-value (also referred to as "LTV") measures how much of the value of the property is eaten up by debt. This is the *only* ratio that a hard money lender will scrutinize. If you will recall the list of ratios above, you will remember that banks also use this as one of several in making their lending decisions. Why is the loan-to-value ratio so important?

Consider Marilyn Jenson's situation. She recently began buying and selling real estate as a step towards her safe retirement. She currently owns a property worth $100,000, and she owes $80,000 in mortgage loans. The loan ($80,000) to value ($100,000) ratio on this property is 80 percent.

Steve Sez:
If you remember nothing else, keep the loan-to-value ratio in mind at all times when dealing with a hard money lender! It is critical to getting your loan application approved!

To further understand how to compute this percentage (or ratio), divide the current loan balance ($80,000) on her property by the total value ($100,000) of her property. The result (80 percent in this example) is the "loan to value" ratio of this property.

If she then went to a bank to borrow additional money, the bank might look at making her a second mortgage loan in the amount of $10,000. By adding the amount of the first mortgage of $80,000 to the $10,000 that the bank may loan as a second mortgage, it brings the total of the two to $90,000 if she takes the new loan from the bank. Marilyn's new *combined* loan-to-value ratio considering all loans is, therefore, 90 percent of the value of her property.

You may hear lenders talk about the "CLTV" of a property. Again, remember that this means "combined loan to value." Now you know this means simply the combination of all of the loans on the property divided by its value (hence: "combined" loan-to-value.) Again, it's quite important that you understand this concept as it will determine your chances of getting a loan.

Steve Sez:
The "loan-to-value" ratio is the rock of Gibraltar for hard money lenders; it is the ultimate measure of the safety of the loan. It will help the lender to determine how much he will lend to you based upon these numbers. Always keep the loan-to-value ratios on your collateral as low as possible in order to get another loan.

It's important to remember that when a hard money lender considers making you a loan, he won't look at your credit, your income, or your employment in making his decision. The most important factor to a hard money lender is always found in the safety and equity position of the collateral. If Marilyn had gone to a hard money lender, he would have taken a close look at the CLTV of her collateral in order to judge the overall safety of the loan.

Let's look at this through the lender's eyes—how protected is he if he makes you the loan? The hard money lender's primary method of keeping his loan safe is to keep the loan-to-value ratio on your property very low. This insures that in the event of a problem, he will have excess value available to allow him to: foreclose; pay all of the legal and holding costs and expenses (insurance, maintenance, taxes and so on); sell the property; recoup all of the expenses and commissions of the sale; and collect the balance of the outstanding loan with a good margin of safety.

Loan-to-Value Ratios (2)

Residential Loans from Banks and commercial loans from hard money lenders are a high risk element for both. As you've read, banks and other institutional lenders all have differing requirements about what they'll accept as maximum loan-to-value ratios. The loan-to-value ratio goes to the issue of safety. Banks making loans on residential property usually look favorably at loan-to-value ratios of 80 percent or less of the value of the residential property. And in the event that you cannot come up with the additional funds in cash, mortgage companies often know lenders who will make second mortgage loans to make up the difference. The higher the loan-to-value ratio for any particular piece of property, the riskier the loan for the lender (any lender).

In the case of commercial lenders, maximum loan-to-value ratios are usually in the range of 70 to 80 percent of the appraised or other value measurement. But, what happens when you're buying a commercial property and you need more than the amount that the bank will lend?

This is where many commercial borrowers run into problems; either they need a second loan (second mortgage) or some other source of capital (or collateral, as we will see) in order to cover this gap.

In the eyes of a hard money lender, this is completely backwards and is a very poor and dangerous business practice. In the commercial loan arena, unlike homeowners, people who own commercial buildings like apartment buildings, strip retail properties, office buildings and so on, have no emotional commitment to their properties. They would easily walk away from their property if it weren't providing them with positive cash flow either now or in the foreseeable future. You can easily understand why commercial loans are much riskier than are owner-borrower's residential loans.

Residential Loans: Banks and Mortgage Companies vs. Hard Money Lenders

Banks and mortgage companies make the majority of residential loans; why can't hard money lenders do the same with their loans?

As you may have heard, banks and mortgage companies will quickly sell the residential loans that they originate and close with their own money so that they can bring their capital back in order to make more loans, and hence earn more fees as fast as possible. The appetite of the buyers of residential loan packages has been exceedingly large because of the lower rates that exist in the marketplace in general.

Because of this, buyers have been eager to purchase these residential mortgage portfolios believing them to be very safe. After all, back to ratios, each loan in the package must meet the bank's loan-to-value ratios, and debt-to-income ratios. If it's a choice between buying larger or smaller pools of loans, they would rather purchase larger portfolios in one transaction. Therefore, the pressure is on the banks to make their pools as large as possible as fast as possible in order to earn fees as quickly as they can sell each new portfolio.

Steve Sez:
Because banks quickly package and sell their residential loans, they compete aggressively for owner occupied loans. The impetus is to allow borrowers to put virtually none of their own money at risk so the portfolio can be enlarged quickly.

Banks actually compete for residential loans that can be packaged and sold easily. It's how they make a great deal of money quite easily. It is this competition that draws borrowers in droves.

The reason that hard money lenders never get onto this merry-go-round is that there is no effective way for them to sell their portfolios. There are many, many reasons for this fact the most common of which is that most hard money lenders make six month to one year loans. And because they can't package and sell their loans to anyone, hard money lenders are much more attuned to making their loans safe to hold, regardless of outcome. And, I might add, that the way hard money lenders do that is to keep the "loan-to-value" ratios on their collateral much more conservative (and realistic, I might add).

> **Steve Sez:**
> **Hard money lenders keep each of their loans until they are paid off. They stand to lose money directly if any loan goes bad and, therefore, they take valuation seriously. Be highly realistic about the valuation of your collateral. Otherwise, you'll waste your time even looking for a loan.**

Commercial and Residential Loans: They Are Quite Different Creatures

The maximum loan-to-value ratios in the commercial lending arena won't be the same as the ratios you'd find in residential lending.

A commercial loan which would be considered by a hard money lender is for a business, investment, or profit generating purpose. With regard to the loan-to-value ratios, most banks' LTV (loan to value) limits aren't as high for their commercial loans as they are for their residential loans. Why is this?

As you remember, residential loan portfolios are popularly resold and quite quickly. Each of the residential loans fits within a "box" of debt to income ratios, loan to value ratios, credit scores, and so on. Banks have no residual liability for a loan that goes bad after it is sold to someone else.

Commercial loans are incapable of being put in such "boxes" because each is unique—completely different from the last or the next loan. This is why most commercial lenders must be prepared to hold the loans in their own portfolios until they are repaid. No two loans are the same.

Most of the time, so goes the argument, a person will do virtually anything to avoid losing his or her home. Because of that, mortgage companies think that high loan-to-value residential loans are very safe. Remember, however, that when the value of the house is actually below the amount owed on the property, the serious motivation for the homeowner to fight to keep the house often rapidly disappears. In these situations, equivalent homes are selling for less as well, and so it becomes a matter of a price spiral downwards. In these cases, this leaves the lender or loan purchaser in serious trouble. Without a borrower who will fight to keep his or her house regardless of value, the lenders are left with a piece of property upon which they are going to lose money.

In the commercial world, you rarely run into instances of losing homes. It's only a matter of losing an investment property. It's far easier to walk away from an investment opportunity that's gone bad than it is to displace your family. Most investment borrowers won't fight as hard to keep their investment properties, so the lender must consider this fact as he builds in safeguards when making his commercial loans.

What does that mean for you? It means you can't borrow as much against a commercial property as you might be able to with a residential loan. The highest bank commercial loan-to-value ratio is in the range of 70 to 80 percent and that's typically reserved for the best borrowers.

You might be saying, "Hey, Steve, that's cool." But hang on. That's the *max*. What do we do about the difference that we also need? We will explore the solutions to this situation in a bit. And, to further complicate the issue, most hard money lenders have found that a loan-to-value ratio of between 60 and 65 percent for improved properties, gives them the security that they need considering the risks being assumed.

How does this work numerically? Let's go back to the example of a $100,000 property. If the commercial property you are offering as collateral to a hard money lender is worth $100,000, you'll be able to borrow between $60,000 and $65,000 if your lender's loan-to-value ratio is 60 to 65 percent. Loan-to-value ratios vary considerably from hard money lender to hard money lender, however.

Hard money loan-to-value requirements are very different from those of a bank or conventional commercial lender. As we have discussed above, hard money lenders prefer a lower loan-to-value ratio for their loans than do banks. The results of this lower "loan-to-value" ratio requirement (meaning, once again, that the loan amount will be smaller), is that if you are unable to make up the difference between the loan amount and the purchase price, the good news is that many a hard money lender will be more flexible and find a way to make it work for you.

Although commercial bank lenders are typically confined to their guidelines and can't vary much in order to stay in compliance with the federal regulations, hard money lenders can be far more flexible. Banks do not have any flexibility by comparison. With a hard money loan, what you give up in loan-to-value ratio (meaning lower loan amount), you gain in flexibility and speed in most cases. Creativity and flexibility are two of the distinct advantages that you will always find with a good hard money lender.

With the creativity of a hard money lender, it's even possible that you can purchase a piece of commercial property with no money out of your pocket for the acquisition. Isn't hard money wonderful! We think so too!

Banks and mortgage companies are both highly regulated institutions. Legislation and policies enacted by both the state and federal governments guide banks lending practices closely. There are literally dozens of ratios banks look at when making loan decisions. Because of these often complex ratios and lending guidelines, securing a loan with any speed at all is now almost impossible.

Steve Sez:
Never do I believe that you cannot get your opportunity financed. If there is a way, an experienced hard money lender will help you find it.

Steve Sez:
With a hard money loan, you gain creativity in getting a loan as well as in its structure, and the best part is that it happens NOW! Your loan-to-value ratio will usually be lower—not a bad tradeoff when banks aren't making many loans anyway, I'd say.

One of the regulations that banks must follow in approving loans is to limit the amount they loan based on the loan-to-value ratio of the proposed collateral.

A hard money lender will also pay very close attention to the loan-to-value ratio. Because they have no regulatory oversight, they can be more creative and flexible in their loan structure without fear of any consequences (but for the loss of their princpal).

Chapter Summary

1. Banks are highly regulated institutions, hard money lenders are not.

2. Banks use a number of ratios in determining whether or not to make you a loan; a hard money lender looks primarily at one ratio: the loan-to-value ratio.

3. Because banks package their residential loans for resale to investors but not their commercial loans, these loans are made very carefully.

4. There are significant differences between commercial and residential loan packages which impact their resale potential.

5. A hard money lender can look at a variety of strategies for augmenting a borrower's collateral. This creativity saves the day for many a borrower. Sadly, a bank cannot do the same.

Next Chapter Preview

In the next chapter, we'll take a look at some ways that hard money lenders can employ creativity and flexibility in their loan structures while discussing why banks are locked into specific loan models.

CHAPTER 5

Let's Get Creative and Help You Get a Loan—FAST!

Positive thinking will let you do everything better than negative thinking will.
—Zig Ziglar

In this era of economic pressure and increased regulatory oversight, creativity is the one ingredient that you truly need—but sadly is largely missing when you turn to your bank for a commercial loan.

Fortunately, hard money lenders are able to utilize their creativity at each step in the application process. In this chapter we will begin to see and understand some of the strategies that a good hard money lender can utilize in order to create a loan package that uniquely fills your needs and allows you to take advantage of great opportunities ... today.

Creativity and flexibility are generally completely missing from a traditional bank commercial loan. It isn't because bankers love to be rigid and structured; it's because state and federal banking regulations make it that way. Finding a banker with creativity is like finding blue apples. They just don't exist in large numbers (OK, so this might be a bit harsh—I'm sure that there are some, and as a matter of fact I would have to say that the president of my primary bank is quite creative).

Hard Money Difference #6: Creativity

Banks are locked into a few distinct loan types. Creativity and flexibility abound with a hard money lender! Two things make hard money such an ideal solution for so many borrowers:

- Creativity

- Flexibility

These elements go hand in hand to help you get the best structure possible for the loan that you need fast.

Creativity and Flexibility

Hard money lenders have a greater ability to think outside the box than do traditional bankers. No federal regulations apply to hard money lenders or the loans that they make. Creativity and flexibility can apply both to the structure of the loan as well as to the loan terms.

Let's take a look at some of the most creative techniques and structures that a good hard money lender can bring to your loan package. As you review this list, consider how beneficial some or all of these techniques can be for you:

- Monthly payments of interest only,

- Deferred interest payments,

- Interest escrow account,

- Partial mortgage release,

- Equity participations,

- Cross collateralizations,

- Limited personal liability, and

- Seller carrybacks.

Let's take a look at each of these, one by one. Before we start, note that even the basic structure of a hard money loan is highly creative even before we start adding other features.

> **Steve Sez:**
> Take advantage of creativity in structuring a hard money loan; the loan can be what you want it to be.

Monthly Payments of Interest Only

In order to fully understand what this can do for your cash flow, it might be useful to describe how an amortized loan (the usual loan structure) actually works. With an amortized loan, each payment includes a payment of principal and interest. Paying the principal down each month results in the loan being paid off over time but makes each payment a little larger to account for this pay down.

The usual payment plan for most hard money loans will require you to make interest payments each month. This works to your advantage because it keeps your monthly cash outflow for loan payments to a minimum. Its only disadvantage (and advantage, by the way) is that you are never reducing the amount you owe because none of the payments you make each month include any principal reduction.

For borrowers whose circumstances require lower monthly payments, interest-only payments will keep your loan payments to a minimum. Let's compare an amortized loan with an interest-only loan:

Numerical Example

If you borrow $100,000 from a bank, and the payments are based on a six percent annual interest rate, the payments for a loan which is amortized (fully repaid) over 15 years would be $843.86 per month, which includes some principal pay down plus the interest on the unpaid balance.

If you borrow the same $100,000 from a hard money lender and the payments are also based on a six percent annual interest rate, the payments for the loan based upon paying only the interest each month would be $500. This is an example of paying no principal down each month. You will save $343.86 each month in principal payments which can go directly into your project.

Steve Sez:
There's no free lunch no matter how you slice it. Be aware of the fact that these creative techniques just change the timing of loan payments and not the ultimate amount due. Timing of cash outflow is critical, however, to most early stage businesses.

No free lunch ... what the heck does that mean? In hard money terms, it means that at the end of the loan (the maturity of the loan), you're still responsible for repaying the full principal balance because you haven't been retiring any of the principal each month with your payments. The final principal payment is called a *balloon payment* where the principal is due in one lump sum at the end of the loan.

The big benefit to a balloon payment is that in the short term, each month that you have the money borrowed, you are NOT paying $343.86 (the difference between the payments to the bank and the payments to the hard money lender). Over the period of only one year for a $100,000 loan, this means that with a hard money loan, you'll have an extra $4,126.32 of cash flow in your pocket to work with that you wouldn't have had with a fully amortized bank loan.

But, don't forget our rule that there truly is no free lunch. You will have to pay the money back sooner or later. The expectation will be that when you do repay a hard money loan at its maturity, your cash flow will have improved significantly, so that its repayment is not a burden that you can't meet easily at that time. While many hard money loans do not include this feature as a matter of standard course, it is still very important to understand how this might be of significant value to you in some circumstances. Understanding this option will give you ammunition with which to negotiate loan terms with a hard money lender that may suit you better.

Deferred Interest

Deferred interest means that the payment(s) of interest is put off for a negotiated period. This does not mean that interest does not continue to accrue. You have, after all, borrowed the funds and interest is the charge for the use of that money over time. Deferred interest means that there is some grace period, usually at the beginning of the loan, when regular interest payments don't have to be made. In many cases, the unpaid and deferred interest payments are added to the ending principal balance. While deferred interest is wonderful in theory, it always raised a red flag with me.

Having warned you about the downside of deferring interest payments, the obvious advantage in those circumstances is that during the early stages of a project, cash flow is not yet established. That's when you need the most assistance from your lender. Most hard money loans (and most conventional loans, for that matter) do not offer this possibility as a regular option. But sometimes, if you ask, you may be surprised to find that the hard money lender will consider it whereas a bank would never go for it.

Critically Important

Again, I would urge you to rethink your project if you need this type of concession. By needing deferred interest, what you are really saying is that the project won't carry itself, and you can't individually make the payments-at least initially. If any of your plans should fail to materialize exactly as you have planned, your property is at risk of foreclosure. You also place yourself at

Steve Sez:
As a hard money lender, I shuddered when I heard that a borrower needed some help with the first payment due after the loan was made. This spoke volumes about how risky this loan was going to be. As your new found friend, let me give you some helpful advice. If you can't make the payments on the loan from the very beginning, *don't borrow the money!* You risk losing everything.

risk of being sued personally. When any payments are deferred, it's always harder to catch up because the first payment that you make after any deferral may have to include all of the previous unpaid interest. Imagine the burden on you if you had to make up an entire year's interest with one payment! If you can't do it, take photos of the property you used to own, as that's all you will have left.

Steve Sez:
Taking a deferred interest loan may only leave you with mere memories of your property!

Interest Escrow

This is another version of an interest grace period. In this variation, you do not have to make interest payments out of your pocket. Rather, you ask the hard money lender to take funds out of the loan proceeds and to establish an escrow account from which interest payments will come each month until the funds are gone.

The impact of the interest escrow structure is almost the same as the deferred interest approach. In the interest escrow variation, the lender does get some monthly interest from each monthly payment. The interest escrow has virtually no impact on the hard money lender so it shouldn't be difficult to get his agreement. This is because the hard money lender will typically only lend funds up to his maximum loan-to-value percentage. To the lender, what you do with all or some of the loan proceeds is not important as long as the overall loan is within the acceptable LTV range.

Financially Important

Another impact of putting funds into an escrow account at closing is that you will net less money from the loan closing. You are actually prepaying some or all of the interest by the amount of funds that you escrow at the loan closing. Be aware that you are paying interest on the money that is being set aside in the escrow account and can't be used for your project.

The additional cost to you shouldn't be substantial, but you should recognize what will happen before you ask for this loan repayment structure. If your hard money lender will not allow this out of the net loan proceeds, you can just compute the interest over the loan term and take this amount and open a savings account to cover these payments.

Partial Mortgage (or "Deed of Trust") Release

A partial release of the mortgage option works well when multiple pieces of collateral are used as security for the loan. The collateral can be in the form of several pieces of real estate all the way to a couple of valuable

Steve Sez:
Taking an interest escrowed loan will have the same impact on your fortunes as a deferred interest loan—don't do either if you like and want to continue to own your property!

paintings. When crafting the loan structure, the promissory note can be written to specify that, as principal payments on the loan are being made and the balance is decreasing, you may request that the lender allow some of your collateral to be released from his lien. Make sure, however, that your agreement for this partial release option appears in the loan documents. A good and experienced lawyer will make sure of this also.

The logic for securing a partial release of the mortgage is fairly straightforward: As your loan balance decreases, the lender needs less collateral to keep within his minimum loan-to-value ratio. (There are those darn ratios again—aren't you glad that you know what they are now?)

Obtaining a partial release clause in your loan documents lets you keep the option of selling or re-mortgaging a portion of the collateral without having to pay off the loan in full first. If you don't have partial releases in your loan documents, you would have to pay off the entire loan before any single piece would be free to sell.

By the way, you'd rarely get approval for a partial release structure from a bank unless you were a real estate developer with great credit and you needed to release each lot from your lenders mortgage in order get a construction loan to build on that lot. In real estate, a release or certificate of satisfaction is normally given by a bank only when the full amount of the loan (principal, interest, costs and expenses) is repaid. It is only then that you get back all of your collateral free and clear without a lender's lien against it.

A hard money lender, who can creatively structure loan terms by allowing you to receive partial releases as you pay down your loan principal, will most certainly add significant value and flexibility to your transaction. In some circumstances, this could make the entire difference between the success and failure of your entire project.

Equity or Profits Participation as an Added Incentive for Your Lender

Offering your lender an equity position in your project can add just that little extra that will encourage a savvy lender to make a loan which they would otherwise turn down. With an equity participation in your project, your success will also become the success of the lender. I have seen many forms of such participations that have been creatively developed in order to convince a lender to make a loan that is on the high side of the lender's loan-to-value limits.

As an example: Steve and Tara Smythe want a loan to start the first leading edge sugar free bakery and ice cream business in their city. They have real estate and other assets to be offered as collateral but right now, their real estate is encumbered by loans in the amount of 85 percent of its current value. This high loan-to-value ratio would normally prevent a hard money lender from approving their loan request. Adding equity participation for the lender just might convince him to stretch his comfort zone and approve their loan request. His potential profits could be very high if Steve and Tara are successful.

Steve Sez:
Giving your lender a small piece of ownership in your project may be far more beneficial, both in the short and long run, than not getting the loan at all.

How does an equity participation structure actually work? Let's take a closer look at the Smythe's project. They have their eyes on an empty storefront in a newly-hip part of town. Amazingly, this neighborhood which enjoys growing foot traffic doesn't have either a bakery or an ice cream parlor. Steve has some experience in this area as he was a product manager for an international foods company for more than 30 years. Tara was the manager of an upscale women's wear boutique in the neighborhood for the past six years. They need a loan to buy and fix up the building, order inventory and do some marketing.

They have marginal collateral because they have recently invested in their daughter-in-law's yoga studio and the building in which it is located opened right up the street. It already has loans against it that are either at the limit or slightly in excess of what most hard money lenders would consider their maximum loan-to-value ratios. (Remember that this is the most important number to a hard money lender.)

They considered offering a hard money lender five percent ownership in the ice cream/baked goods store to keep him fat and happy in exchange for making a loan that he may not have ordinarily approved. That way, they get their money and the lender becomes their biggest cheerleader because he is participating in the eventual success of the store.

In order to illustrate how profitable this can be for a lender and how it may easily influence him to approve a loan, consider the case of profit participations in the motion picture industry (often referred to as "points" in a movie). An actor might choose to take "points" in a film in exchange for a lower salary (the same thing as a lender taking points in exchange for making a loan that exceeds his safety zone, to you). A point is equal to one percent of the gross or net profits (you can define it almost any way you want). If it's a blockbuster, this could turn out to be a shrewd business decision for the actor (or lender in our case)!

Can you imagine walking into your bank and suggesting they take points in your project if they would only make a loan to you? What do you think their response would be? Would it be, "No, thank you"; would it be, "Are you crazy?" or, "Don't let the door hit you on the way out!" My vote is for the last.

Just as the movie star taking points in a film, a hard money lender can reap a much greater reward than just the interest being charged on the loan by taking a position in the business. It can become a terrific incentive for the lender to step outside of his comfort zone and convince him to say yes to your loan request.

This is where hard money lenders can really shine if they are creative thinkers. You'll know if you have a good potential lender if you get a positive response when you ask if he would consider taking a piece of the project that you're financing in exchange for a loan approval.

This doesn't always mean that you have to give the lender equity participation in order to get your loan approved. It's only one more creative technique to help you get the funding you need.

If the lender is amenable, you should also consider raising your loan request. Exercise great caution and make sure that you're getting enough funding for your project with the first loan so that the granting of the equity participation will be worth the extra cost. Once you've borrowed money and given equity in your project, you don't want to go back to the lender until you're up and running, and profitable. Otherwise, you may have to give away more equity in your business than you may have wanted.

An equity participation loan is like a combination of getting funds from a venture capitalist and a hard money lender. It can be the answer to your dreams if you structure it right. But do it right the first time because once you start down the equity participation road, it's hard to get off without giving up much more of your project.

Critically Important

Make sure that you have a person with experience in these types of transactions to help you put numbers together for any equity participation offer to a hard money lender. You don't want to give away too much or too little.

Cross-Collateralization

Cross collateralization is one of those areas of lending that you would think you would see every lender offering as a regular course of business. Cross collateralization is a strategy that combines many different pieces of collateral in order to qualify for a loan. For example, if your primary collateral for the loan already has a large mortgage on it, you can add additional property to the package in order to meet the loan-to-value requirements of the lender. Simple, isn't it? More collateral translates into easier loan approval. It is

> ## Steve Sez:
> Adding equity or profits participation to your deal with a hard money lender may be just what the doctor ordered to get a larger, more flexible loan.

called cross collateralization because the equity from more than one property will be used as the security for the loan.

Numerical Example

Let's look at some numbers behind this strategy; it will give you a good understanding of this technique which is used by creative and flexible hard money lenders.

You own a piece of real estate that is worth $250,000, and you already owe $125,000 in mortgage debt secured by this property. You need to borrow $100,000 in order to take advantage of the opportunity to purchase the office building next door to your office, but the seller needs his money badly and has to close by next Tuesday. If you ask your hard money lender to put a second mortgage on your property, he will be in a 90 percent combined loan-to-value (remember CLTV?) position.

The formula for loan-to-value is total loans over the value of the property (the total of the first and the proposed second mortgage loans, or $225,000 in this example divided by $250,000). If the lender in question requires a maximum of 60 percent loan-to-value, then there is only $25,000 of additional loan value in this property (60 percent of $250,000 is $150,000; and there is already $125,000 owed on this building, meaning that there is only $25,000 left which can be borrowed).

What a creative hard money lender will allow is the addition of more collateral as security for the loan, in order to bring the combined loan-to-value ratio down to the acceptable limit of 60 percent in order to be able to advance to the borrower the $100,000 that he needs. Therefore, if the borrower owns a second building worth $200,000 upon which is owed $40,000 as a first mortgage, there remains $80,000 which can be borrowed on this building (60 percent of $200,000 is $120,000 but there is already a $40,000 loan, so the maximum additional amount that can be borrowed is $120,000 less $40,000 or $80,000).

Therefore, if you add the $25,000 in lendable value on the first piece of property, to the $80,000 of lendable value on the second piece of property, the borrower can get the funds that he needs by allowing the lender to put mortgages on both pieces of property (hence, "cross collateralization).

The lender now has two pieces of collateral for his loan, which should make him feel safer and the borrower now stands to lose his two pieces of property if he fails to make his payments when due. In this case, the flexibility to allow cross collateralization makes the loan work.

Imagine what a traditional banker would do if the two pieces of property were in Louisiana, and in New York State? Do you suppose a regular banker would ever entertain such a loan structure? I would bet not. What about you? The answer leaves the borrower with nowhere to turn for his money except a hard money lender. A good hard money lender can add the creativity, speed, ability and experience necessary to close within the time required by the borrower.

Steve Sez:
Cross collateralization can work magic on your loan application. Therefore, don't overlook any collateral that you may own in order to ensure that your loan will be approved.

As the fact pattern gets more complex with numbers and varieties of different properties in different locations, a borrower is even less likely to find a bank or even a hard money lender who can successfully close such a loan. I have seen loans with properties in five different states close, even though all had different values and different laws because the lender was able to think outside of the box in order to help his borrowers. The lender felt better because he had more collateral, the borrower felt better because he got all of his money when he needed it, and the seller of the building felt better because he got the funds at the closing.

An Actual Experience

This Is The Story of Dr. Ted Who Needed Our Help Badly!

I once helped a very nice oral surgeon by the name of Ted who had his office in Irvine, California. The good doctor wanted to purchase two apartment buildings in Denver, Colorado. By the time he and I met, he'd already negotiated an incredible deal with the seller. But, because Dr. Ted lived and worked in Irvine, no local bank in California would loan him any money on apartment buildings in Denver. And no bank in Denver would loan him the funds because he lived in Irvine. A bit of a dilemma, don't you think?

He came to me with great collateral but no place to turn with a closing scheduled next Tuesday. After some discussion, I shared with Ted the fact that the loan-to-value ratio didn't work for me if the apartment buildings were his only collateral.

His mother owned a house in Grass Valley, California, however, that was free and clear and that she was willing to add to the picture just to get the loan done quickly for her son. I immediately flew to Grass Valley to confirm that his mother's estimate of value was realistic. Within hours I knew her valuation was accurate so I ordered title work and the legal work be done immediately in both places, and closed a loan to him by the next Monday, leaving an entire day to spare. Needless to say, he was thrilled to have discovered hard money as a creative resource for him.

Who Signs on the Dotted-Line?

A hard money lender may not make your spouse sign on the loan documents but you can bet that your bank will! How many times have you become involved in a business transaction which required your spouse sign the documents as well as you? Doesn't the deal immediately get much more difficult to do because of your spouse's reluctance to sign personally? The result is that you risk not being able to close your loan because your husband/wife doesn't want to sign the loan documents personally. A hard money lender will probably allow you to close the loan with only your signature on the loan documents. Why? Remember, a hard money loan is collateral based. It's not about people. The only way that the lender might require your spouse to sign is if you are in a community property state, or you have put all of your assets into your spouse's name leaving you with no assets. This reminds me of a thought first expressed by Bob Dylan: "When you have nothing, you have nothing to lose." As applied here, if you are the only one signing the promissory note, and you have already put your assets into your spouse's name, then you just might develop an attitude of "who cares if I pay timely, or even at all? After all, my assets are completely safe, and the lender can't sue my wife/husband as they haven't even signed on the loan documents."

Steve Sez:
If you want to stress your spouse, just ask him/her to sign on the dotted line with you. Sadly, it adds anxiety every time and always kills your loan application.

A bank will almost always require a spousal signature as well as yours because it is about the borrower(s) when you go to the bank. An unintended benefit of using a hard money lender is that you can keep your assets and liabilities separate from your spouse's comments and possibly criticism and disapproval.

I cannot tell you how many times I've reviewed collateral, and heard from the borrowers that their wives were absolutely unwilling to sign anything to help their good-for-nothing, wheeler-dealer husbands borrow money. I, of course, responded by letting the wife know that I had never even thought about having her sign anything. In most cases, this restored marital harmony and the husband went merrily on his way doing what he wanted to do anyway.

There is nothing here to imply that husbands should keep information from their wives or that all wives are critical and disapproving. It is just a trend that I have noted when a married person applies for a loan. You are always much better off telling your spouse everything, but this is not a book about marital harmony. It's all about money.

Seller Carryback

If you are in need of a loan to purchase a piece of property, the expectation is that you will have the cash necessary to meet the shortfall between the purchase price and the amount that you can borrow. In many, many cases, however, you won't have that kind of cash just hanging around for this transaction. One of the solutions with which many sellers will agree, especially in a slow market, is to "carry back" some or all of the difference between the purchase price and the loan amount, which is then secured by a second mortgage on the property being sold.

The net result of this act of "generosity" by the seller is that you need less cash in order to close your purchase. And, after all, who would know more about the property than the seller, so he should feel safe in carrying a second mortgage on what was his own property.

Banks want you to have your own money in the deal, which they think makes you more likely to do everything you can to avoid losing the property in a foreclosure action. It makes you more serious about making your loan payments on time, so they say.

Hard money lenders also want you to remain committed to the project and to make your payments on a timely basis. They recognize, however, that if they are in first position (holding the first mortgage) at or below their maximum acceptable loan-to-value ratio, the worst that can happen is that they will end up owning and selling your property in order to recover the loan balance. In this case, unless the holder of the second mortgage (in this case, the seller) steps in to pay all of the amounts due to the first mortgage holder, he will lose his mortgage position on the property and be left in an unsecured position and only able to look to you personally for the repayment of his loan.

Chapter Summary

While banks and other commercial lenders are forced to remain fairly inflexible in their loan structure decisions due to complex state and federal regulations, hard money lenders are much more flexible. As we have seen, there are a number of strategies that can allow an "iffy" loan to move forward successfully.

There are several creative structures available through a hard money lender that may get your loan approved much more easily.

The loan may provide for interest-only payments monthly, with a balloon payment of all that is then owed when the loan matures. The loan may alternatively allow the escrow of interest payments or deferral of interest payments until later in the life of the loan.

Occasionally, the seller will carry back a portion of the selling price which has the effect of requiring less money from you at the closing, and thereby placing the hard money lender in a safer position.

Some hard money lenders might be willing to take an equity position in your project in exchange for approving your loan request.

If the loan-to-value ratio is insufficient, some lenders will allow cross-collateralization with other assets in order to make the LTV work.

Because hard money lenders look primarily to the value of the collateral, they are much less likely to require others to sign your loan documents. Commercial lenders will frequently require spouses to sign all loan documents as well.

Next Chapter Preview

At this point, some of you may be wondering if it would just be easier to get a business partner with money to join you in building your dream instead of borrowing the needed funds. Well, sure, you could, but ...

CHAPTER 6

Nightmare on Partnership Street

It is rare to find a business partner who is selfless.
If you are lucky it happens once in a lifetime.
—Michael Eisner

I've met a number of skilled and successful entrepreneurs who, when faced with an inability to get a bank loan, make the decision to take on a partner who can infuse the necessary cash to make their project go forward. Unfortunately, many of these otherwise successful entrepreneurs grow to regret their decision almost immediately. In this chapter, we'll look at some of the reasons why taking on a partner is a bad idea and propose some alternatives that are less permanent and certainly less painful.

An Actual Experience

Did I Miss Something Here, or Do I Still Own My Business?

You'll love this one: I had a borrower a number of years ago who wanted to open a pharmacy in Los Angeles. In all states there are significant restrictions in place regarding those who can have physical access to prescription drugs and particularly the "scheduled" medications containing narcotics. My client was not a pharmacist. He needed money to hire a registered and licensed pharmacist and to open his store, but he was uncomfortable with the cost of a hard money loan.

Instead of borrowing the money that he needed, he found a pharmacist who agreed to become his partner in the store (without any investment on his part). Not only did this solve his regulatory issue as a pharmacist can obviously have access to all medications, it also temporarily resolved his need for a loan as well.

However, the seemingly nice pharmacist quickly started to take control of the business and shortly thereafter, moved my borrower out of control of the very business that he had started. At this point, the non-pharmacist realized what a bad deal he had made when he couldn't even get into his own store (California's laws don't let the owner of the store be alone with drugs without having a licensed pharmacist on premises). He was literally and figuratively locked out of his own business.

The sad and ultimate resolution of this dispute was to close the doors of the pharmacy resulting in the loss of over $100,000 because of BPS (bad partner syndrome). Remember this story before you bring in someone to be your partner that you don't know very well. It can come back around to hurt you significantly! And always make sure that you have a very tightly written agreement with your partner so that in case things do go wrong, you have a relatively pain-free way to get out of the situation. Make a good lawyer your friend throughout this process.

A Hard Money Loan Is Far Cheaper than a Bad Business Partner

Let's compare the additional dollar cost of a hard money loan against something less tangible: an equity partner. Someone who invests money into your project for a percentage of the ownership instead of interest on his money is referred to as an *equity partner*.

An equity partner will probably bear the financial burden of your project—solving the immediate monetary needs—but only for a short time. Because he has put up the money, he may feel like he has a right to be "in control" until he gets his money back at a minimum.

But who is this person anyway? Choosing a good business partner is as critical as finding a compatible spouse. In order to make it work, the two of you can't be too far apart in your thinking and must be a close match in the visions each of you has for your individual and combined future. Make no mistake about it, partners can be great; but if not, then getting rid of a bad partner can be worse than a nasty divorce.

The difference between "divorcing" a bad business partner and a spouse is that it is frequently much more difficult and much more costly to divorce the business partner. That's because, typically, during the marital divorce process you can keep working. A bad business partner can shut down your operation by tying you up in lengthy and costly lawsuits; or worse.

Linda Bartlett recently became accredited by the Council for Interior Design. She marked the occasion with the decision to open her own studio. Unfortunately, the time that it took to gain her accreditation had seriously depleted her savings; she'd even gone so far as to take a second mortgage on her townhouse in order to complete the coursework.

Rather than seek help from a lender who had expressed a willingness to loan her the needed funds to start her business down the road to success—Linda really is a talented designer—she decided to enter into a partnership with another designer she'd met in class who had the financial wherewithal to finance the studio launch.

Eight weeks after the studio opened, Linda fully understood that she had made a terrible business decision. Not only did her partner regularly miss appointments with clients, she was ordering new furniture and artwork for her own home while leaving the invoices unpaid.

In a few short weeks, Linda's partner had drained the studio's funds and hopped a flight to Jamaica where she now planned to open a rum bar with a man she'd known for just a few weeks. Not only was Linda now broke, her business reputation and credit rating had gone down the tubes. And to make matters worse, she could not even pay her bills—including salaries—nor could she even get papers served on her partner because she's where? Jamaica! (oye vay)

Steve Sez:
Imagine what can happen if your "partner" suddenly takes your business over. Don't let this happen to you. Enter into a partnership with your eyes wide open and a great written agreement in place. It's a real leap of faith. Good luck!

Just for the sake of this discussion, let's say you take on a business partner to fund your venture. Certainly, the monthly cash outflow for debt repayment will or should be almost zero. With a partner, all you do is sign over some of the ownership in the project to the person who puts up the money with no muss, no fuss ... or so you think.

In the case of a loan from anyone or any bank, you'll be paying interest. When considering whether or not to take on a business partner, the question in your mind usually is: Is it better to pay nothing each month at the start of your relationship because your partner is putting equity into the kitty, or to make monthly interest payments to a lender regardless of when your business starts generating positive cash flow? Note that this self-talk is all about cash flow. Why stop your thinking there?

Many forces are at work here besides the immediate cash flow impact on your new business. With a partner, you don't have to worry as much about when positive cash flow will be achieved. But then you are stuck with the partner, be he good, bad, or even ugly.

Why choose a hard money lender over business partner? Two reasons:

- Freedom of choice: you can choose the right lender for you and extricate yourself from the loan simply by paying it off; and,

- Control: with a lender, there is no need to run any business decision by a partner first. And you won't risk being left out of the loop on your partner's business decisions because you have no partner; the business is all yours!

> **Steve Sez:**
> Without a partner, you are the captain of your own ship! Isn't that what you had envisioned when you first thought of starting a new business?

When my borrowers have done their homework and the associated math, almost universally they've discovered some fundamental truths about banks, hard money lenders and their loans, and business partners:

1. Seeking a bank loan is not a good answer to the need for money. If a borrower is turned down by his bank, the time that it took for this decision is precious time that shouldn't have been wasted. Had the borrower done his homework before approaching a bank's loan officer, he would have known that his credit rating and income made it virtually impossible that the bank would loan him any money at all.

2. The best investment opportunities at the best prices are available for those with the cash to spend *now*. Rarely will the seller of a piece of real estate say, "Close on this transaction whenever you like; just take your time and find the best loan you can." Sellers of investment opportunities don't wait. Sellers are always motivated to make the transaction happen immediately. Wouldn't you? When sellers decide to sell, it's often because they want their cash now for some reason.

3. When expressed in monetary terms, the "costs" of bringing in a partner are far greater than the amount of extra interest that would have been paid to a hard money lender. The cost and pain of a bad partner can be forever. Bad partners do not just fade into the sunset; they will be an owner like you are in your project or company. The hidden cost of a partnership includes aggravation, anger, negative energy, sleepless nights, and any legal fees that must be paid to get out of such an arrangement. The "aggravation cost" of having to dance to a partner's tune will always be more than the amount that their capital contribution was worth.

4. And, let us not forget the hidden cost of focusing energy on negative things like litigation, arbitration and the like. When you are spending time on your "de-partnering" activities, you don't have time to focus on the business and its care and feeding. And, this winding up process could result in a lengthy unwinding process which could include litigation, mediation or arbitration, collection or discussing payment terms. And, as if this isn't enough (and believe me, it is), you now have a collection issue when your ex-partner fails to live up to the terms of the settlement agreement. Thereafter, you will experience the joys of aggravation and additional legal activities and costs. But, not to worry, sometimes you can litigate your way out of a bad business partnership in only a couple of years or three. And who knows, it may well cost you less than $100,000 in legal fees before it's all over—is that a problem for you?

There are lots of great business partnerships out there. But if you'll ask your circle of friends and business acquaintances about their business partners, you'll inevitably hear examples of large amounts of money in legal fees and years of litigation to complete a "partner-ectomy." There are those who swear never to have a partner again because of the bad experiences they've had.

By the way, before we move on to another interesting topic, there is still one more bit of information that you should understand.

Most borrowers with whom we have worked over the last three decades never consider what the impact of a bad partner could be on their own personal situation as well. The unspoken cost to your relationships and your peace of mind as the result of litigating and fighting for potentially years will absolutely take its toll on you personally, while your business success will be derailed until your problems are resolved. Therefore, if you like or love your spouse, stay away from partners. Over time, partnership dissolution can break up even the strongest relationships.

The impact a bad partner can have on your *personal* credit rating cannot be under-stated! There are a number of early-warning signs that your partnership is about to go south: Checks for your payables don't get sent when they are supposed to; rent or mortgage payments become late; payments and distributions to you start to slow down as does your business cash flow. This disrupts the overall profitable operation of your business very quickly. Finally, dis-

> **Steve Sez:**
> It takes luck and good planning to develop and train someone to be a great business partner. Many have tried and it's only the lucky few who have made it work for extended periods of time.

agreements between the two of you accelerate. Generally, every aspect of your business starts to suffer as a direct result of the growing disagreements between partners.

Because you are a significant owner of the business, when your business debts don't get paid in a timely fashion, credit reporting agencies will note this on your personal credit record even if you are not directly responsible for the company's cash flow management. Often, whatever happens to the business will impact your own credit report regardless of how much you own or what your position in the business may be.

Additionally, because you will have to sign personally on most, if not all of your business debt if the business fails to make its payments when due, its creditors may turn to you for payment. Now there's a great idea: NOT!

Chapter Summary

Hopefully, you now have a better understanding of the real opportunity and hidden costs of taking on a partner. When eagerness to launch a new venture combines with stress over cash shortfalls, many otherwise skilled and knowledgeable entrepreneurs take on a partner he or she knows little about, especially if they have only been "dating" for a short time. Sadly, this is often a recipe for disaster. Before taking on a partner, take a close look at what it could "cost" when compared with the extra interest you might pay for a hard money loan.

1. Choosing a good business partner is as important as choosing a good spouse. But in the case of a business divorce, the final decree will not happen quickly or inexpensively if things turn bad in your business.

2. Ask yourself if you are willing to share the decision-making process for *your* business—that's exactly what will happen when you take on a partner.

3. You may be personally responsible for your partner's failure to pay business obligations in a timely manner as it will affect your own credit worthiness in the short-run.

4. It can take years to dissolve a complicated business partnership which gives you more than enough time for your business to completely fall apart.

5. If you are uncertain about the pros and cons associated with taking on a business partner, ask your friends, neighbors, lawyer, banker and rabbi—all of them undoubtedly will have had at least one business partnership nightmare to relate.

Next Chapter Preview

Now, it's all well and good for me to sit here and tell you to be watchful of whom you choose as your business partner. Obviously, if you need capital fast, I'm suggesting that you should seriously consider a hard money lender because it makes more sense in many circumstances. But, you can't just look in the Yellow Pages under "Hard Money" or "Fast Cash." Where do you go to find one? Let's head to Chapter 7 to find out.

CHAPTER 7

Let Me Help You Find the Right Hard Money Lender

The darkest hour in any man's life is when he sits down to plan how to get money without earning it.
—Horace Greeley

Because most banks across the country are governed by the same federal bank lending regulations regarding cash flow, credit scores, debt to income ratios, and so on, you can feel fairly confident that if you have been turned down by one bank, it's probably going to happen to you at all other banks too.

The same is not true, however, for hard money lenders. As you learned earlier, hard money lenders are not subject to state and federal regulations as are commercial banks. As the result, each hard money lender has developed his own criteria and preferences for making loans with which he feels most comfortable. With this in mind, not every hard money lender will be interested in your particular project. Certainly don't take it personally, however.

In this chapter, we'll take a close look at what distinguishes one hard money lender from another, and which is the best for you in your specific circumstances. And, of course, once you can generally identify which type of hard money lender is the best for you, I'll help you with some instruction in how you can find him.

Let's move into a discussion of how hard money lenders differ in their business orientation, and how you can find the good ones more easily and more quickly.

Don't Look in the Yellow Pages for Hard Money Lenders

To start this discussion, you know that hard money lenders do not have their own category in the Yellow Pages. There are no newspaper ads for "hard money lenders," and there are no national or even regional industry associations or directories that are available to search. Everything has moved to the internet.

I know that many of you are thinking, "But I am not web-savvy so what am I going to do? I have no idea how to deal with the internet." Please keep the faith and believe that if I can do it, anyone can. I know a great deal about hard money lending, but not much about computers and the internet. I don't want you all to start thinking that it's time to bail out on this topic because you just don't get it. It's very easy actually, and you'll be glad that you take the time to follow us through the process.

Please remember that search results can be very dangerous to utilize if you don't know what you are looking for. So "sit tight" and let's let you in on some tricks of the trade as you search for hard money lenders.

Critically Important

First, let's get you on your favorite search engine whether it is the ever-popular Google, Yahoo search, or whatever else you might prefer. If you don't know how to do this, ask any person under 20 for some help, and I'm sure that he or she can teach you to understand basic search engines and how to deal with each of them.

When you search for "hard money lenders" in your favorite search engine, you will come up with more than a million search results.

When you are searching, use your imagination in entering the search terms that best describe your personal circumstances. The following discussion applies to any company or person who is claiming to provide hard money loans to qualified takers.

I'm going to teach you some tricks to separate potential lenders from brokers. I'll tell you how devastating brokers (and bad lenders) can be for you, your project and your financial health.

Having said these things about most loan brokers, let me explain why. What you need from a hard money lender is fast, honest service that hopefully results in a loan at the end of the process. A broker has no money. End of story. All they do is look for an appropriate lender (or not), and charge you fees up front.

Did you ever hear about the theory of "low hanging fruit?" Let me briefly explain it to you. If an average person has five projects that must be completed, which one will most people do first? The answer, as you can guess, is that you (and most people) will complete the easiest one first. It takes the least time. It is the easiest to complete. And you probably know how to do it the best.

Steve Sez:
Always, always, always be alert for loan brokers who represent themselves as hard money lenders. If you fail at this task, you will lose time, money, and maybe even your opportunity or your property! Remember that brokers have no money! Lenders have the money! This is advice that you cannot ignore!

In the world of loans, if a broker has five loans in front of him, which one will he usually do first? You're right of course: it would be the easiest one. He gets the loan done fast, he knows exactly where to go, and he gets his fee quickly.

Where does your loan fit within this search process? If your loan is not something that is easy to do, it will fall to the bottom of the list, and will probably only be worked on after all of the easier loans to place are completed. But, the broker who doesn't want to give you back any of the funds that you have already paid him will continue to tell you that he has many potential sources of funds. This is usually so, even after your loan has been turned down by the few places that he actually goes with his loans. This is a very unethical practice if he has no real lenders to go to for your loan. But when times are bad, brokers have to earn their money wherever they can. And that "where" is sadly from your pocket, unless you are an educated borrower.

The very success of your project, the saving of a deal, the payment to someone who is selling something that you want, and the other needs for which a hard money lender is the perfect answer, is going to be in the hands of your broker. Doesn't that make you feel swell? Me neither!

To avoid this problem, remember that the broker has no money! The lender is the one with the money.

After saying all of the above, borrowers are drawn to brokers because it is certainly much easier to use a broker if he actually has sources of capital. But it certainly has its costs. Among them, you will probably add some additional time to process your request before you close on your loan by a number of days, weeks or even months.

If you are not dealing directly with a lender (the actual person or company with the money), the introduction of a third party in the form of a broker will slow things down enough for you to possibly lose your opportunity.

If you use the services of a broker, he will need extra time to shop the marketplace with your loan if he has integrity. The response time will be slower with a broker than by going directly to the lender. Remember that it is not the broker's project. It's all yours. Therefore, he will never be as anxious to find the right lender for you as you are. He's not the one losing the deal if the money isn't found quickly.

There are other serious drawbacks to using the services of a hard money loan broker. Virtually all of the brokers with whom I have dealt over the years have required their clients (translated into: borrowers in need of "yesterday" financing) to pay an advance fee to "cover their costs" in locating the appropriate source of capital for your loan. And this fee is to cover what exactly?

Well, I've never figured this one out. There is absolutely no logic to this statement. The broker never goes to look at the property. The broker really never has to leave his house in order to shop around (usually on the internet, just like you are doing in your search). All the broker has to do is to pick up a phone and dial ten easy numbers to call a lender. And, therefore, the broker has absolutely no substantial expenses at all that I can identify.

Brokers are merely independent contractors who locate something for you for a success fee. When you list your house with a real estate broker, do you pay him/her a fee when you sign the listing agreement? Of course not. Who would do that? The broker knows that when the house is sold, he will get a commission. It certainly keeps the broker more mentally involved. Without any sales, the broker gets no commission. Try to explain this to a loan broker and see what you get.

The standard line from brokers is that you have to pay some money in order to prove that you are serious about obtaining your loan. The second standard line from brokers is that he has a lender who will be perfect for your situation. All you have to do is just to pay his advance fees, and he'll pick up a phone and get your loan placed. Isn't that silly to even consider?

If it's that easy, why does he need the advance fee? Why not just place the loan and get paid a short time thereafter? Because I hear it continually from borrowers who have dealt with brokers, I know that it is a big problem out there in the real world. And due to almost no regulation, brokers slip through the cracks with your money in hand.

You should always ask the broker if the advance fee is refundable if he doesn't find an appropriate lender for your request. If he says yes, then get it in writing! If he says no, then politely say goodbye, and call the next possibility.

Let's cut to the chase on this issue: you can use a broker, but my advice is to stay far, far away from them, especially if you value your money, your time, and your peace of mind. You can do just as well if not much better than a broker can in a shorter period of time. You have the motivation that they don't.

Having now warned you about loan brokers, in reality they can sometimes actually help you find a good hard money lender. There are some great brokers out there who actually try with integrity to locate a lender for you.

It will, however, take quite a while to separate the best brokers from all the rest. Of course, you only have one million brokers to try in order to get an idea of who is and isn't real and honest (hahaha).

Dealing with a broker instead of a direct hard money lender means that you won't develop a relationship with the lender as quickly.

Steve Sez:
I'm negative on brokers in general. They add a layer of complexity, added time and expense, and stress that you don't need at a time when you need performance. All you are paying them for is a hope and a fantasy that they can help you quickly in most cases.

There are actually many benefits to establishing a personal relationship with a hard money lender, and you may well be missing out on one of the most important of them as the result. Brokers play very close to the vest and hate to reveal their sources to anyone, preferring to control the entire transaction until the very end of the process. In all likelihood then, you will only know the name of your lender at the closing table or shortly before.

An Actual Experience

The Story of the Greedy Broker
Who Lost the Deal for His Client!

I received a call from a loan broker in Honolulu, Hawaii, regarding a borrower with a dramatic need for capital in a matter of days. After hearing about the collateral (remember, that's the most important thing to a hard money lender), I determined it was a loan that I could probably complete fast if the values were as represented. Furthermore, I really liked the other attributes of the loan which made me want to make the loan all the more.

I proceeded to negotiate the costs and expenses of the loan with the broker (our interest rate, our fees, our closing fees—exclusive of his broker's fees and so on) over the phone. Note that he never disclosed the name of his borrower to me, nor my phone number to the borrower. I then asked this broker what his broker's fee was in the event we can get this done for his client. His reply nearly knocked me off my chair.

The broker calmly explained to me that he has to live also, and that he really wanted to make $50,000 on this $450,000 loan in fees. To put it a different way, for his part in making the loan happen (putting us and the borrower together), he wanted to earn approximately 11 points (that would be 11 percent of the gross loan amount) on this transaction at closing. When I heard that, I was breathless and at a complete loss for a civil response to him.

I asked him what he had in writing from the borrower authorizing him to charge this large fee. "Well, it turns out that it was a handshake agreement," he confided in me. "But the borrower is OK with a charge of that magnitude." I was relatively certain the borrower didn't know that every dollar that goes to the broker is money he doesn't get out of the loan proceeds. Otherwise, why would he have told the broker that 11 percent was acceptable to him? Maybe he told his client that the 11 percent was inclusive of our fees as well as his compensation which was clearly not the case. The broker wanted to earn the entire 11 percent for himself to make matters worse in my mind. After all, he said, he has been turned down by all of his other loan sources so he has really done lots of work on this application.

In my entire hard money lending career, I knew that charging the borrower such a huge "finder's fee" or closing commission was completely beyond the scope of what is reasonable, responsible and ethical. I just wasn't going to allow the poor borrower to be robbed in this way. I wanted nothing to do with the loan if he stuck to his guns about his fee.

As part of a normal loan application on a potentially interesting piece of collateral, typically, I travel to the property, I inspect it, I evaluate the condition and value of the building(s), acreage, mineral rights, access, easements, and so on. Ultimately, it is my decision to recommend the loan or not. If it's a go, I also orchestrate the lawyers and title companies, I review the documents, I oversee the loan closing, and the biggest deal of all is putting my company's money at risk. In exchange for all of this work and obligation, I get closing fees that are extremely low compared to this broker. All the broker had to do was just make the phone call to me. How can that be worth two or three times the amount of our fees with all of the work that I have to do to get a loan approved and closed? Don't know? Neither do I.

I told this broker in no uncertain terms that I considered his fees more than excessive; that normally, a broker's fees would be two to three percent of the loan amount. He told me that it was 11 percent for him or he would take the loan elsewhere. End of story! I told him to try his best to forget our phone number. Greed is a killer! Sadly, it not only killed his income (11 percent of nothing is nothing), but it hurt his borrower, to whom he owed a very high standard of care.

Here is another piece of the bad news. The broker's expectation that he will be your sole and exclusive representative in the search for your hard money loan presents another drawback to using such a service. It is not uncommon for commission based brokers to want to work on a project that pays them a success fee only if they know that the project can't be stolen from them at any minute. How would you like to work on a project and get close to success only to be told in the final stages of your search that your client found someone who would solve their problems and they don't need you anymore?

Therefore, I don't believe that it is inappropriate for brokers to ask you to sign an engagement agreement granting them exclusivity in searching for an appropriate hard money lender for you. But, how scary! You don't know these people at all, and here you are being asked to throw your business future with this project to them without knowing anything about them. All you did was to find them on the internet with no ability to assess his credibility.

My best advice is to seek the advice of a great attorney who can review the broker's agreement and negotiate the right terms on your behalf. Ideally, you want a provision in the broker's agreement that allows you to terminate the agreement at any time for any reason.

Financially Important

There are some smart ways to find a good hard money lender—without resorting to the services of a broker. Use the same tools you use when you're looking for a good mechanic, hair stylist, or plumber: research, word-of-mouth, and interviews. You can easily outperform most loan brokers and save yourself time and money in the process.

Research

The best and most efficient research tool is the Internet. If you're connected to the Internet, go to a good search engine like Bing, Google or Yahoo! And enter one of the following (or get creative ... it doesn't cost any more):

- Hard money lending,

- Hard money commercial loan,

- Hard money business loan,

- Hard money lender,

- Hard money loans,

- Hard money,

- Bridge lending,

- Bridge loan.

or any other combination of those words. You'll get millions of hits. The trick is to sort them out according to your unique needs and to do it quickly.

As you look through the list generated from your Internet search, your goal is to find a lender that you're comfortable with, one who understands your loan and collateral circumstances and one willing to put in the effort that it takes to close it on your time schedule. Obviously you can't tell from a website who is and who isn't good for you; at this level, you can't really even tell the brokers from the lenders, either. So, you begin drilling down.

You should plan on spending quite a bit of time on the phone after visiting the available web sites. Talk to as many people as you can in the business. Read the information on the sites, research the links on the site to past clients and references, call and ask questions, use what you learn to conduct further research, ask more questions and only then, start to narrow down your choices.

A word about web sites: if a site seems poorly written, it may be a sign that this is either not a true lender or is a broker. Think of the website as your opportunity to "interview" a company before the first phone call. They should always have to rise to meet your standards.

You certainly can't always tell the lenders from the brokers immediately. Let's say you that you find a few websites that look interesting and seem to offer the scope of services that you need for your project. Hopefully, you keep in mind why or why it would not be wise for you to work with a broker. But how do you tell the difference?

The answer is amazingly simple and direct: look for *honesty*. What a concept! If the description of the services offered on the website seems like an honest disclosure and description of their process and track record, then they have passed the first test: the "gut test."

In your search for a hard money lender, trust your gut (women call it intuition; men call it vibes). If a company or individual doesn't feel "right," listen to yourself. They probably aren't for you.

You won't find a broker's web site with flash media in big block red letters pulsing "Broker! Broker! Broker!" But, you will uncover some subtle but important telltale signs that can guide your identification of brokers from lenders. Take a look at these examples and let your instinct guide you:

Steve Sez:
Web sites are almost always enticing until you look "under the hood". Take a minute to *drill down* looking at links, the site map and the wording and representations being made.

- **Loans from $50,000 to $50 Million:** If you find such a website that proclaims that the alleged "hard money lender," will consider loans from $50,000 to $50 million, almost certainly you've stumbled on to a broker's site. Genuine hard money lenders will never establish a loan range that extreme. Hard money lenders are always constrained by their capital base unlike banks that actually can make large loans within these limits by joint venturing with their upstream correspondent banks. You have either run into a bank website (unlikely unless they identify themselves as such) or a broker's website. Beware!

- **We Consider Collateral Located Anywhere:** If a website indicates that the company considers all collateral, any location, all borrowers, any amounts, and other overly broad and far-reaching statements, be on the alert for brokers. No lender can possibly consider all collateral, in any location, in any amount. It is simply not possible for one lender to understand all types of collateral no matter where it's located in any amount. This language is the representation of a broker, fishing for any deals he can get. All he wants are phone calls and front money. From there he will choose the easiest ones to work on (the low hanging fruit), leaving the other prospective clients hanging higher and dryer.

- **Come to Us for a Quick Closing:** This one sounds tempting, doesn't it? But beware here as well. This could well be another imposter looking for front money. The best way to weed these possibilities out is to ask for references. References will be the key here because, without being the lender, you will hear stories of longer closings than expected, or more complexities and paperwork than anticipated as well. By the way, this could be the website of a bank offering fast closings. Search the site and all of its pages carefully to identify "bank giveaways." Banks will have to identify themselves someplace in the site, and most likely it will be on the home page.

Three Warning Signs That You Have Found a Broker

Let's assume for a moment that your initial review of a website passes the gut test. So far, everything appears to be on the up and up and you believe you are contacting a hard money lender directly. Here are three additional warning signals that you should still watch for:

- **"Tell me all about yourself."** If your call to the potential hard money lender quickly turns to questions about "your" credit rating, "your" income, "your" outstanding debts, and "your" employment, you are definitely not talking with a true hard money lender; you have just met a banker disguised as a hard money lender. Or, you may have found a broker who deals with bankers. Hard money lenders don't ask questions such as these when interviewing borrowers. These questions will ultimately lead you through a lengthy bank process that will result in a probable turndown of your loan request. This is the very reason that you want to avoid bank loans when you are in need of fast funding. Don't be fooled by banks that advertise they can close loans fast. Underneath it all, they are still banks with regulations and requirements.

- **"I'm sorry, Mr. Brown, Ms. Green and Mrs. White are all in a meeting and are currently unavailable."** If the staff at the office claiming to be a hard money lender is large and you can't get the same person twice in a row when you call, you're probably dealing with an institution or bank trying to offer "look-alike loans" in order to increase their business. Most hard money lenders are in business by themselves, or at most, with just one partner.

- **"Just FedEx five years of tax and employment records to me and we'll get started on your loan application."** If the application process requires you to provide income tax returns, projections, formal appraisals, an analysis of bank balances, a verification of your income or employment, then run, don't walk to the next exit. You are clearly on a lengthy road to a potential turndown and the result: the loss of your opportunity.

What then, you might ask, *are* you looking for in website research? What are the telltale signs that you might (notice I said "might") have found an actual hard money lender and not a broker?

I would certainly start by looking for a clear description of how the business is limited by loan size, geography, property type, or some other criteria on their website. Anyone who admits to being limited in the types of loans they will consider is probably honest. Take it as a positive sign if the website includes a description of their property evaluation process.

Property evaluation is always a difficult topic because it involves a payment to the lender for an inspection trip, up front. But, didn't I tell you not to pay up-front fees? Why am I violating my own rule, you may ask? It is because in some way the potential collateral will have to be inspected and valued by the hard money lender in order to verify that it is as you have described. And do you think that he is going to take these expenses out of his own pocket for your loan?

Word-of-Mouth

Another good way to research good hard money lenders is by word-of-mouth referrals. How many times have you talked to a friend to find out if Bernie is a good: plumber, lawyer, therapist, photographer, painter or ...? Positive word-of-mouth advertising is one of—if not the most—important marketing tools any business can have.

Ask friends and relatives, as well as coworkers and business partners if they have ever borrowed money from a private source or if they have ever heard of anyone doing so in a successful transaction. If they answer, "Sure, someone borrowed money from a guy named Uncle Bruiser," then keep asking other people; and keep asking until you begin to find the same people mentioned again and again.

You're looking for a firm or individual who privately lends money on a regular basis. As I mentioned in the very first paragraphs of the very first chapter of this book: money is a touchy subject. It doesn't matter who you're talking with—it's touchy for you, me, Oprah, and even The Donald. But, remember: you are not asking questions to be nosy or intrusive; this isn't about someone else's financial situation. It's about choices—your choices.

If you find a friend or two who have borrowed money from sources other than a bank, get names, numbers and recommendations. Ask if you can use your friends name when calling to interview the potential lender. And remember that you needn't restrict your search to your own backyard; lenders located in other cities, counties, and states often consider making loans in geographic areas other than their own. We will cover that later.

This may seem to be common sense, but make sure that you ask your friends about their experiences. What did they use as collateral? How did they find the lender that they used or heard about? What were the terms? Was the lender easy or hard to work with? How long did it take them to close? How hard was the process? And then just let your friend ramble on about his/her experiences and make sure to take notes.

That is why you have two ears and only one mouth. You have to listen twice as much as you speak in this adventure. You'll acquire a significant amount of information by just listening and absorbing how others are treated by a particular lender.

As the lender, I can tell you that nothing opens a door faster than the recommendation of a good client. But you, the borrower, still need to decide for yourself—that's where intuition comes in. Word-of-mouth recommendations in my opinion are the most important marketing tool any business can have and hard money is certainly no exception.

Interviewing

Interviews? Yes, I do mean good old American interviews. This is where you decide who is going to lend you money. I don't mean interviews like the old 20 questions in a locked room under a bare, hanging light bulb. Take the time to think about what you'd ask bank representatives if they were all flocking to you for your business—play Donald Trump for a while. Here are some potential questions that may interest you.

Twenty Seven Questions and Answers to Discover with Whom You Are Dealing

As you begin questioning potential hard money lenders, be especially clear about identifying and weeding out the brokers from the lenders. Here's a starter list of questions that will help get you the results you need:

Questions	Answers
Will you fund my loan internally?	No, our loans will be funded from a distance and serviced locally. (broker)
Do you participate in the loan? If not, who does?	We don't need to participate in your loan; our loans will be funded by our investors. (broker)
Do you refer the loan out to someone?	Of course; we place all of our loans with the appropriate investor(s). (broker)
Do you obtain credit reports on your borrowers before you make decisions?	We will obtain your credit report as a matter of standard policy. (not a hard money lender)
Do you review tax returns to determine the income history of the borrower?	We will be looking at your tax returns to make sure you have the income to service any loan we may make to you. (not a hard money lender)
Do you use recent appraisals in making loan decisions?	We'll order an appraisal of your property and will tell you more later. (not a hard money lender)
Who does your appraisals?	Our appraisals are done by MAI appraisers in _____ (the city in which the property is located). (not a hard money lender)

Will I have multiple loan quotes to choose from?	We will have loan quotes to you shortly and you can choose the best one. (broker)
Do you make the final loan decision? If not, who does?	The final loan decision will be made by our investor(s). (broker)
Who services the loans that you make?	The investor who makes the loan will service your payments; in the alternative they may let us (referring to "us" the broker) service their loans. (broker)
To whom do I make my monthly checks payable?	You will make your monthly payment checks out to the investor who makes you the loan. (broker)
What is your approval process?	Our loan approval process will be explained to you when we have the interest of a specific investor in our group. (broker)
How many parties will participate in the loan?	We never know going into an application. It could be anywhere from one to a small group of our investors. (broker)
How long does it take for loan approval and closing?	Our loan approval process requires us to follow the requirements of the investors we choose to use for your loan. (broker)
Do you physically inspect the proposed collateral?	Sometimes we physically inspect the collateral and sometimes we rely on our MAI appraisers to complete the inspection. (could be lender)
Do you charge for this inspection?	If we do the inspection, the fee for this process will be set by the investor who is interested. (broker)

What is the size of your loan portfolio?	We can't tell you about the size of our portfolio. That is confidential information. (could be anyone)
What is the average size of your loan?	I can't disclose the average size of our loan. That too is confidential information. (broker)
What are the property types that you especially like?	We like all property types. (broker)
What are your geographic preferences?	We have no geographic preferences. (broker)
What is the dollar range of your loans?	We make loans from $25,000 up to $100,000,000; how much do you need? (broker)
How long have you been a lender?	There are members of our investment group that have been in the lending business for over 40 years. (broker)
Do you have loan officers who evaluate collateral?	Each of our investors has its evaluation committee. (broker)
Do you have a loan committee through whom you must submit all packages?	Each of our investors has its own loan committee process. (broker)
Can I take a look at a package of legal documents that I will be asked to sign at the closing?	The package of legal documents will be available for your review when the investor's in-house or independent counsel prepares the same, prior to closing. (broker or bank)
What is your loan-to-value preference (to be discussed shortly)?	We are flexible lenders; our loan-to-value requirements are set by our investors and can be at any level where they feel comfortable. (broker)

| Do you have references that I could call? | No, we don't have any references for you to call. They are very private and don't want everyone to know about their businesses. (broker) |

Once you've whittled your choices down to some true hard money lenders, it's time for references. Just as you've provided references to prospective employers at one time or another in your life, it's now time for a business to prove itself to you. And if they really are a lender who has been around for some time, they should have no issues with allowing you to talk to one or two of their references unless they have something to hide.

References

You would not let someone care for your home, your pets, or even your plants, while you were away on business without getting references first, would you? Why, then, would you ever consider taking a loan from someone unless you were confident that he has integrity and is honest?

Always ask for references. While some hard money lenders may try to hide out and tell you that this information is confidential, a good and reputable hard money lender will consider calling a few of their clients to ask if you can talk with them. If the lender or the borrower doesn't want to divulge client's phone numbers, ask if the hard money lender would share your phone number with his clients and offer to reimburse those clients for the calls if they are long-distance.

If the hard money lender balks at any of this or suggests that you need to apply and be a client first, RUN! You do not want to do business with anyone who won't let you check their integrity and honesty first by calling or at least hearing from a few of their clients. Some might hide behind the shield of not wanting to "disturb" their clients, and in that case tell the lender that you must have a way to verify their business ethics, their reputation, and their ability to help you as they say they can. This is an important key to finding the right lender for you.

> ## Steve Sez:
> Caveat Emptor! It's your loan, it's your personal liability, it's your collateral. Therefore, BE CAREFUL! There are many sharks in the water, all waiting for YOU to fall in! Do your research carefully and completely before you select one lender over another.

If you have any doubts about particular hard money lenders, check with the Better Business Bureau. You can also research lawsuit filings. Frequently, entering the name of the largest (or capital) city in your area with the words "district court" or something similar, into a search engine is sufficient to bring up a link to any online court filing websites.

If you find a lender who's been sued over and over again, I would run, not walk away. What an obvious red flag. This is true even if it's the lender who is suing. Check to see what the lawsuits are about. Whenever possible, try to determine who won each suit; this information can often be incredibly valuable—particularly if the lender you are considering has been sued for taking money up front and then not performing. Another cause borrowers have for filing suit against a lender centers on promises made to that borrower that are not being fulfilled.

If the lender is the one filing the suits, it probably indicates that the lender is exceedingly aggressive with his own borrowers. This is not a situation that I would recommend either. Either of these situations should be like huge flashing neon signs telling you about the character of the person with whom you are about to do business.

A Note of Caution

This is just a quick note to the cautious: In some instances when your vibes or intuition tells you to be careful—that you may be dealing with someone who is not all he says he is—it might be prudent to call a private investigator and order a preliminary, fast background check on the "lender." You would be surprised to see what a good PI can find out with very little effort or expense. You might be able to find out about civil and criminal litigation, criminal issues, and other items that could give you a greater insight into the person.

Wouldn't you spend a few hundred dollars to make sure that you are in good hands? I certainly would. All this checking and research is called "due diligence," and it's something you should do regardless of whom you hire. Reputation is everything. Investigate each prospective "lender" thoroughly before you decide to use his services.

Chapter Summary

Your project is important to your monetary success and future; don't gamble with them. Take the time at the beginning of the project to find the right hard money lender—it is far less expensive than getting tied up in court or finding that you've spent time and money only to get no results. Make certain that the person with whom you are dealing is as he represents himself. Be on the lookout for loan brokers disguising themselves as lenders always. When in doubt, research, interview, ask questions and get additional help finding out with whom you are dealing, if necessary.

1. Unless you don't have the time or patience to search for yourself, find a broker with integrity (possible I guess, but hard to find).

2. Use the Internet to search for hard money lenders that do business in your area and specialize in the type of project you are launching.

3. Be on the lookout for loan brokers disguising themselves as direct lenders—your interview should bring out the imposters.

4. Ask for references! If the lender tells you that he or she will not release the names of clients that you can call as references, then this is not the lender with whom you want to be doing business.

5. Ask friends, family and other business people in your community if they can recommend a good hard money lender.

Next Chapter Preview

In the next chapter, we'll take a look at what you can do to make the application process with a hard money lender easier and more successful. Getting a hard money lender to say, "Yes," to your loan application will be a major milestone toward your ultimate success.

CHAPTER 8

How to Increase Your Odds
of a Loan Approval

*The brick walls are there to stop people
who just don't want it enough.*
—Randy Pausch

What wall will you break through today?
—Tony Robbins

Establishing a good personal relationship between you and a potential hard money lender is important for a number of reasons. First, you naturally want the lender to say, "Yes," to your loan request. That's probably not too likely if he finds working with you difficult. Second, and mostly overlooked by borrowers, has to do with future projects. If you are successful with your first loan, your lender is far more likely to want to work with you again in the future. This relationship can be particularly important during periods of economic downturn when you may not have all of the resources you need to secure a loan from a bank or other sources. This chapter discusses how to build these positive relationships. Few people give much thought to making certain that their bank is happy. So, why then should anyone care if their *hard money lender* is happy? After all, do you think that both are merely just lenders? Do you think that they have no heart, no soul and certainly no feelings? Or, do you think that they are machines kind of like robots who act uniformly each and every time.

Hard Money Lenders Are Not Constrained by State and Federal Regulations

Of course being a lender, I would never suggest that good lenders are anything less than human and out to provide a benefit to you as the result. I would, however, point out again that in their business practice, commercial lenders are constrained by state and federal regulations; hard money lenders are not. Because hard money lenders make all of the lending decisions on their own or with the help of their loan committees, use their own funds to make loans, and are personally hurt financially when a loan is not repaid, there is every reason to make certain that this person is happy. Your financial future may be literally in their hands.

I know for certain that hard money lenders are in fact human beings with feelings, compassion (often buried deeply), a heart (sometimes faintly beating) and a soul. So then, what does make a hard money lender happy? I would bet that it's the same thing that makes *you* happy when you are getting ready to review a potential transaction. If you have a person who is completely ready with all of the honest answers that you need, it makes your analysis so much easier. And it raises a trust level that is hard to get any other way.

What does that mean for you? You as the borrower need to be as ready as you can be with a complete package of information regarding you and your collateral. Do as much advance work as you can. Your role—*before* you approach any potential hard money lender—is to be as well prepared as possible. You now know that to a large extent, each potential hard money lender will want the same things from you as part of their application process.

If you're planning to use real estate as collateral—and this is the most common form of collateral—there are several documents you'll want on hand as you begin the application process. I devote some time to this issue in Chapter 15 of this book.

Have you heard the phrase "time is of the essence"? In the case of securing a loan for your project, you can interpret that expression literally; time becomes money. You must meet a certain date set for performance or lose your deal.

Paul Simmons was a flight surgeon with the U.S. Air Force for nearly 20 years. Last summer he began planning his transition to civilian life.

Steve Sez:
Be Prepared! You'll make it easier to say YES to your loan request. Hard money lenders are only people and what makes you happy will make them happy.

Last month, he got a hot lead on a piece of real estate—a small four-plex located less than a block from the largest V.A. hospital in the region. The price was really a steal because the owner was moving out of town soon. If he could open his medical office nearby, he had the opportunity to pick up a number of patients on the very first day of his practice. The four-plex would be an ideal location not only for his medical practice but for the immediate revenue stream that the other three rentals would provide.

Lynne Goldberg is the seller. She is also an Air Force veteran, genuinely likes Dr. Simmons and would love to sell him her property. But, friendship and common history aside, business is business. Ms. Goldberg has also spoken with a number of other potential purchasers with regard to the sale. Intent on closing by the end of the month, Lynne places a "time is of the essence" clause in the real estate purchase contract.

This provision starts the doctor's clock ticking down. If Dr. Simmons fails to complete certain items by the set dates in the contract, he has committed a default under the terms of the original contract. If he doesn't close by that date, not only will he lose the chance to buy the four-plex at a great price, he also stands to lose the earnest money deposit that he has tendered to Lynne with the contract.

Fortunately, Ms. Goldberg did not include a "specific performance" clause in the contract, which would have compelled Dr. Simmons' to close on the date set for closing in the contract. In hard money lending, you trade a higher cost for very fast property inspections and equally as fast closings. This is worth it all when in fact time is of the essence. You want to be prepared to close as quickly as possible—that means having all of the documents related to the collateral readily available. When you know that you are ready to secure a loan, it is a good idea to start building a separate file for each piece of property that you own. In these files, put every receipt, every appraisal, all bank deposit slips from the rental income that you have received, a copy of the purchase contract if that is appropriate, a copy of leases if there are any, and so on. It is this preparation that will make a path to your loan closing as easy and quick as possible.

Some Things to Keep in Mind

As you read this book, make sure you are making note of items that will be critical to have before you apply for a loan with a hard money lender. Take your list of information and use it as a checklist for the material that you should have ready to produce if the lender should ask. Make a photocopy of these items and put the list on the inside cover of the file folder. Next to each item, make sure to make a note of the date upon which you obtained the item, and check it off. If a lender or anyone for that matter sees that list and isn't impressed with your organization, then you have the wrong person.

And, if you don't have certain items, the time to worry about it is *not* when the lender asks; then it's too late. Some items take preparation, ordering and the time for delivery; others require inspections to be conducted, environmental reports to be prepared and assurances to be drafted. You can't afford to procrastinate. Get it done now! You're bound to need it sooner or later anyway, so why wait.

By the way, so that you don't get too anxious about this one, in the 30 years that I have been a hard money lender, none, yes that's right, absolutely none of my borrowers have ever done this exercise. I believe that I would have been so impressed that I would have fallen over, and upon getting up, I would have done everything in my power to get the loan closed for them. That type of organization indicates people who are serious about their loan.

What Pricks Up the Ears
of a Hard Money Lender?

I'll answer that question with a question: What would you want to hear if you were the lender? Would you be comfortable working with a borrower who really doesn't know the value of his collateral, who hasn't made a personal inspection of his property in years and whose only interest in that property seems to be directly related to getting the loan? Most hard money lenders wouldn't want to work with that borrower, either. Most hard money lenders are more interested in hearing statements such as:

> I feel so comfortable with the value of my property that I'm ready to get you to the property as quickly as you can be there.

Or,

> My loan-to-value ratio is currently 34 percent and the loan that I want just takes that up to 51 percent.

Or,

> I can make the payments easily; a saving account I've had for years is available to help me pay off the loan if need be.

As long as you have acceptable collateral (we talk about the meaning of "acceptable" later in our book) with the appropriate level of equity, then your hard money lender is ready to listen.

Okay, you've done the research and found a couple of lenders that you like. You want to make this experience as good and profitable as you can for both of you. You are anxious to make your ultimate lender very, very happy to have met you.

An Actual Experience

Heads, It's Lender #1; Tails, It's Lender #2.

I once had a borrower who had called me while doing his research—just as he should be doing. When it came time for me to tell him how I evaluated his real estate upon a physical inspection, (of course including the inspection trip's costs, expenses and timing), he proceeded to tell me that he had found a lender who had advertised quick closings, no up-front costs, and fast decisions and closings.

Of course, I do not want to make a loan when the borrower will resent my terms, nor when he can get it for a lower cost. In this case, I suggested to the borrower all of the reasons why the other lender's (or broker's) program sounded too good to be true, particularly after our borrower had told me that he had been turned down by two previous lenders.

The borrower called me back the next day to tell me that, after thinking it over, he was going to go with the other lender. After all, the prospect of paying very little front money was quite attractive. I wished him well, and went on about my business.

Not even a week passed before I received a call from the same borrower who wanted me to fly out immediately to review his property. It turns out that the other lender was ordering a commercial appraisal that cost more than my entire inspection trip. Additionally, the commercial appraiser's schedule was backed up; it would be six weeks before he could even start on the appraisal. My question to the borrower was why did the other hard money lender need a formal appraisal? I think that it was a broker who was going to shop it around to his contacts.

This is more proof that if a deal sounds too good to be true, it ALWAYS is!

Chapter Summary

Do yourself a huge favor: invest the time necessary to make certain your hard money lender is happy and comfortable with your working relationship even before you actually start the process. Do whatever is necessary to make his loan decision easy—and affirmative. Create a file that contains all of the information, documents and valuations he will need to review when determining whether to extend a loan. If there is anything else that he needs to know, then tell him up front. Always be honest with your lender.

1. Having all of the appropriate documentation available for your hard money lender when you first meet is an essential step toward building a long-term relationship based upon trust and respect.

2. Get a sense of the approximate "loan-to-value" ratio of your collateral.

3. If you have a contract for the purchase of a piece of property, take note of any clauses that are time sensitive.

4. A "time is of the essence" clause in a real estate contract emphasizes deadlines for the completion of specific actions. If you fail to meet these deadlines, not only might you lose the opportunity to purchase the property, you might also lose any deposits you've paid as well.

5. A specific performance clause in a real estate contract legally requires you to move forward with the purchase of the property regardless of an inability to find the funding. You should definitely heed this warning. Finding money is never an easy process so plan accordingly.

Next Chapter Preview

How do you pick the right hard money lender? Chapter 9 will help you with that decision.

CHAPTER 9

How to Find a Lender Who Understands Your Collateral

Do not be fooled into believing that because a man is rich he is necessarily smart. There is ample proof to the contrary.
—Julius Rosenwald

Commercial bank lenders consider a wide variety of loans in a wide variety of circumstances. Hard money lenders, on the other hand, do not; they are specialists. Some hard money lenders make loans only on collateral in a specific geographic area; others may only make loans using restaurant buildings as collateral. It is in your best interest to make certain that the hard money lenders that you approach will be interested in your project. Once again, research is your best tool.

When you think of specialization, loans don't immediately pop into your head. You won't see a bank advertising that it only specializes in jumbo residential first mortgages—that would drive a lot of potential business away. But, hard money lenders are a different breed and can afford to specialize with their money. That's a tremendous benefit for you, as you'll soon see. Doing business with a lender who prefers your type of collateral will raise the probability of a loan and will make the process as seamless as possible.

Difference #7: Lender Specialization

Banks rarely specialize in loan types (which is good news and bad news). Hard money lenders do specialize in making specific types of loans. And, because of this specialization, you can limit your search to relevant lenders and avoid the incredible waste of time it is to sort through the millions of results on the web.

Steve Sez:
Know what type of loan you are seeking and what type of collateral you have. It will make finding a lender many times easier.

One of the first things you'll need to decide when choosing a hard money lender is what kind of loan you're looking for.

How do you do that?

Defining Your Project

Look at your project. Then, take an inventory of all of your potential collateral. This will help you determine what kind of a lender you need to approach. Perhaps it's even a specialist with sub-specialties. For instance, some lenders are looking only for artwork as collateral (a subspecialty would be French Impressionists); others prefer apartment buildings (a sub-specialty would be those who like buildings that are 100 units or more with no amenities). There are hard money lenders who only look at non-residential real estate in Lafayette, Louisiana, and others who prefer loans on any kind of real estate that is under $250,000.

Banks, on the other hand rarely have a specific specialty. They are general lenders who loan on everything from generic real estate to standard construction projects; from cars to student loans and so on. Finding a bank that will consider your type of loan is reasonably easy. Finding a bank that will loan you funds is an entirely different discussion (and is the reason for this book).

But, if your loan is at all out of the ordinary, commercial loan officers tend to shrug their shoulders and send you away without so much as a referral. They just don't understand unusual collateral (or loan circumstances).

Max and Dave Barber own the Brothers Garage, a successful chain of repair shops serving exclusively recreational vehicle enthusiasts. When they decided to expand by building a headquarters and "test" shop in Del Mar, California, and six new shops in Arizona, Nevada, and Oregon, they first approached their bank with which they had been doing business for several years. Max and Dave were surprised when the loan officer turned down their application for the expansion project because he was uncomfortable with their existing collateral—properties in four different states.

Every other bank they approached thereafter turned them down as well. One lender suggested they drop the idea of borrowing money from a California bank for the entire project and find banks in each location instead. But, think about that. Banks are most interested in their borrower, and secondarily about the collateral. So, if the borrower lives in California, and the collateral is spread out between Nevada, Arizona, California and Oregon, how do they establish relationships in the other states quickly? This is a perfect, hard money scenario, however.

The first filter in picking a hard money lender is to find one who specializes in your type of collateral. Think of all of the possible types of collateral.

Frequent Hard Money Collateral Specialties

Specialties for hard money lenders are as diverse as the assets they get offered as collateral. There are real estate specialists, local and national specialists, and oil and gas, intellectual property and mineral specialists. And, this list is far, far from exhaustive. Naturally, the more precise your asset description—like intellectual property for musicians'—the harder it will be to find the perfect hard money lender. But when you find just the right lender, it will all be worth the effort. He'll immediately understand what you have and know how to value it easily. You will know that you've found the right lender because it will feel right.

Let's take a look at some of the major areas of specialization in hard money.

Real Estate

The majority of hard money lenders are real estate specialists. Does that mean that's the only kind of collateral they accept? No, it means that they look at a wide variety of real estate, from residential property to rehab property, industrial land to warehouses, strip commercial property to multi-family residences, and unimproved land. And, they look at other types as well. Each lender will define his area of interest when you call. Or, if they are smart, in order to generate the type of business that they like, they will list it on their websites.

Real estate is a popular category with most hard money lenders because it is also what most borrowers have. Further, real estate values historically fluctuate very slowly making this form of collateral among the safest available. The specific hard money lender that generally works with real estate collateral will further focus on certain dollar amounts, types of property, and location (remember location, location, location?). This is one of the many reasons why it pays to start your search for an appropriate hard money lender *before* the need arises.

> **Steve Sez:**
> Most hard money lenders are real estate lenders—end of story. Some of them will consider loans outside of this "box." There is a great lender who is perfect for you and the type of collateral that you may have out there somewhere. Keep searching and don't give up. Success is closer than you think.

As we have seen above, specialties frequently include subspecialties. Because hard money lenders do focus on specific types of property, most of them further narrow their portfolio of loans to certain property types and locations and maximum dollar amounts. When you locate the lender who specializes in your property type, you are half way to your funds, all other things being equal.

Consider the wide range of sub-specialization within the broad category of real estate loans as you are searching the web. There are some who only look seriously at apartment building loan requests and others who'll only consider loans for triple net leased, stand-alone commercial property. Some lenders only look at unimproved land as potential collateral. Some lenders will only look at loans in Atlanta, Georgia and suburbs. I have even run across some lenders who focus only on construction loans to builders. The sub-specialty possibilities are nearly endless; but, you get the idea.

> **Steve Sez:**
> Make sure to describe your collateral to a prospective lender early in your conversation. You'll find many lenders who will and many who won't be interested in working with your type of asset. This will save you untold hours of time in your search activities.

Special Purpose Real Estate

Many hard money lenders will often consider special purpose real estate. These are properties that have only a few limited number of logical uses because of the cost to modify them accordingly. Let's look at motion picture theaters for an example. If you can remember as a child going to the movies, you may remember that the ceilings were high and the floors were sloping down towards the screen. This enabled people to see over the heads of those in the rows in front of them. Great idea, and by seeing the screen, most people liked their movie-going experience that much more. But, that particular interior design placed limitations on any future uses for the building.

As a lender, if I ended up with the property, what would I do with it besides put another movie theater in that space? The cost of leveling the floor, adding windows, adding new air handling systems into the building, putting new electric service into the building, lowering the ceiling and changing the interior configuration of the walls, bathrooms, and so on, is so expensive that it is a collateral class that I never considered. There are motion picture theater hard money lenders who know what the costs are, and how best to reconfigure these properties as a last resort. These are the guys to use.

The same issues exist with bowling alleys and big box retailers like K Mart or Albertson's—locations that now stand empty. There are hard money lenders who are experienced at resolving the problems associated with these types of properties, and again, these are the "go to guys" in this circumstance.

Bank Turn Downs

There are some hard money lenders that specialize in only bank turndowns which are loans that were almost approved by a bank but, for some reason, were ultimately denied. Some hard money lenders do set lower interest rates and associated costs for these types of loans.

Critically Important

If you are working with a lender on a bank turndown, make sure you are not dealing with another bank in disguise. If the lender asks you for credit reports, income tax returns, appraisals, verifications of employment, verifications of deposits, and the like, once again, you are in the wrong place. All you have done is to replace one bank with another bank.

Steve Sez:
Find Bankers who are willing to give you hard money referrals. Keep asking until you find the right lender for you. And remember, these lenders can be located anywhere. There is no requirement that they be located in your back yard.

Hard money lenders who specialize in these loans are easy to find quickly. Merely ask your banker who he refers his "turn down" loans to and you'll have the answer. And keep asking until you find the best lender for your collateral. If he says he doesn't know anyone who can help in these circumstances, ask other bankers. Or, ask the bank's loan officers and not the vice president or president of the bank. The loan officers who man the desks and meet with borrowers will often know more people in the community than the bank manager who does not often deal with the real world of the others in finance who are out there. They are really the best resource in this area and they often have a referral pool of alternate lenders.

An Actual Experience

*In Life, Isn't Who You Know Much More Important
than What You Know? In Mine It Certainly Is!*

Years ago, I had carefully developed a wonderful relationship
with a bank loan officer who liked my philosophy of making
loans. He continually sent me his turned down bank loan
applications; most of them, however, had too much debt
against the collateral for me to do any good for the borrowers.

One of the reasons that he sent me his turned-down
borrowers, however, is that he knew that I wasn't about to
steal his customers. I don't offer checking accounts, don't
have a drive-through lane outside of my office (I am on the
third floor of an office building), and was not offering any
banking services.

In one case, however, which was indicative of the types of
loans that I love, he sent me one loan turndown on a piece of
property only because the credit score was below the bank's
minimum requirements. Everything else was acceptable (as
it was for me too).

His suggestion to me was that I make the loan to the
borrower who needed his money fast, collateralize the loan
so that it was comfortable for me, and once the borrower's
credit score improved sufficiently, to refer it back to his
bank (and to him in particular) for refinance. Of course, the
banker was correct and within six months, the borrower's
credit score had improved, and I referred the borrower
back to the original banker for his permanent financing.

It was a complete win/win for all of us. I got a great loan
out of this referral, the borrower got his money fast, and
the banker got to "control" his customer. The borrower was
the complete winner as he got his money fast, didn't have
to pay much more than the bank was going to charge him,
and had a ready and willing banker to ultimately pay us
off in the near future.

In this case, I was acting as a bank turndown specialist because of my close relationship with the bank loan officer. It's great work if you can get it. (You probably have already guessed the rest of the story: my wonderful friend at the bank was moved to another branch, wasn't making loans any longer, and what was previously a great relationship was over in a flash ... isn't that just like a bank?)

Local vs. Non-local

Another decision you'll face when searching for a hard money lender is whether to stay in your local area or look to lenders across the country. If you've worked with a large nationwide bank or residential mortgage company before, you know that it doesn't much matter where you are in the country. This is even more true with the increasing number of owner-occupied, residential loans being done over the Internet.

Every hard money lender defines his portfolio parameters. Hard money lenders tend to specialize in either local loan requests or in regional or national requests. Just as large commercial lending institutions are doing more frequently, many hard money lenders are increasing their service area, stretching across the city in which they live, their state, region or throughout the entire country. You don't want to necessarily confine your search to local lenders; you might miss out on finding the right lender for you ... in Paducah, Kentucky (go figure).

An Actual Experience

This Is the Story of a Lender Who Turned Down Great Loans Because of Their Location and Type.

I once had a relationship with an occasional lender in Denver who continually turned down loans with very low loan-to-values (a hard money lender's ideal loan conditions) because the potential collateral wasn't located within driving distance of his house. One instance that stands out involved an apartment building in Kansas City—worth $1.4 million—with a current first mortgage of only $200,000.

The borrower needed only a $200,000 advance, secured by a second mortgage on this building, which is a complete dream come true for a hard money lender.

Unfortunately, my portfolio was completely in loans at that moment, and I went to this gentleman for his participation. He turned me down because the location of the collateral was not to his liking. Secondly, he really only wanted warehouses in Denver as collateral. He didn't understand apartment buildings and therefore wanted no part of these loans. I thought it was pretty short-sighted, but the golden rule prevails: "He with the gold, rules!"

Again, remember this lesson: Start your search early to find the right lender for your circumstance. I think that I've said this before ... many, many times. Believe me in this case and just do it!

If you find that the best vibes you get are from a lender in Colorado—and you're in Virginia—then, by all means, go with the lender in Colorado! Remember that this is a relationship that could last a life time. Finding the right hard money lender will take you farther and faster in your business than any bank could ever hope to do. Most hard money lenders have specific cities or states in which they are most comfortable

---

Steve Sez:
Keep a nationwide frame of reference when searching for a hard money lender. Out-of-state lenders can be the most flexible, most responsive, and the best alternative to local lenders.

---

and interested in making loans; very few actually have a national (or international) focus. Hard money lenders define their own "market area" and rarely, if ever, make loans beyond these borders. It's easy to understand how someone who has lived in Tampa, Florida, and suddenly comes into enough money to become a hard money lender will prefer to make loans in his immediate area. Other lenders—I was one such lender—are up for a bit of travel and will go to places they can fly into and out of in one or two days. Nationwide lenders are the best sources for you.

Loan Size

The size of a loan is another way in which hard money lenders specialize.

Some lenders will only consider very small loans while others will go to the edge of their comfort zone. In order to save time, ask about the lenders preferred loan size and whether he will accept larger and smaller loan applications. The answer to this question will assist you in weeding out the lenders who don't fit your monetary needs; you will be able to quickly move on and find the lender who is the right fit for you.

Steve Sez:
Line up potential lenders in advance—you don't want to scramble when you need to find money fast. Give yourself enough time to find the perfect lender for your circumstance.

Financially Important

If the loan you need is $50,000, most lenders located on the other side of the country will consider this loan amount too small to seriously consider; the cost of the inspection and the time for the trip will be out of balance with the loan request. If, on the other hand, you are looking for a $2 million loan, you are faced with the opposite problem: this loan will be far too big for most local lenders. The lender who will consider a loan of this size will have a portfolio many times this amount. Why? Because it isn't prudent for a hard money lender to make a $2 million loan if he has just $2.5 million in capital to lend.

Chapter Summary

Although large banks and other commercial lenders consider themselves to be "generalists," able to make loans on a wide variety of properties and projects, hard money lenders are not generalists. Hard money lenders are true specialists; they will define their own market criteria and make loans on properties and projects that fall within their area of interest. In the weeks and months before you need to secure your loan, begin looking for *and interviewing* hard money lenders. Find the ones making loans in your area and begin to get to know them. Don't wait until the day before you need to close in order to start the process; by then it will be too late.

1. Most hard money lenders who specialize in real estate will be willing to consider anything from residential properties to commercial buildings to warehouses.

2. Some hard money lenders specialize in bank loans that were turned down. If you are in this position, ask the banker to refer you to a hard money lender he knows in the area.

3. Don't necessarily limit your search for a hard money lender to your own neighborhood or community. This is true particularly if you are seeking funding for a large project. There may be a lender in a distant city with more experience in and more focus on your type of project.

4. If your loan will be relatively small, limit your search to your community or state. It doesn't make sense to pay a hard money lender to travel thousands of miles to inspect your property if you can eliminate these costs by working with a local lender.

Next Chapter Preview

In the next chapter, we'll identify and analyze the costs that you'll encounter associated with hard money loans so that you better understand how it all works. Let's take a look at some hard money loan cost basics: prime rate, interest, and origination fees.

CHAPTER 10

What Does a Hard Money Loan Cost?

*Save a little money each month and at the end of the year
you'll be surprised at how little you have.*
—Earnest Haskins

You can already guess that hard money loans are more expensive than bank loans—the interest you will pay is higher than what a commercial lender will charge. Then again, the value of a hard money loan can be so important to your business success that this extra cost can be meaningless in the short term. In this chapter, we'll take a look at hard money costs and expenses.

We know that interest rates on hard money loans can be in the range of 10 to 15 percent annually. This range of rates will always fluctuate with market conditions. However, no matter what you do, you'll never get a hard money loan at bank rates. No hard money lender will look at collateral only and give you fast cash for 6.0 percent interest and 1.5 points.

One of the primary reasons that banks can lend money so inexpensively is that they offer depositors a relatively low interest rate on their CDs, checking accounts, savings accounts, and other bank instruments. What they pay to their depositors is their cost of funds. When banks "borrow" from their depositors at these low rates, they can turn around and lend that money at slightly higher rates, and merely earn the "spread" (which is the difference between the interest they pay their depositors and the interest they charge their borrowers). Many people are willing to put their money into their bank accounts even though they pay relatively low returns because those accounts are insured by the government's Federal Deposit Insurance Corporation (FDIC) for balances of up to $250,000 each.

Hard money lenders, on the other hand, get their money from individuals, small pension and profit sharing plans, IRAs, inheritance, and the proceeds from the sales of businesses to name just a few common sources. For these lenders there is no FDIC security blanket; understandably, they want to be paid for taking a risk and lending their money. Therefore, the cost of funds for a hard money lender will always be higher than that of a bank.

Another reason that hard money is more costly than a bank funding is that these loans are perceived as more risky due to the fact that there is no analysis of the borrower. In addition, their funds cost them more because they have no depositors, as a bank does. And, a third reason that these loans cost more is that hard money lenders are only broadly regulated by state and/or federal law. Therefore, private lenders are free to charge whatever the market will bear within limits, which is always greater than a bank.

Steve Sez:
Investing in hard money loans is perceived to be risky, so lenders charge more interest to balance this "risk." Look at the value to you instead of the extra cost to accurately tell if a hard money loan is right for you. It's not what it costs that makes the difference; it's what you can make by using it that is the determining feature.

Because there is no organized "industry" of hard money lenders, no hard money industry associations or groups, and no directories or listings in the Yellow Pages, it follows, then, that there is no uniform way in which the pricing of interest rates gets communicated from one hard money lender to another. This brings new meaning to the term "your rate may vary" as it is definitely true when applied to hard money loans. It pays to shop around to find the best lender keeping in mind that the best lender and the best rates may not always occur together.

That's why I can't tell you exactly what rate you can expect to pay with a hard money loan. The best I can do is to describe the most current range of rates in today's marketplace. Don't necessarily take an individual lender's word about prevailing rates as they have recently fallen toward the lower edge of this range. It always pays to shop around. Remember that just because a lender is on the high side of this range does not necessarily mean he is a bad lender and vice versa. Do your due diligence carefully, and don't be persuaded solely by a lower interest rate. Always, however, be prepared to pay more than a bank loan.

> **Steve Sez:**
> Hard money lenders don't talk to each other (pretty unsociable, don't you think?) So check 'em out and play one against the other to get the best price possible for your loan.

It's All Tied to Perceived Risk

You know what risk is: it's the chance that something or someone will or won't work out the way you expect. The risk of any hard money loan, then, is a balancing act between the borrower and the collateral. When you don't judge a borrower based upon his credit report, payment history, and debt load (remember the debt-to-income ratio we described earlier?), you must increase the costs and fees to justify the risk of not really knowing the borrower.

The Greater the Perceived Risk, the Higher the Interest Rate and Fees

Put yourself in the hard money lender's shoes: he will want to have as many safeguards as possible when making his loans. What's the lender's best safeguard for a real estate loan? Clearly, it's to have a mortgage on the property as well as a nice yield on his loan. Before beginning our discussion of the various costs you'll encounter when closing on a hard money loan, let's first review "prime rate" and "origination fees" (also known as "points").

The *prime rate* is the starting point used by most lenders—hard money and banks alike—to help them determine what rate of interest they will charge for their loans. The prime rate is typically defined as the lowest rate of interest charged by a bank to its best customers. Where do you find out what the prime rate is at any given time? Easy. It's published in the *Wall Street Journal* every day in the section entitled "Money Rates." The prime rate is always on the move in order to reflect changes in Federal Reserve monetary policy to increase, decrease or keep interest rates steady at their periodic meetings.

Origination fees are often referred to as "points." One point is equal to one percent of the gross loan amount—one point (1 percent) on a $100,000 loan would be $1,000 for example. Don't worry, you'll understand the math easily here.

In the marketplace for loans, interest rates are often tied to the prime rate. By way of example, if the interest rate on a loan is "prime + 5" it means that the effective interest rate is the prime rate of interest on the date of the loan closing plus 5 percentage points. Origination fees may be as high as three to six points (three to six percent) themselves.

Steve Sez:
A helpful hint: In many cases, you should be able to negotiate a reduced origination fee merely by asking your lender. Don't be intimidated because you don't completely understand the language.

Bank's origination fees, by comparison, will often be in the range of one to two points (one to two percent) of the loan amount. Some lenders (even banks) will charge no points in exchange for a higher interest rate. Banks may also lower their costs if you bring significant deposits with you; they often view loans as a way to build their customer list. Hard money lenders obviously can't do the same thing because they are not banks.

Financially Important

Some loans are considered "floating rate" loans. This means that if your interest rate is tied to the prime rate, each time that rate goes up or down, your interest rate varies by the same amount. You will find these types of loans from a bank, a mortgage lender, and occasionally from a hard money lender. As you might imagine, a loan with a floating interest rate creates uncertainty and risk for you in the future. This is true particularly in periods of economic instability. With a floating interest rate loan, you will never know what will happen to your interest rate in the future, and therefore, a good guess is that it will go—up. What a surprise! Plan accordingly.

As hard money loans are intended for relatively short periods of time (on average, one year), if rates go up, you will only be exposed to this increase in rates for the balance of your loan term. Try a little exercise. If you project what interest rates will be in a year from today, do you think that interest rates will move wildly? In a stable economic period these shifts in rates are relatively slight; but, as the economy slowly recovers, you can expect more dramatic shifts in both directions. Still, it's the 20 and 30 year loans that are the most exposed to rising rates. One year is foreseeable; 10, 20 or 30 years are clearly and completely unpredictable.

> **Steve Sez:**
> Interest rates and origination fees for hard money loans are often tied to the prime rate (meaning that they "float"). Hard money loans are usually made for short periods of time so it shouldn't represent too much risk for most borrowers.

After yelling "Yikes!" think about your hard money loan. You need the money *yesterday* but you don't want to go through the hassle of providing a lot of documentation to your bank because you don't have the time. And what is worse yet, if the proposed security that you have to offer is a second or even third mortgage against your property, there isn't a bank in the world that will look at you.

If you were presented with this situation, what would you do? You would do exactly what the hard money lender does—price your loan with origination fees and an interest rate that reflects the level of service that he is providing to you. I speak with the voice of experience here: my borrowers weren't always thrilled with any costs and expenses that were higher than those of a bank. However, they definitely got a higher level of service, turnaround, and performance than they ever would have had with a bank, other commercial lender or most other hard money lenders. My higher fees and those of other hard money lenders, who also maintain an absolute commitment to integrity and service, will allow borrowers to close on loans that would be otherwise "uncloseable" by a bank. Think of the opportunities in which they could participate!

An Actual Experience

Here's What Hard Money Can Do for You: The Story of a Loan Application I Received and Closed on the Same Day.

There I was, enjoying my usual daily, early morning coffee in Cherry Creek, a very "coffee shop friendly" section of Denver, when I got a call from a fellow in St. Joseph, Missouri. He was requesting a loan on a "fix and flip" property in his city. The collateral sounded excellent so I told him that I was interested in helping him. He then proceeded to tell me that the loan had to close *that afternoon*. I quickly told him that a loan closing that day was almost impossible because I personally inspected every property upon which I loaned money. In addition to the inspection, my needs were many: I had to review comparable properties in the neighborhood; I needed a title insurance commitment to review, I needed a property insurance binder to review, and I needed legal documents to be prepared that were acceptable among other items. At that point, he told me the loan documents and title work had already been done for another lender, and if I would get on a plane within the next two hours, he would get the property insurance binder by the time I got there. His lawyer just needed to change the name of the lender and change the terms to mine.

After a lengthy discussion with him, I decided that if I saw the house, and saw the comparable properties that established the value, I just might be able to do it. In order to be prepared to close the loan when I got there if it was as good as the borrower represented to me on the phone, I went to the bank to get certified funds in the amount of the gross loan, payable to the title insurance company. Within two hours of the phone call, I grabbed a flight to Kansas City, rented a car, and drove the 45 minutes north to St. Joe. The borrower met me with a realtor in tow, and whisked me to the property where I did a walk through. As soon as we finished the property inspection, the realtor took us to four different properties that confirmed that the estimated value of this property was indeed correct. Next, we went to the lawyer's office in order to review the loan closing documents that had been pre-prepared to reflect our loan instead of the prior lenders terms. Then we went to the title insurance company to see what and how the closing process was coming. And, at 4:00 p.m. that afternoon, darned if all of us weren't at the title insurance company's office for a closing— an actual experience.

What's the silver lining to this increased expense for hard money?

Fast Money "Yesterday," With Very Little "Out of Pocket" Cost!

Hard money loans are relatively easy on the "up-front cash" front if you are dealing with a good lender. All of the loan fees and costs will usually come directly out of the gross loan proceeds. Borrowers won't have to pay these items out of their own pocket, however, as long as they can live with a smaller net disbursement for their project.

If you said, "But Steve, it still comes out of the borrower's pocket even if the costs are taken out of the loan proceeds," you'd be right. The major advantage here is that borrowers can finance virtually *all* of the loan costs if they have a flexible and cooperative hard money lender with whom to work. Yes, they still have to pay it all back sooner or later, but they get the money they need, fast, with a minimum of out of pocket costs.

In Hard Money Lending, It's the Price of Speed!

Now we've come to the part everyone wants to know about: How much interest is charged on a hard money loan and why? We know that interest on a hard money loan is greater than the interest charged on other commercial loans. We've briefly touched the surface in our discussions of this higher interest, but let's really dig in to *why* these loans are more expensive.

> **Steve Sez:**
> Hard money lenders trade cost for speed—there is significant value to getting your money fast! And it happens with little money out of pocket. What could be better?

At the beginning of the chapter, we discussed how banks are able to loan money at relatively low rates because they don't pay much for their funds.

Hard money lenders, because they cannot take deposits, do not have the same easy access to inexpensive funds for their loans as do banks. When a hard money lender chooses to extend a loan to a borrower, he is loaning you money that he could have invested somewhere else at the same or higher rates of return. That's just one reason why a hard money loan is more expensive. There are three other factors that drive up the cost of a hard money loan:

- **Speed:** You are trading cost for speed when you take a hard money loan. In almost every arena of life—from dry cleaning to package delivery—if you want it done today, you will always have to pay a premium. In this case, you are not getting your shirt cleaned faster; you are getting your money *faster*! How much is this worth to you? Within limits, a higher price is the way life works for performance.

- **Risk:** Risk is related to rate. Remember, the hard money lender doesn't follow the same procedures as a bank. This is fortunate for you because it allows the lender to act much more quickly than the bank. But, in bypassing a thorough review of your financial strength, the hard money lender has little information that might have alerted him to the risk and probability of default. Imagine the anxiety of lending money to someone and not knowing anything about their judgments, the liens on their property or even their bankruptcies? Unlike banks which thoroughly research the borrower's credit worthiness, hard money lenders look at property. By focusing only on the collateral, the loan inherently gets riskier, and the higher interest rates and all of the other loan fees are what compensate the lender for this added risk.

- **Little Regulation; No Uniformity:** The hard money business is largely unregulated throughout the United States. There are laws in each state that prescribe the maximum interest rates on commercial and residential loans (known as usury laws). In addition, *all* lenders are bound by loan laws in each state that may require licensing and oversight of lenders. Because most hard money lenders are individuals, they act in their own self interest, pricing their loans for as much as the market will bear. This type of lending is below the radar of most state's lending laws. Additionally, remember that the most heavily regulated part of the market is for owner-occupied residential loans and not commercial loans made by hard money lenders.

  This means that hard money lenders escape most of the governmental lending laws. Most state legislatures believe that if you are doing something with a profit motive, you should be able to fend for yourself. Sadly, I've seen many lenders, knowing that people come to them at a time when money is needed fast, charge excessive amounts of interest and origination fees. Additionally, borrowers often exhibit some indifference to higher rates; faced with the loss of very profitable opportunities, they are willing to pay more for immediate access to money.

We have discussed average interest rates for hard money loans—currently anywhere from 10 to 15 percent annually. It is important to understand that as certain as the sun will rise in the East each

> ## Steve Sez:
> We all know with certainty that interest rates will continue to change constantly ... and forever. Accepting a floating rate loan is nothing but a crap shoot that rates will be the same or lower through the life of your loan.

morning, interest rates will change. If you had the ability to peer into the future, undoubtedly you would see rates rise, fall or remain the same. If you looked twice, however, rarely would they be the same for long.

Banks can lend money at lower interest rates because the traditional bank loan carries all of the traditional safeguards. We've already discussed the security the FDIC affords. But, there are other safeguards for lenders. There are governmental programs that will insure portions of residential loans. Then, there is the bank's insistence that a borrower demonstrate sufficient cash flow coverage for the debt service (monthly payments), multiple sources of repayment, good credit, a good job and overall stability in their lives. In short, banks are well protected—in many ways.

All of these protections are missing from a hard money loan; that, in and of itself makes a hard money loan a greater risk to the lender and therefore, more expensive for borrowers. These missing requirements are what allow hard money lenders to get loans closed fast.

Critically Important

Please keep in mind that these safeguards exist only in the world of traditional bank owner-occupied residential lending, and not hard money commercial lending. With that said, let's briefly look at some of these bank safeguards:

- **FDIC:** The Federal Deposit Insurance Corporation (FDIC) insures deposits in national banks, most state banks as well as some other types of financial institutions such as credit unions that apply for special coverage from the FDIC. The current limit of this insurance is $250,000 per account. This means that the average owner of a checking or savings account covered under the FDIC has up to $250,000 of government insurance against the failure of the bank. This is about as risk free an investment as one can find anywhere in the world. The banks know that they are offering the ultimate in risk free investments to their depositors, and therefore, they offer the lowest interest rates possible on their deposits. If you don't believe this, just note how much interest the bank is paying you on your checking account deposits right now. This is the same for savings accounts as well. If they're paying very little for their money, they can afford to lend it at lower rates because they still earn a good return between their cost of money and their earnings on these funds.

- **Freddie Mac/Fannie Mae:** In this case, the government purchases first mortgages from members of the Federal Reserve System and the Federal Home Loan Bank system. When mortgages are purchased by Freddie Mac or Fannie Mae in groups from banks, borrowers benefit from lower interest rates. Think of it like group health insurance—your premium is usually lower when you participate in a group than when you purchase insurance as an individual.

- **PMI—Private Mortgage Insurance:** When a borrower needs a higher "loan-to-value" loan, banks require the borrower to secure private mortgage insurance. The traditional thinking is that if a borrower needs a large loan amount relative to the purchase price of the property, this person is a higher default risk than one who needs less, so this added insurance is needed for the bank's safety. This fee is paid to private mortgage insurance (PMI) companies like MGIC (Mortgage Guaranty Insurance Corporation) in your monthly mortgage payment. The length of time for PMI can be anywhere from five to 15 years and can add an extra $50-$150 or more to a monthly mortgage payment.

- **Multiple Sources of Repayment:** Banks hedge their bets on loans by requiring their borrowers to have multiple sources of loan repayment. That's why my friend Frank couldn't get a loan from the bank he'd been with for over 20 years. He quit his job to start his business if you will remember. Many of the rigid requirements imposed by banks on their borrowers are the result of the strict guidelines of federal banking regulators. They are charged with the responsibility of making sure that the national banking system is sound and fiscally conservative. They don't want banks making risky loans with funds that are being guaranteed by the federal government; this really isn't unreasonable if you think about it. Therefore, this requirement is an attempt to keep its loans safe. If you lose your job and want to start a business, or you are a commission earner (a real estate broker, a car salesman, a stock broker, etc.) and don't have a predictable source of income, it will be difficult if not impossible for you to get a bank loan. This requirement is often a killer for borrowers and is one that hard money lenders never consider.

- **Good Credit/Good Job:** A borrower with good credit and a good job is golden to banks. This means that the borrower has a track record of making payments on time and the wherewithal to make these payments. The bank remains within the federal banking examiners' guidelines by making loans to these types of borrowers. Hard money lenders don't look at a borrower's credit and income in most circumstances. The time that it takes the bank's loan committee to evaluate these criteria can add precious time to the closing schedule. The process of verifying income, reviewing tax returns, ordering credit reports, ordering formal appraisals of borrowers property, and reviewing financial statements and projections, as well as verifying all of this information is lengthy and can add weeks onto a bank's loan application process. This is one area in which hard money shines. These verifications, appraisals, and document reviews

Steve Sez:
In hard money lending the measure of the strength of the loan is in the value of the collateral; it's not about you. Banks are in a regulated environment for all of the right reasons. Hard money lenders are entrepreneurs largely unregulated by anyone.

are not part of the typical hard money process, and hence cut weeks off of the application process.

How to Make Your Loan Costs as Reasonable as Possible

Hard money loans are inherently more expensive for the reasons we've discussed; but, is there any way to lower the costs? Actually, there are many ways you can lower the risk of your loan and, therefore, possibly lower the interest rate and/or origination fee being charged to you by your hard money lender.

Seven Critical Factors that May Lower Your Loan Costs

If you understand and apply the following suggestions, I believe that, in a significant number of cases, you will lower the pricing of your hard money loan. These factors are truly where the "rubber meets the road" in pricing hard money loans! Read and study them carefully:

1. **Add extra collateral to your loan application:** Increasing the amount of collateral and the number of properties that you offer to a lender may run counter to your instinct of keeping as much collateral out of the hands of the lender as possible; but, after all, it's only a loan. You are putting your property up as collateral; you're not selling it or permanently transferring the collateral to the lender. After you pay your lender back, the lien is released from your property. If the hard money lender is only looking at the collateral as the measure of how much to loan you, the more collateral the lender has as security, the safer he should feel. Often, safety is directly related to the interest rate on your loan.

   While there is no guarantee that providing more collateral will lower your cost, it *will* at least make the hard money lender more motivated to make the loan quickly. Do not wait for the lender to offer to reduce costs. Why would he do this on his own? Ask! You are in a great position to expect a lower interest rate and a lower origination fee with more collateral. Go ahead—try it. You could be pleasantly surprised.

2. **Reduce the loan-to-value ratio as much as possible:** In this case, by adding collateral to your loan request with few if any loans attached to it, you are lowering the critical loan-to-value (LTV) ratio. That is the single most important ratio to a hard money lender. Lenders are in a much more secure position when the loan-to-value ratio on the collateral is lower. Because collateral is the primary measure of the willingness of the hard money lender to make you a loan, a lower loan-to-value ratio will significantly increase the odds of getting your loan approved quickly.

   Let's look at an example of this: Shelly Fulbright is an investor; she is interested in purchasing a small boutique in a rapidly-redeveloping section of southeast Washington, D.C. She intends to seek a hard money loan with a low loan-to-value (Shelly is a smart cookie). She has a $150,000 piece of property that is free and clear of any other mortgages and knows that the less she asks for, the lower her loan-to-value ratio, and hence, the better her loan looks to a hard money lender. The lender in this circumstance would rather loan her $50,000 on this property than $90,000. This will certainly raise the interest (not the interest rate) of any lender in closing her loan fast. It may even lower her interest rate and origination fee as the lower the loan-to-value ratio, the lower the risk.

3. **Bring a co-signer:** Another way to add strength to your loan request and possibly lower your loan costs is to attach a strong co-signer to your loan application. A hard money lender will not directly evaluate the additional signer on the loan. Why? Because he's focused on collateral. The thing he will notice is a strong financial statement that further ensures that, in the event of any loan default, there is someone to legally look to who can

make the payments and even pay off the loan if need be. In a way, this actually brings the loan-to-value ratio down (not really, but it is more collateral in a human sense). This additional financial strength should translate into a lower interest rate and/or origination fee because your loan is safer.

4. **Increase your cash flow:** Add as much cash flow to your loan application as you can. By doing this, you'll prove to the hard money lender that you can make the loan payments with ease. Once again, this may not directly translate into a lower cost loan, but it will certainly make the hard money lender feel better about making you the loan in the first place. If speed is what you're after, the more you can do to make the lender feel comfortable, the faster (and hopefully cheaper) the process will be.

   There are a couple of things you can do to add to your cash flow:

   Pledge something you own that pays you a monthly income (or at least show the lender your cash flow asset that provides periodic checks to you). If, for example, the building you are pledging as collateral is rented to a tenant and the lender can easily see that the rent payments may cover a large part of the monthly payments due him, he will be more inclined to move forward with the loan at a lower cost.

5. **Build on the relationship:** Keep doing business with the same hard money lender over and over again, because, as you make your payments on time, the lender will begin to feel comfortable with you. You will become a known borrower with a known track record and he may make exceptions in the form of lower rates and fees to keep you happy. Believe or not, some hard money lenders actually have a heart and will like the feel of having a tested borrower who pays his loan on time. This may be reflected in faster service as well as exceptions to his other

requirements—the ones imposed by the lender on his
unknown borrowers.

6. **Limit the term of the loan:** Take a loan for the shortest
   term that seems reasonable for you. The shorter the term
   (for example, take the loan for six months instead of one
   year), the lower the interest rate and origination fee may
   be. Don't, however, make yourself crazy with a short loan
   maturity that is impossible to repay just to make the loan
   a bit cheaper. You'll ultimately only hurt yourself. On the
   other hand, don't take the loan for an excessively long
   period of time because the costs will be at the higher end
   of the scale. Be realistic about your loan term.

   Most hard money lenders like to turn their money as
   often as possible because they earn a new fee each time
   they originate a new loan. Knowing this, do all you can to
   assure your lender that you will have the loan repaid in
   the shortest possible time in order to accommodate the
   desire for a fast turnaround of their capital. If you can
   show the lender that this is a realistic expectation on your
   part, he may show mercy on you with lower loan costs.

7. **Insure the loan for your lender:** Get some insurance for
   your lender. This insurance can take many forms and will
   be determined to some extent by the type of collateral you
   have or the type of business you're in. The objective here
   is to make the lender feel as comfortable as possible so
   that, if he can offer you a lower rate, he will. Examples of
   what might qualify for insurance would be actual life
   insurance on you as the borrower. If the repayment
   depends upon you and your income producing capacity,
   then life insurance or disability insurance might be just
   the thing that makes the lender feel comfortable.

   Other examples might be a guarantee of a property
   purchase by an independent party. You may have someone
   who will put into writing a guarantee that, at the end of six
   months or a year, he'll purchase an asset from you in an

amount that will pay off the loan. It may also be that this guarantor will agree to purchase the collateral at enough to repay the loan in full if you default on your loan obligations.

While any, or all, of these strategies won't guarantee that you'll end up with a lower interest rate on your loan, they will encourage your lender to act quickly in large measure because he will view the loan as being much safer.

Hard Money; Why Not?

You are the best person to answer this question. You should sit down with a projected balance sheet and income statement, and look at hard numbers. Compare, contrast and then answer this question: Can you afford *not* to get a hard money loan? Remember, you aren't signing up for this loan forever. It's within your power to repay or refinance the loan whenever you want. And, with the terrific terms you've negotiated by listening to all of this sage advice, your hard money loan will be a great deal; it can make your opportunity just that much more profitable.

An Actual Experience

The Story of a Stinky Deal Our Borrower Almost Got Into.

I was contacted about a development property in Memphis, Tennessee, upon which 20 houses could have been built. The borrower was obviously very excited about the profit potential for the land and the planned houses.

I reviewed the paperwork that the borrower had forwarded to me and felt fairly comfortable with the overall theory of the transaction; so I decided to go to Tennessee for a site inspection. After reviewing the results of my due diligence, I became very uncomfortable with the loan application. A number of projects in the immediate neighborhood were lying vacant, with both completed and uncompleted houses sitting unsold. Market conditions were weakening rather quickly, and I believed that soon there would be no buyers at all for the planned housing project.

My philosophy is always to tell my borrowers when I discover facts that they should consider before they borrow money for their project. I could have made a great deal of money on interest and fees if I had only made the loan at a much lower dollar amount, and kept my mouth closed. But, in the end, karma *will* come around to get you. I told the borrower the deal was a bad one from my perspective and why. After he had completed his due diligence, he agreed with me completely and terminated the transaction. I didn't make any money on the loan, but by letting the borrower know how speculative his deal really was, he respected my honesty and came to me for more loans. Karma lives!

If you've compared the cost of a hard money loan with the potential profit that you'll make on your project—and you determine that the profits far outweigh the costs of the loan then the answer to the question of hard money—why not—is really very easy. The answer can be found by answering this question: Will I make more than I'll spend by enough of a margin that it makes sense to take this new loan?

Pretty easy, isn't it? If the project is questionable, then your profits will be too small in comparison to the loan costs, making the loan risky for both you and your lender. If any little unanticipated costs appear, you could be in for trouble. And, of course, remember that the famous fellow named Murphy (of Murphy's Law—whatever can go wrong, will) is always your partner whether you want him or not. Therefore, in this case, you may want to rethink your need for any loan at all.

Steve Sez:
An incredible unintended benefit of using a hard money lender is that you will quickly find out what the "true" value of your property is today. It's like having a confidant without the obligation or the payment.

This is really a good exercise to evaluate strength of the underlying project and its profit potential before you get involved with a marginal deal. I have always been sensitive to this equation, and when a project doesn't make economic sense to a borrower, neither does the loan for a lender. In these circumstances, the responsible lender should always recommend that you NOT take the loan.

How High Can the Interest Rate Go on Hard Money Loans?

Interest is the reward to a lender for the risk, use and the time value of money. However, the law does protect you somewhat. Almost every state has what are known as usury laws. *Usury* is the body of law which makes it illegal to charge interest above a stated rate. The maximum rate is determined on a state-by-state basis. Therefore, what is usury in one state may not be usurious in another.

Actually, some states do not have any usury laws. In the states that do, the law places a limit on the amount of interest a lender can charge on your loan. In the non-traditional money lending business, there are always going to be those who operate on the fringes of the law, and even some who operate outside of those boundaries. Make certain that the person or company with whom you are doing business comes recommended and that you have done research into who they are.

> **Steve Sez:**
> Thinking about the fees, interest expense, and due diligence costs of a hard money loan forces you to think about whether the project makes sense for you in comparison to its cost. When an "opportunity" fails to make monetary sense in light of the costs, then the loan doesn't either.

As the result of this research, discussion, referral and investigation, you should feel comfortable with the lender before you go forward with anyone. If, however, any part of the due diligence process seems unusual or raises red flags within you, then back away from the lender ... now! Do not work with just any lender because you need your money fast. The ramifications of taking a loan from a bad lender are not pleasant.

Eleven Indicators of a Shady Lender (or maybe not even a lender at all) are presented below. Be wary of the following:

1. **Lenders with little concern for your collateral:** Lenders who are not concerned with your collateral, are too anxious to make you a loan, or offer to dispense with the formalities of due diligence in order to lend you money are probably not true hard money lenders. They are in it to own your property. Beware!

2. **Lenders who want to be paid frequently:** Lenders who want weekly or irregular payments are not operating in a typical manner and you should use extreme caution before signing any agreement with them. Doesn't it sound like a "bruiser" loan? Beware!

3. **Lenders who are attorney averse:** "We don't need no stinkin' lawyer! We can draft the closing documents ourselves!" Lenders who don't use a lawyer to prepare their loan documents not only place you at risk for poor drafting. They aren't exercising prudent lending policies. Beware!

4. **Easy lenders:** Lenders who offer to lend you money more easily than it should be, when others have turned you down, should be an immediate concern. Also, be very wary of a lender who is willing to lend you more than the security on the loan would suggest appropriate. Who is this guy? Obviously not a legitimate lender at all. Beware!

5. **Lenders who want to know more about you than is appropriate:** Lenders who ask for personal documents that seem unusual (like birth certificates or credit card applications) may be more interested in assuming your identity than in loaning you money. Beware!

6. **Lenders who speak at the speed of light:** Hard money lending is a serious business for serious investors; fast-talking used-car salesman types who fail to adequately describe the loan to you, including its costs, when and if you ask questions, do not make good resources. Beware!

7. **Lenders who don't want you to read the loan documents:** Here's the approach: "Just sign here; trust me, these are our standard loan documents." Lenders who don't allow or discourage you from reading the loan documents but say to just trust that the loan is a standard loan, done all the time, are not being truthful. You should know that there is no such thing in the world of hard money lending as a "standard" loan or a closing that has "standard loan documents." Beware!

8. **The "take it or leave it" lender:** Lenders who claim that they offer "one size fits all" loan terms or who don't give you a choice of loan terms should be avoided at all costs. Beware!

9. **Overnight lenders:** Lenders who ask for loan terms such as, "We give you $1,000 today and on Friday, you pay us back $2,000," are not hard money lenders. Those who offer loans in very short increments only—for example, loan maturities each week, or each month—can sink you and your project in a very short period of time. Remember the days of cement overshoes? Beware!

10. **Lenders who don't need collateral:** Hard money lenders expect collateral—always. Run, don't just walk away from lenders who claim, "We don't need collateral. After all, we have a life insurance policy to protect ourselves." Those who require you to put life insurance on yourself as an element of "additional safety" for the lender (there are times, however, where life insurance is actually a critical element of a good hard money loan) have a repayment formula that could likely prove very, very unhealthy for you. Beware!

11. **Lenders who want their payments made in cash:** Here is an obvious sign that you are not dealing with a real business person. Are they actually money launderers? Are they drug dealers? Are they tax evaders? In any case, stay far away from people like this. Beware!

In general, listen to your intuition when it comes to people. Borrowers who need money are probably less discriminating in their times of need. Money needs can take precedence over other aspects of the loan and cause a borrower to fail to pay attention to important details. Be on your guard! Don't do business with people who can harm you financially, or even worse, physically.

Listen to your "gut"; ask others to meet the lender with you and help you evaluate the people with whom you are considering doing business. If you have any doubts, it's better to find a new lender than to do business with a bad person. I know it's hard to walk away from the lure of a loan, especially if you needed the money yesterday. And lenders are not easy to find. But, if you get into the clutches of a bad guy, you'll regret the day you signed up to do business with him. He'll make your life miserable. You can lose your property, spend small fortunes on legal fees, and/or pay outrageous amounts just to get out of the deal (much, much more than you ever bargained for).

Steve Sez:

If a hard money lender suggests an interest rate in excess of the legal limit: It's, "Feet, don't fail me now!!" Run, don't walk away! Report the fraudulent lender to the Better Business Bureau, your state's attorney general, your city's district attorney, your attorney and the FBI if the lender is out of state. Here an ounce of prevention is truly worth a pound of cure!

Another way to judge the legitimacy of the people and the transaction is to review the loan documents before you close the transaction—better still, have a lawyer review the documents. If the loan agreement doesn't pass the "smell test," then by all means, take steps to get out of the loan as quickly as possible *before you close*. If you have any doubts about the people, the terms or any other aspect of the loan, notify your local police department, your lawyer, your accountant, or any other business professional in your life. Don't play with fire.

Chapter Summary

There is no one description for a hard money lender. There is no one form of a hard money loan. And, there is no one set of rates and expenses you can expect to pay. Hard money lending is a highly individual process; in essence, a hard money loan is an agreement between two people—you and the lender. This gives you a high level of flexibility and, at the same time, a lot of things to consider before closing on that loan.

1. Search carefully for the right hard money lender for your project.

2. If your project—or the risk—is large, expect to pay a higher rate of interest as well as fees.

3. Hard money loans typically carry a higher rate of interest and associated costs than a commercial loan. Make sure that the value of the opportunity is there for you before you sign your loan documents.

4. Banks can afford to make loans at a lower rate of interest because they have a larger reservoir of "inexpensive" money from which to make these loans. Hard money lenders are using their own funds in most cases. This is one of the primary reasons for the higher loan cost.

5. There are strategies you can use to lower the cost of a hard money loan; consider every alternative as you negotiate the terms of the hard money loan.

Next Chapter Preview

In the next chapter, we'll explore acceptable forms of collateral including 29 different kinds of real estate you can use as security for your loan.

CHAPTER 11

The Heart of Hard Money: Acceptable Collateral

Success seems to be connected with action. Successful people keep moving. They make mistakes, but they don't quit.
—Conrad Hilton

Without question, hard money lenders are most interested in the quality and value of the collateral you bring to the table with your loan application. While it is natural to think first of real estate, there are actually a number of forms of collateral that many hard money lenders will also consider. Earlier, we spoke of hard money lenders who specialize in lending funds for certain types of projects. We have also now seen a bit about lenders who will consider non-real estate collateral as well.

As we saw in Chapter 4, flexible and creative loan terms are much more plentiful when you're working with a hard money lender than with most banks. Hard money lenders are much more flexible about your collateral as well.

Acceptable Collateral

Acceptable forms of collateral for a hard money loan include, but certainly aren't limited to: real estate, stocks and bonds, accounts receivable, pre-public and public company stock, and, in some circumstances, even the assets of a bankrupt company.

As promised, I'll run through a partial list of acceptable real estate collateral for a hard money loan. Some lenders will have collateral preferences that aren't listed here, therefore, you'll have to do your homework to find those lenders who will consider your specific collateral.

Steve Sez:

All types of real estate are acceptable collateral to a hard money lender somewhere.

Real estate is by far the most common form of collateral offered, because it is the asset that the largest segment of the borrowing population owns.

Thirty Three Common Types of Real Estate Collateral

We'll talk a lot about real estate in Section Two but this is a starter list of property that can be considered for a hard money loan (it's far from exhaustive—it's just meant to give you some ideas):

- Residential property,

- Commercial property,

- Industrial property,

- Undeveloped property,

- NNN leased real property (This is referred to as "triple net leased property" which is, typically, leased property with tenants who pay all of the costs of taxes, insurance and property maintenance.),

- Multifamily residential property,

- Manufacturing facilities,

- Time share properties,

- Condominium properties,

- Co-op properties,

- Damaged properties,

- Warehouse properties,

- Recreational properties,

- Environmentally contaminated properties (yes, you heard me),

- Partially constructed properties,

- Mini warehouse properties,

- Airport hangar properties,

- Single tenant properties,

- Lakeshore properties,

- Hotel/motel properties,

- Entertainment venues,

- Vacant properties,

- Strip commercial properties,

- Mixed-use properties (like mixing an office with a residence in one building),

- Rural properties,

- Urban properties,

- Foreclosed properties,

- Properties in need of rehabilitation work,

- Special-purpose buildings,

- Agricultural properties,

- Mountain properties,

- Internationally located properties, and

- Boat harbors.

Non-Real Estate Collateral

We'll describe non-real estate forms of collateral in more detail in Section Three, but here's a taste of three types of collateral that can be used to secure your loan that are not real estate: stocks and bonds, accounts receivable, and the assets of bankrupt companies.

Financial Collateral Including Stocks and Bonds

Some hard money lenders will make loans on both restricted and free trading shares of common stock and bond issues. Here's a partial list of this type of collateral.

Ten Varieties of Financial Collateral

1. Traded and listed stocks and bonds,

2. Shares in mutual funds,

3. Asset-backed, secured preferred stock (public or private),

4. Shares of stock and/or bonds in companies that are about to go public,

5. Restricted stock (or stock that can't be sold immediately),

6. Bonds or other debt instruments of private companies, and

7. Limited partnership interests or shares in REITs (real estate investment trusts) that generate real estate income,

8. Interests in oil and gas royalty programs,

9. Over the counter traded stock, or

10. Stock traded on foreign exchanges.

This list is far from being a complete list of the various types of financial collateral. Hard money lenders will consider many types of non-real estate collateral as long as you can prove the value in a verifiable way.

Accounts Receivable Financing/Factoring

Accounts receivables are monies owed to you because you sold a product or provided a service to a third party. Accounts receivable financing is exactly what it sounds like: You are using a company's accounts receivables as collateral for a loan.

Factoring of accounts receivable, on the other hand, is a technique that transfers the title (the ownership) of your account receivable from you to the "accounts receivable factor." The accounts receivable factor is actually the person or company who is purchasing your paper (as it is known) and providing you with funds as the result. You are actually selling your account receivable to the purchaser (the factoring company).

Steve Sez:

An acceptable account receivable is one that is due with finality by a company with great credit. An account receivable is an unequivocal obligation to pay someone or a company for what was received by the obligated party.

When you sell your account receivables, you will have a right to repurchase the account(s) at a higher price, the difference being the amount of profit (or interest) charged on the transaction. This is often the financiers preferred method as it yields much more income to the factoring company. It's outside the usury laws because it's not a loan. It's a sale. Therefore, it takes the receivables off of the company's balance sheet so that if a bankruptcy arises before any receivable is repaid, it isn't "owned" by the bankrupt company and is thereby protected from the reach of creditors.

Some hard money lenders develop custom programs for their borrowers with specific goals in mind. It is important that selling or borrowing against accounts receivable is not seen as a sign of weakness to your customers or to your competition. Accounts receivable financing and factoring can be designed by a sophisticated hard money lender to provide that:

- Your customers think that it's your own finance division doing the collecting,

- The account receivable factor (i.e. lender or purchaser) will never call your customers,

- Sometimes you can negotiate to have even marginal receivables allowed as collateral for a loan,

- The transaction is structured as financing instead of factoring in order to save you money and to keep the transaction as simple as possible. In addition, factoring is a special type of "financing" about which few understand fully.

Be aware of the power of borrowing on your accounts receivable. You should only offer your good accounts as collateral for an accounts receivable loan. If you try to pass off only the accounts about which you are nervous, a smart hard money lender is going to be uncomfortable about loaning you more money if they think that you have no ability to distinguish between honest people and the bad guys.

Debtor-in-Possession Financing

A *debtor-in-possession* is a term of art for a management team of a company that may have gone into a Chapter 11 bankruptcy filing (reorganization). They still may remain in possession of its assets rather than having to liquidate them to pay off debts.

Many times a bankruptcy court will allow the current management to remain in control of the operations until they come up with a plan of reorganization. Other times, the creditors prevail and a new court-appointed management team moves into the control position, with court oversight, in order to preserve what's left for the creditors, or to try to reconstruct the operations of the company so that it can move forward and become profitable.

A few hard money lenders specialize in debtor-in-possession financing and this specialty sets them apart from the majority of other hard money lenders. These lenders can provide financing in many creative ways to a company after they have filed in bankruptcy court. By blending more common collateral categories with the fact of the bankruptcy, a hard money lender can typically develop a means of providing funds to a company that would otherwise not be able to obtain money elsewhere.

One of the things that make this type of financing so attractive to a hard money lender is the fact that loans to companies that have filed bankruptcy have to be approved by the court. Therefore, a loan on collateral owned by the company in Chapter 11 will be "sanctioned" by the court. In effect, the court confirms the rate and other terms, but also places the hard money lender's indebtedness in a senior position. Usually, this security is more senior than debt, equity, and any other securities issued by a company. It gives a troubled company a new start, albeit under strict conditions.

Chapter Summary

Although you may naturally think of real estate as the collateral of choice for a hard money lender, that is not always true. There are a number of lenders who actually prefer collateral to be in other forms such as collectables, rare automobiles and technology, accounts receivables, stock and other financial instruments.

1. Consider your options in terms of the collateral you can pledge before you approach a hard money lender.

2. Real estate collateral can take many forms. Look for hard money lenders who are willing to consider other real estate such as vacation homes, warehouse or other property you may have.

3. If your company has been in business for some time and you have outstanding accounts receivable, speak with a hard money lender who is willing to accept these as a form of collateral. This may be your key to getting the money that you need.

Next Chapter Preview

There are two final items to cover before we leave Section One and go on to the real estate section: establishing a relationship with your hard money lender and how to be on the lookout for some of critical danger signs. Danger signs of what? ... (Review the next chapter with regard to this question.)

CHAPTER 12

Relationships and Warnings

For me, life is continuously being hungry.
The meaning of life is not simply to exist, to survive,
but to move ahead, to go up, to achieve, to conquer.
—Arnold Schwarzenegger

Although today's banks are probably multi-state if not multi-national, their advertisements always seem to harken back to an earlier time when someone in business actually knew and had a long-standing positive relationship with his or her banker. While this may still be true in some of the country's smaller communities, it is unlikely that this is the banker who will be in a financial position to lend you hundreds of thousands of dollars to launch your next venture. Picking the right lender for you and your project is critically important to your long-term success. Let's review this area carefully.

One of the most striking differences you'll find between banks and hard money lenders is that a hard money lender is someone with whom you will be working each time you have a financing need. It is this long term relationship potential that will become a highly valued asset if you repay your loan on time, are always honest with your lender, and are always entirely up-front in communication with your lender.

Steve Sez:
Developing a personal relationship with a hard money lender is one of the benefits of using one lender over and over again. It'll make future borrowings much easier. This is as close as you can come to the days of old local banks with familiar and stable local bank officers.

Naturally, it's a gross generalization to say that every bank has enormous turnover in staff and executives. It's likely, however, that when you are working with a large national bank, the opportunity to work with the same loan officer for more than a few years is usually slim to none ... and slim left town. That is clearly *not* the case with a hard money lender.

Okay, you've whittled down your selection of hard money lenders by completing your research, checking references, and fitting your loan within the specialties of each particular lender. The two acid tests—the same thing you use to choose anything of value—are relationship and perceived value. My advice is, don't let this decision be driven exclusively by cost alone. There are many bad hard money lenders out there who can cut their rate to you a small amount just to get your business. Once you have signed the loan documents, however, it's then too late to get out of the loan without incurring the attorneys fees, the origination fees, the title insurance fee, and all of the other closing costs. If you have regrets thereafter, it's like divorcing your spouse immediately after the wedding. It will be a complex and long row to hoe. And, this is not to even mention the costs and expenses that come your way, plus the inevitable legal fees.

Difference # 8: Relationships

You want a relationship with your lender that extends through the entire life of the loan at a minimum. With a national bank, you'll be lucky to deal with the same person from the loan closing to the payoff of your loan. You can easily, however, build a lasting relationship with your hard money lender; he'll be there for you time and again. What does relationship mean in this context? It means a comfort level, someone with whom you communicate easily, and a lender who gives back the respect he expects from his customers.

Have you ever met someone and found that individual so easy to talk with that you feel that you've known him or her all your life? That's also the kind of feeling you want from the hard money lender you choose. It's not that you are borrowing money to make a friend, but you do want someone with whom you believe that you can work over the years. You want someone who knows that you are a person of your word and that you will never purposefully fail to perform on your promises.

Critically Important

Remember: You decide on who you want to work with to secure a hard money loan; this is *your* choice. If you don't feel comfortable with any of the first set of hard money lenders you interview, keep looking. It is important that you recognize that your position is one of need, and in these times, you could be vulnerable to hearing only what you want to hear from just about anybody. Because of this, you don't want to opt for the first lender you come upon because "you have no other choice" and besides, he said that he could help and make you a loan with a great deal of assurance.

At the end of the day it is ultimately how you and the hard money lender relate to one another. This is a transaction between two people who need to communicate with each other. It is not about you dealing with a loan servicing person who is employee number 12,439 in Charlotte, North Carolina, where your lender is headquartered, who couldn't care less about you. Actually, most of the time, employee number 12,439 will view dealing with you as a nuisance rather than as a help to their customers.

Now this next sentence isn't quite as true for bankers in small towns as it is for cities: The bigger the bank, the quicker the banker leaves. In a normal time, bankers are always seeking positions with better titles, more responsibilities and bigger salaries, of course. Bank officers are an upwardly mobile group in general, which increases the chances they will jump to another bank at the drop of a better offer. And then where are you?

It's unfortunately all too common to be in the middle of a loan application process to find that the person you began dealing with

152

When the Bank Says No!

at the start of the process isn't the person now reviewing the loan application. Your loan officer gets booted upstairs or out the door and you have to start all over again building a new relationship. Sadly, you can't build trust overnight. That takes years of experience in living through good, bad and ugly times with that person.

Bankers are a disposable commodity in large national banks. Locally owned and operated banks seem to have the formula for keeping loyal and good employees over the years, but national banks don't have it down just yet. This hurts you as a borrower because each time you go back to a bank for a loan, you have to reintroduce yourself to a new loan officer, explain your business, and walk them through your needs and requirements. You can rest assured that the loan officer with whom you have just met at a national bank couldn't pick you out of a lineup 30 minutes after you walk out the door. They're just not as customer oriented as a local lending officer. Their salary continues whether or not you get or take a loan. There is no accountability with most national or regional banks.

Can I guarantee that this won't happen with any hard money lender? No, of course, I can't. But I can say with certainty that it doesn't happen often. Hard money lenders aren't going to be carried away by mergers or acquisitions as are banks and mortgage companies. As your experience grows with your hard money lender, you'll become comfortable with what he will need to look at each time you need more financing. Your hard money lender will also become comfortable with the types of projects or property that you bring to them. Most important to your relationship going forward is how you perform on your commitments to him and what you do when you are having a problem making your loan payments in a timely fashion.

Most hard money lending companies are owned and run by one person. That person is typically "the company." Even if the business is being run by a few people, the odds are in your favor that every time you call, you will get the same people that have been there for years. By selecting the right lender at the outset, you'll be developing the relationship that was so valued by clients of small banks in the good old days.

You may say, "But Steve, first you said bank decisions were personal, soft, all about me, and a hard money lender would just look at my collateral. Now you're saying it's important to establish a personal relationship with my hard money lender. What's up with that?"

Simply speaking, *the hard money relationship is all about you, individually; the loan decision is all about your collateral.* Relationship lending is a term bandied about by bankers who make a big point of developing a "relationship with their borrowers." What this most often means is that they want your complete financial relationship to be with them. They want all of your individual accounts, your children's accounts, your spouse's accounts, your business accounts, and those of your cousins, uncles, nephews and nieces. It's banker code for wanting all of the deposit balances that they can get from you (which doesn't even count their very profitable safe deposit boxes, debit cards, credit cards, and online banking).

> **Steve Sez:**
> A significant benefit to using a good hard money lender is that you will always have someone to call when you need money *fast*! Remember that you are borrowing money from a person just like you. Treat him with respect and you'll have funding for years to come.

An Actual Experience

High Blood Pressure and How to Prevent It.

For no other reason than to prove a point, I'll share a very current story about how a little communication from a borrower might have led to a much better relationship with his lender—and to much greater financial success.

I once made a loan to a fellow in Diamond Lake, Michigan, using various parcels of real property as the collateral. After the loan was about three or four months old, the borrower stopped paying. My repeated attempts to call him were futile. Just as I was getting ready to leave for a dinner engagement one evening, this borrower called me after no communication for quite some time and begged for more time to get his life straightened out. What can you think about someone who doesn't keep in touch on a regular basis and then becomes radio silent for weeks or months at a time? Silence always causes the other party to believe the worst, and then to act on it.

The point about the blood pressure is simply that after an extended period with no communication whatsoever, how could I ever trust that he would do what I asked him to do again? And how could I ever trust that he would make his future payments on time? How could I believe in his integrity? Was this the way to build up trust in anyone? I think not!

What was the ultimate result? I was forced to sue him on the promissory note, and commence foreclosure on all of the properties. And, each of these actions could have been avoided by simple and regular calls each week to just give me an update on his progress in bringing the loan current.

Sadly, this borrower never learned the simple lessons about relationships.

Let that be a lesson for you in terms of how to work with *your* hard money lender.

As we have seen, banks want your entire financial life to revolve around their bank. It's not about you as a person; it's about your dollars. Occasionally referring one of your wealthier friends with big cash deposits to the bank doesn't hurt either. This is how bankers define "relationship." Are you surprised?

A relationship with a hard money lender has nothing to do with deposits. A hard money lender is not a bank and therefore couldn't take your deposits even if you wanted him to. What a good hard money lender wants is a good person as a borrower, one who will deal with him in an honest and straight forward manner. It is this honesty that will cause your hard money lender to respect you and want to help you each time you call. Most hard money lenders we know wouldn't mind a good referral from time to time either, just for grins. This isn't to say the hard money lender doesn't care about whether or not you pay the loan back. He cares very much and having a good track record makes it easier for him to lend to you in the future.

I believe that the biggest killer of relationships (or in the alternative, the biggest builder of relationships) is how and when communication occurs. I can't emphasize enough that a simple call from a borrower each month will make any lender feel comfortable and certain that the borrower is there and intent upon making the loan work as agreed. In this manner, after a one-year loan, the lender will have had at least a dozen calls from the borrower and have a good sense of the level of integrity that the borrower has (or not). By doing this repeatedly, your lender will feel comfortable lending you more money in the future.

Steve Sez:
This should be common sense, but communication with your lender is critical to building that prized relationship you want and need. Not only is it the right thing to do, but it is also the key to your monetary future. With this relationship firmly in place, you have access to "yesterday money"— that pot of gold that everyone in business seeks. It's yours for the taking!

Chapter Summary

When banks speak of relationships, they are usually referring to your cash relationship with their bank. If you think that you are cared for as a person by a large bank, think again. Nothing could be farther from the truth.

A hard money lender, on the other hand, can't take your deposits even if he wanted to. He is not a bank. The best relationship to a hard money lender is with a borrower who communicates often and openly, shares important information relevant to the loan and makes his payments as agreed.

1. If you are securing a loan from a large bank, don't be surprised if you have to deal with different loan officers from start to finish—loan officers are commodities to large banks.

2. A hard money lender is usually working alone or in a very small firm. It is common for a borrower to work with the same person not only through the life of the loan but over the course of several loans and potentially several decades.

3. A good relationship with a hard money lender will make subsequent loans from that same lender easier to close.

4. Communication is vital when working with a hard money lender. You are using their money to launch your project and they have an interest in your success. Keep in touch with your lender with any news, be it good or bad.

5. If you find that you cannot live up to the terms of your hard money loan, do not run and hide. Open communication with your lender might just result in accommodation and an eventual solution to your cash flow problem.

Next Chapter Preview

There are good and bad borrowers, and good and bad hard money lenders. What can you do to protect yourself from the charming bad lenders? Turn the page and I'll tell you.

CHAPTER 13

WARNING: Danger Signs of a Bad Hard Money Lender

The starting point of great success and achievement has always been the same. It is for you to dream big dreams. There is nothing more important, and nothing that works faster than for you to cast off your own limitations and then to begin dreaming and fantasizing about the wonderful things that you can become, have, and do.
—Brian Tracy

Everything is not always as it seems—this should be one of the first rules of business. The statement is, however, relevant to the practice of magic and to the magic of hard money lending. After all, isn't it a bit of magic that if you meet the requirements, you can have money "yesterday?" In spite of this magic, you should always heed the signals that this may not be the ideal relationship for you. In this chapter, we'll talk about those warning signs.

All right, let's put the cards on the table: Not all hard money lenders are monetary fairy godmothers; nor are they all nice guys. There. That said, let's look at some warning signals showing that you may be heading straight into a storm.

As I've said before, trust your gut. You know what it feels like: uneasiness, maybe even queasiness, and some lingering uncertainty.

Maybe it was just that you didn't get a good feeling after you spoke to the potential lender. Two and two didn't quite add up to four.

Maybe your instinct is telling you that the hard money lender is moving in too fast. Maybe the lender is asking for a great deal of money in advance of the loan as a "commitment fee" for agreeing to loan you money (call your lawyer or other advisor immediately, by the way). Perhaps he is pushing you too hard to take his loan. Maybe he is telling you that he can do anything for you but you know that your loan is a difficult one to complete. Maybe he says that your loan is "no problem" and all he needs is a little time and a little money from you to put it together ... which might mean that your "lender" is really a "broker"—not someone who even has the funds to close a loan to anyone.

Steve Sez:
Your instinct is your best friend and your biggest protector. Listen to it. A trusted advisor who can add his input and validation of your feelings is your second best resource. A second pair of eyes can be invaluable for your assessment of the voice on the other end of the phone.

The needier you are for a loan, the more desperate you become and give yourself less time to "take it all in" and to focus on how it felt to talk to your potential hard money lender. My best advice to you in these circumstances is that you really need someone who has had a bit of experience in this area in one way or another. You need to talk to someone who is not driven by the same monetary need as you are. Their assessment of the lender could save your monetary career from great loss especially if it helps you to identify even one bad person.

Nine Important Danger Signs to Recognize Before You Say "Yes" to a Lender (and Remember to Trust Your Gut Instinct)

1. **"I require advance fees in order to process your loan."**
   These are the guys who are out to get money upfront and then move on immediately thereafter. Like a bank, a

reputable hard money lender will never ask for money upfront for commitment fees on a loan they haven't even researched yet.

2. **"You don't need to review the loan documents."** These are the lenders who want to keep you uninformed and confused and therefore more vulnerable to creating a default or breach of your loan terms unintentionally. If you don't know what is in your documents, how can you comply with all of their terms? If you remember what happens when default interest and penalties start to add up, you will recall that at the end of the story, you had one less piece of property. Bad result! These lenders want your property, not your money.

3. **"I can't really answer that question."** Lenders who stammer when you ask them questions and who never seem to come up with the information that you want, probably don't have any information to give you. If they were really honest with you, they would have to say that they are really just after your front money.

4. **"Privacy prevents me from giving you references."** Lenders who won't give you references when you ask for them are not worth the second phone call; my strong suggestion to you is that with no references—there is no business to be had from you!

5. **"Voice mail; voice mail; voice mail; is anyone home?"** Lenders who never answer their phones probably have already collected their up-front fee from you and have moved on to the next poor soul. The wonder of caller ID now works against you. Don't sign anything—particularly a check—until you know that you are dealing with a reputable lender.

6. **"All of our correspondence goes to our post office box; we would have way too much mail at our office otherwise."** Lenders who use a post office box, and won't give you a

physical address even when you ask for it are probably not going to be around in the future. They need a post office box so their local district attorney can't find them easily. Find someone who is real.

7. **"I can't show you the loan documents before the closing; you would only be confused."** This item is a kissin' cousin of item number 2. above. A lender who won't let you see the documents before the closing is hiding something that is very detrimental to you. Actually, he is just telling you what you should do; you definitely will be confused about how dishonest the lender is after all he has told you thus far. Step away from the lender and then move on to someone honest.

8. **"Whoops, did I tell you that; I really didn't say that. You must have misinterpreted what I said."** Lenders who change the terms of the loan at the closing table when it's usually too late for you to back out of the loan gracefully, are going to be trouble for you in the very near future. If you feel uneasy, don't go through with the closing! It doesn't matter that it is awkward to leave the closing. I would suggest that you drive straight from the failed closing directly to your lawyer's office. Whoops, did I also tell you that you will lose your property if you sign his loan documents?

9. **"Take my loan; it's the best rate and term that you will find; and, I'm almost out of funds, so you should accept today."** Hard sell lenders or highly aggressive lenders are more than likely to be "loan to own" guys rather than real lenders. What are "loan to own" lenders? They're the loan sharks I've warned you about. "Deez guys" (as they said on the Soprano's) want your property at a wholesale price; they don't want their interest rate. Run directly to the district attorney as fast as you can.

If a hard money lender says that you don't need to worry about reading the loan closing documents, take the time to let that soak in.

If you let desperation make you ignore this warning sign, you're "crusin' for a bruising." These lenders know that you are ripe for the kill. These signs are definitely problematic and are signs that the lender is not dealing with you fairly. Obviously, you want to read *all* of the loan documents—this is an absolute necessity for you, your lawyer, or other trusted advisor. And furthermore, you want to read them well in advance of the time when you will be required to execute them in order to get your money. At that time, you are too unlikely to do anything that will interfere with your closing proceeds.

Steve Sez:
If you are feeling unable to say no for any reason, let someone else do the negotiating for you. Hard money lenders generally have strong personalities. Don't let embarrassment get in the way; protect yourself or you will end up being a story in a future edition of my book.

These documents define your costs, obligations, and responsibilities. You must know what is contained in each and every document associated with your loan in order to be aware of your commitments. In addition, if you have questions about anything in these contracts (all of the loan documents are really contracts between you and the lender), the hard money lender must answer them to *your* satisfaction. Anything less is bordering on being unethical (if not worse). You can't agree to anything if you don't know that to which you are agreeing.

Critically Important

Remember, loan documents are legally binding and anything that you sign can and will be held against you in a courtroom. You must read and understand the terms of the entire transaction. Make sure that the terms contained in these documents are the same as the ones quoted to you earlier by the lender. Don't accept stories about the reasons that the terms may have changed dramatically to your detriment. Ethics are ethics and if the lender stated it and then he shows up at the closing with documents containing different terms, I would say this is one of those strong signs to run the other way! It portends of his honesty and integrity on all of your issues with him going forward. *You won't be able to believe a word that he says!*

Evasive answers are another sure sign that something is wrong with the lender that you have selected. Questions about the process, the costs, the type of collateral that the lender prefers, the terms and so on, are so basic that an experienced hard money lender could answer these questions even if you woke him from a deep sleep at three a.m. Anyone who is unwilling to answer basic questions about his loans or his processes is to be avoided at all costs. What is he hiding?

Think about this situation: What if after you've borrowed money, you need to get answers to questions and the lender is evasive? Then, because you don't get the answers that you need, you are late with your payment because you didn't have the correct information. Many, many lenders who have bad motives will be intentionally evasive. They believe that they may be able to cause a default to occur which in turn gives them the rights to impose default interest and penalties. As these two items cause the amount due to grow quickly, you continue to fall farther and farther behind on your payments which ultimately causes a foreclosure on your property. And, sadly because you chose the wrong lender, you could lose your property. Pretty incredible result, don't you agree? Especially when a review of the history of dealing with this lender could have tipped you off much earlier.

Trust Your Instinct

This is the kind of thing that probably won't happen with a bank loan. There are far too many regulations protecting you. And, to ease the situation for you, there is always someone higher up to whom you can complain if there are abuses of the system by your banker. One of the primary danger signs with respect to a banker is a loan officer who says, "Yes, we can do that; no problem" too quickly. In my experience, it causes most borrowers to rely too heavily on this statement of "quasi approval," resulting in severe stress and anxiety when the loan fails to pass the bank's approval process at the last minute.

Yes, the relationship with a hard money lender is all about your collateral. But this time it's about how you feel rather than how you look on paper. You have the power to assess the person on the other side of the transaction. Nice change, don't you think? It gives you the power instead of the other way around. Treat any suspicious hard money lender as you would someone calling to tell you that, as a result of being entered in an international sweepstakes contest, you've won a million dollars. All you have to do to claim your prize is to send a check for $50,000 to a foreign post office box in order to cover taxes in a foreign country.

And, of course, then there is the scam regarding Uncle Mbutu in Nigeria who has $28 million and just needs an American account into which it must be deposited. In exchange for allowing the use of your account, he'll let you keep half of these funds, or $14 million. All you have to do is to send him $100,000 to show that you are sincere in your desire to help him and to earn $14 million as the result.

The pathetic thing about this is that I actually know someone who fell for this one and actually sent $100,000 to Nigeria. You can probably write the ending yourself: three minutes after the $100,000 was sent, Uncle Mbutu disappeared. Where-oh-where could he have gone? I just don't understand ... do you?

And of course, there is an Easter Bunny.

Ask many, many questions. The thing that bad hard money lenders like to do is the same thing that predators do: they prey on (and pray for finding) those who can be easily intimidated. You won't want to hear the rest of the story.

> **Steve Sez:**
> Always, Always, ALWAYS trust your gut. If you think that there is something wrong, there probably is!

Loan to Own: I'll Make You a Loan, the Loan Will Make You Fail and Then I'll Take Your Property

The old gangster movies with Acey and Joey, the Knee Breaker, are examples of "loan to own" lenders. The scene is set as follows: A charming gentleman—usually wearing some kind of fedora—listens patiently and endearingly to your desperate tale of woe, lends you money, and then whacks you with expensive and rapidly escalating interest. You don't have this week's payment (yeah, weekly not monthly), too bad. What do you think happens next?

The whole goal is to foreclose on your property in exchange for this inflated amount due on your loan. The result of this foreclosure is that they have then taken your property at a very low price (the loan amount), in order to resell it at a great profit. The profit on this transaction is far greater than the interest and penalties that they are accruing on your defaulted loan. What a racket!

And, if they are really bad dudes, they will end up not only owning your property, but with a "deficiency judgment" against you after all is said and done. That's a personal judgment against you for the amount of the loan that has not been deemed to have been repaid to them in the foreclosure process. What a joke! But it's the law in many states. Beware!

Steve Sez:
Stay far away from "loan to own" lenders. They are very bad for your financial and emotional health.

What does a bad loan structure look like on paper? How can a lender draft his promissory note and other loan documents to take advantage of you? Here are a few items to be aware of in your document review:

Six Telltale Signs of a Bad Loan Structure

1. **High Default Rate:** Take a look at the default rate of interest; if it's nearing the top of the state's usury limit, watch out. What the lender may be trying to do is to make the loan's principal balance grow so fast in the event of a default that you will never be able to catch up and bring the loan current. Say goodbye to your property as the result.

2. **Short Loan Maturity:** Take a look at the maturity or due date on the promissory note. You know what the length of the loan was to have been in your early discussions with

your lender. If it's substantially shorter in your final loan documents, this is a major red flag. Most lenders know that it's hard enough to repay a hard money loan before a year in most cases, so by shortening the term they may be forcing a default when you can't repay the loan quickly.

3. **Short Payment Due Dates:** Next, take a close look at the payment terms. If the promissory note requires weekly or semi-monthly payments, be highly suspicious. This type of payment structure is not a common practice in the legitimate lending world. It is meant to add additional stress to a borrower who probably can't easily keep up with a more regular payment schedule anyway. Again, say goodbye to the property that you wanted so badly.

4. **No Title Insurance Commitment:** Make sure that your loan documents include a title insurance commitment or policy. No reputable lender would ever consider making a loan using real estate as collateral without getting a title insurance policy for the safety of the loan. If your lender doesn't give you an opportunity to review the title commitment, there is something that is in your favor in the report that he doesn't want you to see.

5. **No Settlement Statement:** You should see a settlement statement which details each of the costs and expenses being charged to you as part of the loan closing. No real lender ever makes a loan without a settlement statement. Reputable lenders will always include this as one of the closing documents given to the borrower. Title companies even require you to sign a copy at the closing, if the closing is overseen by a title company agent. Make sure, by the way, that these itemized costs are the same as what was quoted to you when you first contacted the lender. Changing costs and expenses that are off by more than a minor amount are a very big red flag.

6. **A Loan Closing that Is Not at the Title Insurance Company:** In the vast majority of loans secured by real estate, some

of your closing documents will be prepared by a title insurance company which will also act as the closing agent for both you and the lender. If the loan is not to be closed at a title insurance company office, the only other regularly acceptable location is at a lawyer's office. In this case, a title agent from the title insurance company will be present to notarize and take the documents for recording after the closing, and to collect good funds and to disburse the net loan proceeds to you.

If the closing is to be at the office of the lender, or another location that seems strange to you, again let your instinct tell you what to do. I will always recommend that if anything seems strange to you either before or at the closing, call someone you trust and preferably with loan experience, and discuss it with them before you sign any documents at all.

One Way to Check Out a Lender in Some States— Do They Have a Lender's License?

In many states, especially after the real estate meltdown of 2008, lenders must now be licensed to make loans in the state. Check with the real estate commission or the state corporation commission in your state. If there is a law requiring lenders to be licensed, and the one you are speaking with does not have a record of having such a license, there is a real problem ahead. Call the state's Attorney General, or the state's Real Estate Commission.

Steve Sez:
Do not go about the process of finding a hard money loan by the "Ready, Fire, Aim" method. It's much easier to stay out of a bad situation than it is to get out of a bad situation.

A Great Solution for Borrowers

Have I raised enough possible warning signs before you go blindly forward with any hard money lender? If so, then I feel like I've done you a great service. I may have saved your property, and your sanity.

I believe that one of the smartest things you can do if you are uncertain about anything in your lender search process, the process of reviewing closing documents, or even about negotiating the final terms of a possible loan, is to hire an expert to be on your team. The money that you will spend for these professional services will be well spent when compared with the potential loss of your money and collateral that an involvement with a bad lender can cause. I have counseled many borrowers with respect to their loan documents, their negotiations with a lender, and about their overall lender search and analysis. Finding someone to help you with these tasks will save you both money and aggravation in the short and long run.

Steve Sez:
If you are unfamiliar with loans, terms, and collateral, find yourself a good advisor to stand by your side throughout the process—you'll be glad you did!

Chapter Summary

Protect you assets! Trust your gut! Ask someone to help you evaluate the loan! Be wary of signs that you may be involved with a bad lender! There are many, many warning signs that can arise as you begin the process of locating and selecting a hard money lender, negotiating the terms of the loan, closing on the loan and the loan servicing process thereafter. But, all of the warnings in the world are useless unless you heed just one: Don't go forward with anything or anybody who makes you instinctively nervous—there is a reason that you feel that way.

1. There *are* unscrupulous hard money lenders; it pays to know with whom you are dealing.

2. Don't enter into any loan that doesn't seem to be on the up and up in terms of loan structure, reasonable terms of repayment, and honesty and openness of your lender.

3. When in doubt, hire a professional to review the proposals, assist you in negotiating the best loan terms possible for your circumstance, help you review loan documents, and help you check out the integrity of the lender—the cost will be far less than the cost of losing your property.

4. Know the usury laws in your state.

5. When you close, be sure to close at the offices of a reputable and licensed title company.

Next Chapter Preview

All right, we've covered hard money lenders and have compared hard money lenders to banks. Now it's time to roll up our sleeves and learn more about real estate collateral as viewed by a hard money lender.

SECTION TWO

Using Real Estate as Collateral for Your Hard Money Loan

CHAPTER 14

Real Estate: Great Investment, Great Collateral

*The turning point, I think, was when I really realized
that you can do it yourself. That you have to believe
in you because sometimes that's the only person
that does believe in your success—only you.*
—Tim Blixseth

This chapter sets the stage for Section 2 of this book which explores the various types of loans and how you can structure your real estate holdings to work for you when in search of a hard money loan. Throughout this section, we'll explore the details of using real estate as collateral for a commercial hard money loan and how these loans differ from residential mortgages offered by banks.

Real estate is and has historically always been the most common form of collateral used by borrowers for both banks as well as hard money lenders. It is certainly the most popular form of collateral that hard money lenders are offered.

Why? Because real property is an asset that a large percentage of the borrowing community owns and its value is typically easier to measure and verify than most other forms of collateral.

Here's one large benefit of utilizing hard money for your funding: The property you use as collateral doesn't have to be owned by you. Take a moment to reflect on how beneficial this can be for your loan request. No longer are you constrained by just what you have. Remember that the hard money loan evaluation isn't about you and your financial worth; it's the worth of the collateral.

This is one of the biggest benefits of working with a hard money lender as opposed to a bank. For example, if your collateral doesn't cover the entire loan that you need, your Uncle Henry or friend Adam can put up some of his property to help you, if either really likes or loves you. And, neither of them have to sign the promissory note, either. This means that there is no personal obligation to repay the loan. It's only *you* who is responsible for the repayment of the loan. Uncle Harry—or Adam—only risk losing their property if you don't repay it in a timely fashion (wouldn't we all like to have an Uncle Harry or friend Adam in our lives?).

Let's talk for a minute about a concept we touched on earlier: all true hard money loans are typically "commercial" loans. It doesn't matter if the property you're using is your old family homestead, Aunt Tillie's waterside condo in the Florida Keys, or a hot piece of land in the Mojave.

Steve Sez:
You can get highly creative in looking for adequate collateral for your loan. It doesn't have to all come from you. Some hard money lenders are very creative if need be.

Hard money lending began with loans to businesses many centuries ago. The loans were often made by individuals wishing to invest their money in areas other than stocks, bonds or savings accounts. This remains true today. Your hard money lender is probably working alone, or with a partner, and focused exclusively on real estate lending.

Banks, on the other hand, often define the nature of the loan that you're getting by the type of property offered as collateral. Bank loans for personal residences are called "residential" loans and loans for business property are called "commercial" loans. In some banks, this is a critical distinction that could make the difference between a loan approval and a loan turndown. Or, it could make the difference in how much money they will loan to you, and on what terms and conditions.

Residential loans typically have a higher loan-to-value (LTV) ratio. If yours is viewed as a commercial loan even though you are using your personal residence, your loan will carry a lower loan-to-value ratio and will have a higher interest rate than a residential loan.

Residential loans from banks and mortgage companies typically have lower interest rates and costs than commercial loans. Competitive interest rates draw borrowers from all over the country to large Internet-based residential lenders, and to multi-state banks like Bank of America and Wells Fargo. When you take a residential mortgage loan, the origination fee that you pay is usually tied to the interest rate and to overall market conditions. For a borrower with a good credit score, credit history, and adequate income, the interest rate can be lowered if you pay more points. Many banks and mortgage companies have even offered "no point" (no origination fee) home equity lines of credit in order to keep their mortgage lending activities at a strong level.

Often, with a borrower who has a so-so credit score, a sketchy credit history, and has jumped from job to job with erratic income, the origination fees (or "points") on his mortgage loan will be higher due to the extra risk of default and foreclosure. He will get the home loan only if he pays higher than usual fees, takes a lower loan amount, and is willing to pay a higher interest rate as well.

The limit on residential loan interest rates are governed by what are known as usury laws. What are considered to be excessive rates of interest varies from state to state as well as with overall market conditions on the secondary market for this mortgage paper.

Remember reading about usury in the introduction? Usury, as defined by Black's Law Dictionary, is "... a profit greater than the lawful rate of interest, intentionally exacted as a bonus for ... a loan of money."[5]

If a lender charges more than the maximum interest rate under the state's statutory usury laws, the lender is "using" the borrower to make an illegally larger profit; and, that's not all. Charging a rate above the maximum allowed by statute is often a criminal offense in some states; it depends on how the individual state's usury statute is written. Even if usury is not a criminal offense in a particular state, it is clearly illegal and will subject the lender to many penalties, fines and other costs.

Does that mean you can never use the residence you live in as collateral? No, not at all. The way to use your residence as collateral and for your lender to avoid violating your state's usury laws is to have him obtain an opinion letter from the closing attorney. The opinion letter should state that the hard money loan that you are taking is commercial in nature and does not violate the state owner-occupied residential usury laws, if such laws exist where the property is located. As always, check with your lawyer wherever you are located; if the residential property that you want to use for collateral is in another state, make certain that your local attorney consults with appropriate counsel in the state where the property is located. If she doesn't, you should find an attorney there, just to cover all of your bases.

In almost all states, commercial loans are governed by different usury limits than are residential loans and lenders. Therefore, a commercial lender can generally charge higher interest rates because the law commonly allows it. In some states, if the loan is made to a business entity (e.g. a loan to a corporation), usury limits do not apply. The theory is that a business entity should have enough information, experience and intelligence to properly evaluate any loan proposal. Therefore, how can an unusually high interest rate be criminal unless the lender is purposely trying to defraud the borrower?

Chapter Summary

Historically and practically, most hard money loans are real estate loans. Unlike banks and other residential lenders that will define the structure of your loan by the property being purchased, by your collateral, and by your credit history, a hard money lender will look almost exclusively at the collateral and the use of the borrowed funds.

1. Real estate is far easier for a hard money lender to value as collateral than art collections, automobiles, stock and other non-traditional forms of collateral.

2. Purchase-money loans for owner-occupied residences which are not commercial in nature and typically have a higher loan to value ratio as the result. We know that these loans are made primarily by banks and mortgage companies.

3. Individual state commercial and residential statutes define how much interest a lender can charge; you should consult with your attorney to determine how usury laws are structured with respect to loans within your state—particularly if the loan will be made to a company rather than an individual.

4. Hard money loans frequently carry a higher rate of interest than a loan from a bank or commercial lender and a lower loan to value ratio.

5. You do not necessarily need to own the property that you are pledging for collateral—family members and friends can help you by pledging their property for your loan. But if you don't make each of the loan payments in a timely fashion, they stand to lose their property in a foreclosure.

Next Chapter Preview

In the next chapter, I will explain the differences between bank loan and hard money loan applications. You'll be amazed at how streamlined and simple the hard money loan process is—and at how little supporting paperwork you'll need for an application. It's what makes the application process so fast.

CHAPTER 15

Loan Applications: the Good, the Bad & the Depressing

The successful person makes a habit of doing what the failing person doesn't like to do.
—Thomas Edison

As we have seen, when you approach a bank or other commercial lender for a loan, be prepared to tell them your life's story in documents ranging from pay stubs to parking stubs. Okay, maybe you won't have to show them parking stubs but you will be expected to clearly show and explain all of the business expenses you've incurred in the recent past.

With a hard money lender, the most important items of information have to do with your collateral. Hard money lenders are not concerned, as a general rule, with you, your income, your lifestyle, your history and the rest of your personal life. All that you need to do is to be prepared to demonstrate that you have the collateral necessary to secure your loan. In this chapter, we'll take a look at a very big difference between working with a bank and working with a hard money lender.

Here's a side-by-side recap of some of the documents you'll need to apply for a loan:

Hard Money Lender	Bank
Property income and expenses	Property income and expenses
Personal financial statement	Personal financial statement
Business financial statement	Business financial statement
Environmental reports	Environmental reports
Tenants' leases	Tenants' leases
Purchase contract	Purchase contract
	Tax returns
	W-2 statements from employers
	1099 statements from payers
	Personal resume
	Verification of employment
	Copies of pay stubs
	Bank statements
	Credit card statements
	Installment debt summary
	Credit report (bank supplied)
	Verification of CD deposits
	Stock broker reports
Property tax statements	Property tax statements
Property insurance policies	Property insurance policies
Purchase contract	Purchase contract
Recent property survey	Recent property survey
Any appraisals of the real estate	Appraisals of all the real estate holdings
	Verification of mortgages
	Source of down payment
Income and expenses of the real estate	Income and expenses of the real estate
	Formal bank loan application

With which set of documents would you rather deal? I'd choose the hard money loan documents any day. No digging around for back pay-stubs, bank statements, or 1099 statements. No searching for old income tax returns. No recaps of income and debt service requirements. When all is said and done, the bank really looks at you like this: You are only as good as your last payment, your last deposit, or your last paycheck.

I listed a personal financial statement in the hard money loan column for a reason: While most good hard money lenders do not base their loan decisions on your personal financial data, they *do* need to get to know the folks with whom they may be doing business. The personal financial statement gives a hard money lender some insight into who you are and how you operate your business life. Do you live with a great deal of debt? Are you debt averse? Do you believe that more assets are better even if you borrowed all of the money to acquire them? Do you believe that less debt is better and safer?

Steve Sez:
Although it may be tempting to do so to improve your chances of getting a loan, do not lie on your personal financial statement by increasing values of assets and decreasing or eliminating any of your liabilities. You will be very sorry (and possibly liable to your lender for fraud) when you do the wrong thing. Always be honest.

Financial Statement Etiquette

There are strategies that you can use to properly prepare your financial statement for presentation to a hard money lender and to anyone else for that matter. The following example should give you a better idea of just how important it is to prepare a financial statement correctly that is not only well-laid out and easy to understand, but is accurate and honest.

Critically Important

Know that when you give your personal financial statement to a lender, you will probably have to sign it, certifying that it is true and correct in all material respects as of its date.

An Actual Experience

My Kingdom for a Drop of the Truth.

I have had many instances over the years of borrowers who must be terribly ashamed of their circumstances in life. I have probably reviewed thousands of financial statements, and when I get serious about a loan application, I always discuss the borrower's situation with him. I've got a number of stories that will absolutely tickle your fancy—in large measure because they *were* fanciful.

I have had many, many borrowers who have put other people's property on their own list of assets. Why would someone do that you may ask? When I finally find out the truth, borrowers tell me that they are planning to purchase the building with the proceeds of my loan and they, therefore, feel like they as much as own the property already. They have it under contract so it already feels like they own it. But, they will always list the asset and forget the fact that they will have to borrow the money in order to complete the purchase. On top of lying on their financial statement which is certainly bad enough, they compound their offense by leaving out the other side of the equation—the liability incurred in order to pay the seller.

The most incredible thing about it is that when they are confronted with this misrepresentation, most borrowers say that they are really sincere about buying the property (which I don't deny), and the omission of the liability is a mere oversight (which I *don't* accept).

Other people have given me outdated appraised values from documents that may be as much as ten years old. Others pull values out of thin air because someone once told them that they would purchase their property for a ridiculous sum, but they were just a little short of cash on that day. Maybe their neighbor once said that they would have given a million dollars for my borrower's property, and lo and behold, the value on the financial statement is, you guessed it, one million dollars.

Or how about borrowers who guess at the asset value—abnormally high, of course, and then round their mortgages down. Sometimes applicants might even forget to list some of their mortgages on the liability side of the financial statement. I really have problems with this one.

One of the worst examples of financial statement fraud happened to me in conjunction with a loan application from a health facility in Puerto Rico. Initially, everything looked to be on the up-and-up and the application even came with an audited financial statement. An audited statement is meant to assure all who see it that an independent accounting firm reviewed and tested the financial statements and found that their financial statements were true and correct to the best of the auditor's knowledge. It's the gold standard of accounting reports.

This audited financial statement, however, had an interesting feature that I had never seen before: On the list of assets, they had listed each of their nursing homes, the furniture, fixtures, and equipment, and so on. When I was reviewing the list of assets, the real estate asset value on the financial statement was written with a different type face than the rest of the report.

Apparently, our potential borrower didn't like the value that the accountant had used, and wanted us to see a larger value. You can't really blame him, can you? How, after all, could he have gotten a loan if he were truthful?

The line item for "Total Assets" had a number that had been treated with white-out, as well. A larger number had been substituted in a different type face that you would have to be completely negligent to miss. And, as if this weren't enough, and just to round out the fraud lest there be a mistake, someone had recalculated the section of the balance sheet entitled "Shareholders Equity," just to make both sides of the financial statement balance.

This is merely **garden variety fraud** pure and simple. If these would-be borrowers would try to pull one over on me *before* I make them a loan, imagine what I could have expected when the payments became due, when they executed their loan documents, when new financial statements were supplied to me, and in conjunction with everything thereafter that was supplied to me. All this is enough to cause even the most reckless of hard money lenders to stop and imagine what else the borrowers are capable of doing.

Anyone to whom you present your financial statements is depending upon your truth and honesty. Loans will either be approved or disapproved based to some extent upon this information. Obviously, the banker will be relying on it much more than the hard money lender. Lying to a federally-insured bank could win you a multi-year vacation, all expenses paid, to a great federal beach resort.

If you haven't a clue how to prepare your financial statements and you want them to be accurate, I recommend that you retain an accountant who can help you prepare your statements in a truthful fashion.

The Application Process

Difference #9: Application Documents

Bank Loan Applications

The goal of a typical commercial loan application from a bank is to better understand your financial world, and how you transact your business. If knowing you better is the goal, don't be surprised when the bank application form asks for your personal information, information about your spouse, the addresses of property you now own, and a list of personal assets including savings and CD accounts, life insurance, and vehicles (and each item's market value).

Typically, a bank loan application will ask for a lot of data as well as many, many attachments. The information that the bank will request after it reviews your application will be used to verify the facts and figures that you present to the bank in your financial statement. The bank may want to see things like pay stubs for at least three months (if not six—each bank has its own requirements) in addition to current savings and checking statements (you need to prove to them that you have liquidity and ongoing cash flow from investments, salary or any other source). You'll be asked to prepare a financial statement that lists all of your creditors, assets, liabilities, and a complete description of each entry in detail.

At the end of the loan application, expect to be asked to respond to a series of personal questions including the following:

- Are there any judgments against you?

- Have you been declared bankrupt within the past seven years?

- Have you had any property foreclosed upon or given a deed in lieu of foreclosure?

- Are you a party to a law suit?

- Are you obligated to pay alimony, child support, or separate maintenance?

- In the case of the purchase of property, is any of the down payment borrowed?

- Are you a co-maker or endorser on any other note?

Wait! You still aren't finished with the loan application process at your bank. Next, the bank will order a formal and independent appraisal of the real estate and a current credit report. You, of course, will be expected to pre-pay for them when the application is ready to be submitted to the banker.

When you start the paperwork process with the bank, make sure to ask the loan officer to give you a copy of the appraisal after it's received. As long as you're on a roll, you should also ask him for a copy of your credit report as well.

Most borrowers are unsuccessful in getting the bank to provide any of the information it collected (and you paid for), but you should always ask. It may be easier to get a copy of your appraisal than your credit report because credit reporting is a "quasi regulated" issue. Credit laws are in a constant state of flux due to the new and trendy crime of identity theft. Everyone is hesitant to release information about their customers to anyone, even to the person in question.

Keep in Mind

Regardless of the outcome of your application, make sure you get back all original documents that you supply to the bank. In fact, don't give your banker any original documents if you can help it— make copies of everything and attach the copies to your application.

Hard Money Loan Applications

You'll be amazed at how easy and efficient a hard money loan application is … if there is even an application to deal with, at all. Hard money lenders are often very informal about their procedures. Because hard money lending is largely unregulated and most hard money lenders are sole proprietors of their business, no one looks at their files but them. Hard money lenders will need some basic personal information like your name, address, phone, e-mail address, whether you found them through a broker, and the purpose of your loan (i.e. starting a business, purchasing investment property, investing in real estate or whatever the reason might be), the amount of money you need, what it's for, and the details about your collateral. But really, that's about it.

To start the application process for a hard money loan, all a lender will typically need in order to initiate the loan application process is property information including the following (note that each hard money lender will have his own list which will definitely include more items than this basic listing):

- Description of collateral and/or other property;

- As-is estimate of the market value of the collateral;

- Recent pictures of the property if you have them;

- Details of all existing debt on your property (outstanding loans/mortgages) including the details of amounts, lender(s), interest rates, maturity dates, collateral, monthly payment, and so on;

- Use of proceeds (how are you going to use the loan proceeds); and

- Your plan for the repayment of the loan that you are seeking (exit strategy).

One of the main distinctions you will see between a bank and hard money lender is that the hard money lender will ask you for an idea of the market value of the collateral at the time you apply. An older appraisal may actually be acceptable to the lender if it's not *too* old. In case you are buying or have recently purchased this piece of real estate, the purchase contract is always an indication of value—unless there are special circumstances. Lenders and appraisers alike will always question whether the purchase and sale transaction is being made "at arm's-length" (which means among independent and unrelated parties).

A bank won't care about your older appraisals typically, as they order their own new appraisal from an independent appraiser. Think time and money in this area and what these items do to your need for capital immediately!

An unscrupulous borrower might have the seller inflate the price of the sale making it appear that the property is more valuable than it really is. The property tax bill doesn't always add clarity to this situation for your lender, therefore. Most tax bills are based on older assessments or sales from the local city or county treasurer's or appraiser's office. These are always estimates which may be either higher or lower than the "real value" of the property.

An Actual Experience

I Want to Know What Planet These Borrowers Came From?

I once received a call from a husband and wife team of real estate investors in Atlanta, Georgia. I got really interested in the loan when the husband Rick told me that his wife, Madison, was a real estate broker with a large real estate firm in a suburb of the city. In theory, so I thought, these people are positioned very well to understand the market and to recognize good values because of their familiarity with the local market conditions. After our phone discussion, we jointly decided that it was reasonable for me to travel to Atlanta to review the property that they had proposed as the collateral for the loan.

Upon my arrival, I drove directly to the property which was a five thousand square foot home in a very upscale suburb of Atlanta. My plan was to review the subject property first, and then proceed to confirm the value of the home. I completed my walk through of the house with Madison, let them describe to me their plans, and bid adieu to my borrowers in order to verify the value.

The first thing that I did was to drive out of this very beautiful subdivision by taking the long road around the interior in order to see what other properties and the neighborhood in general looked like, and to see if any other homes in the area were for sale.

As luck would have it, I stumbled upon an open house about two blocks away with a very bored real estate salesman sitting inside watching a soap opera while killing time. After a quick look around the house, I stopped to chat with him briefly on the way out, about real estate values in the neighborhood. He knew almost every home in the entire subdivision as he was with the original sales team that marketed all of the homes when they were first built. I told him about the property that I had just reviewed, and he promptly told me that I should look across the street at the home for sale because it was the best comparable property. I told him that I didn't see a sign in the yard so could he please pull the listing information up on his computer, which he graciously agreed to do.

The listing information showed that the house directly across the street was about 200 square feet larger than the house in question, and was being offered at a price that was more than 25 percent lower than my borrower's estimate of the value of their house. This very helpful agent continued to tell me that the condition of each of these properties was almost exactly the same having been inside of each quite recently.

In addition, I found out that the property had been on the market for over one year with no offers and a history of a dropping price each three months. When I drove back to the house in question, I noticed that the "for sale" sign had been removed and placed on the back side of the garage, hopefully never to be seen—by me.

My next meeting with the borrowers later that afternoon was to discuss my observations about the results of my investigation thus far. I decided, however, to call them in advance of our meeting, and to ask Madison to please pull the comparable sales and current listings for properties in the immediate neighborhood and have it for me at our up-coming meeting.

Later when we met, Madison gave me the list of comps (other properties that were recently sold and everything that is currently for sale in the neighborhood) that I had requested, and ...you guessed it. The house across the street was nowhere to be found on the list of properties for sale.

Coincidence with the missing sign, or just garden variety attempted fraud? You pick it. Either way, I turned the loan down so fast that you could have seen me at the airport getting back on the plane while I was saying goodbye to them at the front door.

The moral of the story is to not lie to your lender, your appraiser, your wife, your children or your lender. And that would be—never!

Difference # 10: Your Business Plan

Banks require detailed business plans if you're starting a new venture. Hard money lenders will only need to know the basics about the business and your future plans. For them, it's the collateral, stupid!

A bank will probably require some sort of business plan, including detailed three or five year projections complete with explanations about the assumptions underlying your numbers. Remember, bank lending is about the borrower while hard money lending is primarily about the collateral (have I already said this over a hundred times? Yes!). Therefore, a business plan or an executive summary is typically required for a bank, and might also be considered by the hard money lender in less detail, as just an added extra with your application if you have one available.

Steve Sez:
Always be truthful about your estimate of the value of your property. The lender will find out the truth sooner or later. You will lose a great opportunity to get your loan done quickly, not to mention the loss of a golden opportunity to develop a favorable relationship with a hard money lender who can be invaluable for your future business.

For your hard money lender, your business plan doesn't have to be lengthy and complex but, rather it should give the basics to the reader about your business and projections. Be prepared to answer some questions about your projections from any hard money lender—no lender wants to make a loan for a business he thinks might fail. You need to have a reasonable chance for success, and be able to convey this to your potential lender. There are many good resources showing how to prepare business plans; your local bookstore or library would be a good place to locate many of them.

I have reviewed thousands of business plans over the years and as far as I can ascertain, the ones I have followed have never evolved as initially envisioned. It's for this reason I typically didn't take much time to review business plans in depth as my time was better spent on what was most important to me: a review of the collateral. Sure I reviewed business plans; I just didn't hold my borrower's feet to the fire when things didn't go as initially planned.

And, yes, I have occasionally turned a loan down when the prospect for success was so low that I felt it would, in all likelihood, become a troubled loan with all of the associated problems. I made this decision even when there appeared to be adequate collateral value for the loan. I don't like to go into a loan when the borrower seems headed for failure. It isn't good business for me and, therefore, not good for the borrower either (although borrowers don't usually see it that way).

Hard money lending is not venture capital. Oddly enough, banks approach the lending process more like venture capitalists than hard money lenders because of their focus on the borrower and the existence of his plans for future cash flow (and hence, loan repayment). A bank's evaluation of a loan application revolves around how much cash flow there will be to service the debt and to ultimately repay the loan. My experience tells me that it is foolhardy to base a decision on something as mercurial as a business forecast of cash flows. The hard money lending approach—oriented toward the current value of the collateral—keeps the lender safe regardless of the ultimate success or failure of the business.

> **Steve Sez:**
> Hard money lenders are always fully secured. It's not venture capital! The evaluation process is more about tangible assets than business plans and anticipated cash flow from your prized new business.

Chapter Summary

Be fully prepared to justify your use of the loan proceeds to either a bank or a hard money lender. The difference that creates opportunities to obtain fast loans is that your plans for the future are really of little consequence to the hard money lender. A business plan with details out five years has no relevance to the hard money lender. Therefore, don't spend your precious time preparing a document that won't even be reviewed by the lender.

1. Banks require volumes of information about you and your financial strength and history when you apply for a loan; hard money lenders want to see as few documents as possible.

2. It will never benefit you to overstate your estimate of the value of your project, the worth of your collateral or any other financial information—such deception is not only potentially illegal, it might cost you far more than had you been forthright.

Next Chapter Preview

Let's move on to Chapter 16 and take a look at the remaining loan documents that banks and hard money lenders review for real estate loan applications: the appraisal and title work. In addition, I want to introduce you to the concept of "quick sale value." It's important to understand the logic of a hard money lender.

CHAPTER 16

Valuing Your Real Estate

Why is it that with all the information available today on how to be successful in small business, so few people really are?
—Michael Gerber

In this chapter we will discuss how lenders determine the value of your real estate. For banks, a formal real estate appraisal is the most common tool. Hard money lenders, on the other hand, use a variety of methods. Which method is used depends in large measure on the type of collateral you have and upon the specific lender.

The need for a formal appraisal is one of the biggest differences between how hard money lenders and banks manage their lending processes. It is also the one item that insures a much slower closing with a bank. It is not uniformly needed by hard money lenders but it is *always* required by banks. Most hard money lenders will review old appraisals if they're available. In the absence of any existing appraisal, they usually won't ask you to spend the money to secure a current appraisal. The reason for this is that hard money lenders require a site visit to personally inspect and value your collateral. Banks, on the other hand, rarely visit the property, relying instead upon the appraisal.

The reasons for this are twofold: First, if the hard money lender makes the loan, the funds for the loan are his. Therefore, the lender himself wants to see the collateral because this is his only security for his loan. How would you like to trust a third party to tell you about the value of your only safety net for the loan using your funds. If the loan turns bad and you ultimately own and sell the collateral, do you think that the appraiser will make up the difference if the net proceeds are less than the loan balance? After all, isn't a loss caused because he said that your collateral was worth a certain amount and it wasn't after all? So, someone else's mistake will cost the lender money.

Secondly, your hard money lender is going to evaluate your real estate differently than a formal appraisal. His methodology will result in a different value from a full fair market value appraisal.

Appraisals

Difference #11: Formal Appraisals

Banks always wait for an independent formal appraisal and are required to do so by banking regulators in most cases. A hard money lender isn't required to evaluate the value of the collateral in any particular way by anyone for any reason.

One of the first steps on the path to valuing real estate is to see if an appraisal exists from any prior time period, from any appraiser at all. An appraisal is a document that usually consists of photos of the property, details about the land, including acreage and information about any buildings or other improvements located on the property.

A formal appraisal will also contain a number of comps (comparable sales)—the most recently sold "like kind" properties in the general area prior to the appraisal's completion. An appraisal, even up to five years old, will give you and your hard money lender an idea of historic value. In an economic environment as we've had from late 2008, an appraisal that is over three to six months old probably won't have much relevance, as values have been consistently decreasing in many parts of the country. At some point, values will stop their downward movement, stabilize, and then begin an upward movement. That's when an older appraisal may assume more value. But by then, it may be too old to matter.

If there is no appraisal, check with your hard money lender to find out if he wants you to order one before you spend money. If your lender is local, he may already be familiar with the property you're offering as collateral and the values of other properties in the neighborhood; an appraisal may simply be unnecessary. You may decide on your own, however, to order an appraisal some time after you've closed on a hard money loan in order to be prepared for a refinance.

Keep in Mind

Hard money lenders and bankers have very different views of appraisals. I can tell you from experience that banks won't accept an appraisal ordered privately by a borrower. Make sure, therefore, that you're spending your money wisely. If the purpose for an appraisal is to refinance, wait until you've contacted a commercial lender to confirm that your appraisal will meet their requirements. They'll often work only with an "approved list" of appraisers, and none other will suffice. They may want to order the appraisal directly from the appraiser so that the opportunity for you to influence the appraisal's outcome is eliminated.

If your hard money lender requests that you order an appraisal, make sure in advance that the appraiser that you select is properly experienced in properties of your kind and your location. If I were you, I would also clear the name and qualifications of the appraiser that you want to use with your lender. He may have a preference unbeknownst to you. I've seen commercial appraisals done by residential appraisers with no experience in the commercial arena at all. Needless to say, their appraisals don't hold much credibility. Be sure the appraiser has the appropriate credentials.

Steve Sez:
Hard money lenders cringe when they hear that you have an appraisal. No appraiser can be as objective as the guy putting up the money.

Since appraisals can be expensive and time consuming, make sure it will serve your purposes—ask your lender about his appraisal requirements before you order one.

Appraiser qualifications vary from state to state. Some states call a highly rated residential appraiser a "certified residential appraiser." A commercial appraiser might be called "certified general appraiser." Check with your state to determine the highest designation for both commercial and residential appraisers. Universally, however, one of the top commercial ratings is that of MAI or "Member, Appraisal Institute." The Appraisal Institute is the leading international organization for real estate appraisal professionals.

What's the difference between Arnold the Appraiser with no MAI designation and Annie Appraiser, MAI? The simple answer is: education and experience. An MAI appraiser is highly experienced and equally qualified to perform both residential and commercial appraisals.

What's the bottom line? If this appraisal is to have any value to you, you must make sure it is of the highest quality from the onset. If you need to hire an appraiser for your hard money lender, find one with an MAI designation (or find a new hard money lender who won't require a formal appraisal).

An Actual Experience

Let's Make Nice to the Appraiser So That You, the Borrower, Will Get the "Correct" Valuation of Collateral for Your Loan.

A number of years ago, I was asked to provide a loan on a 160 acre piece of unimproved and undeveloped land in South Carolina, 45 minutes south of Charlotte, North Carolina. The loan request was for $1.8 million, and the proposed collateral was to be developed into mid-priced single family homes; not a bad idea actually. The property was close to downtown Charlotte, and the commute wasn't that terrible.

The appraisal, done by an MAI appraiser within the past six months, valued the land at $8,000,000.

When I arrived for the site visit, I met the broker and borrower at the hotel and they handed me the MAI appraisal itself. Given the hour, we had just enough time to do our preliminary site inspection before the sun went down. In the early morning we would get a jump on the day and review the comparable properties as shown in the appraisal, talk to brokers, and so on.

Later that evening back at the hotel, as I was reviewing the lengthy (and complete, might I add) appraisal, I noticed some interesting things. First of all, the appraiser for our South Carolina property was from Atlanta, Georgia, some 270 miles away. I was there from Denver, so I can't be too harsh on the appraiser, but I did note that it was odd that they wouldn't have used someone local for the appraisal.

Next, I noticed that there were nine comps included in the estimate of value in the appraisal. Of these nine, four were from the Atlanta area and the remaining comps were from properties both within the same county as our land, some comps were in rather distant counties in and near Charlotte, and at least one was from another location in South Carolina that was in a completely different economic area.

Of the five comps from North and South Carolina, only one was from the county in which our property was located. This comp showed that a sale had occurred on a much smaller piece of property within the prior six months at a price that suggested a value of $1.8 million on our property given the difference in size.

The other four comps were from the Charlotte area and elsewhere in South Carolina. And, I'm sure that you will never guess the results of those sales. The other properties had each sold at actual values indicating that the value of our property was $1.1 million. When we actually drove to these properties, it was like we were in a different country. One of the comps was a seven-acre piece of property located in the middle of a development. Another was 14 acres with all of the streets and utilities already completed. I wondered how the appraiser arrived at our $8 million value.

As I read further, the "comparable" sales from the Atlanta metro area showed that the value of our land was $8,000,000. Values in and around a major metropolitan area are quite high. Values 45 minutes away from a major city like Charlotte and in a very rural area are quite different. "What was this all about?" was my major question? I have never, ever heard of an appraiser using comps from 270 miles away and in a different state entirely, with different demographics, different demand for housing, and so on.

I can only guess what happened. The borrowers spent some "quality time" with their appraiser before he began his formal appraisal procedures. At some point, they must have agreed that the local comps were completely inaccurate because of the uniqueness of this parcel of property. Possibly, they suggested to the appraiser that he use comps from other "similar" areas that got the appraisal to the value needed to get their loan.

I know what you're thinking: How could anyone be that dishonest? How could anyone try to alter the value of their property just to get a silly loan? That's what I once thought, too.

After having seen these comps, and re-reviewing the appraisal, I firmly believed the property would bring $350,000 on a good day on a "quick sale" basis, and that's only if the seller was lucky. The borrower's loan request of $1.8 million just wasn't going to fly.

There was, in truth, no quick sale value for this property. You would have to be exceedingly fortunate to find that one special buyer in the proverbial haystack to even get the property sold at $350,000. Also, there was no real development potential that any buyer would ever notice. The cost of utilities, roads, zoning and permits would have been so disproportionately large for this parcel that you could have never sold the finished homes for enough money to recover your costs. And, that's not to mention that it would have taken years and years to get the property completely built out and sold.

Although I was fairly certain they would reject my offer of a substantially smaller loan, I felt I needed to better understand the appraiser's logic. I decided to give him a call to inquire about his evaluation technique. His answer was truly unbelievable. He said that the values were similar because our property was 45 minutes from downtown Charlotte, and so were the properties that he had located in Atlanta and used as comps (also located 45 minutes from the downtown Atlanta area.) Did I understand this logic?? I certainly didn't!

Out of a feeling of mercy, I offered them a loan of $100,000, which they didn't take, of course. Remember that I had concluded that our estimate of value was only $350,000 if you wanted to sell the property quickly. After many years, when I spoke to them again, they still had not obtained their $1.8 million loan. Imagine my surprise!

It is in the borrower's best interest to be as candid and forthright as possible in all cases. Do not ever try to inflate the value of your collateral, overstate your financial strength or embellish your ability to repay the loan when it comes due. Such deceptions, whether or not they are initially successful, will inevitably come back to create larger problems for you in the future.

Critically Important

A word of caution: Many hard money lenders won't accept an outside appraisal. Appraisals can be manipulated, and appraisers will always know the purpose for the appraisal in advance of arriving at a valuation. If you call the appraiser and he knows that it's for a loan, do you think that he will come in with a value that is high or low? I'm sure that you can guess the right answer.

Remember that there are no formal training programs for hard money lenders. As the result, anyone who goes into this business has his own ideas about what to require for due diligence activities, charges, costs, fees and interest rates are going to be and so on. Each lender is very different in what they require you to provide in terms of paperwork and how they treat your loan application thereafter. Therefore, if you are asked for a formal appraisal by someone purporting to be a "hard money lender," it should be obvious you have run into someone who has a sub-conscious, unfulfilled desire to be a banker. If it's speed that you're after, I'd look elsewhere, and quickly.

How Hard Money Lenders Evaluate the Worth of Your Collateral

Why would your hard money lender want to visit your property personally? Generally, real estate holds its value and will, more than likely, increase as the years go by (with the current economic climate aside). The lender could just as easily look at the assessment records for his evidence of value. But, think about this: tax assessments and appraisals are the opinions of others, concerning values. Assessors and appraisers may or may not be looking at the same factors as a hard money lender. For instance, the assessor's office won't know if the property next door has gang graffiti all over it, or that, two doors down, the property is boarded up and decaying. What if the plant two blocks away is planning a large layoff? How would the assessor's office know that? The same goes for an appraisal that was completed some time ago.

Most assessors' offices simply take the public records of the sales in the immediate neighborhood, compare square footages and zoning categories and extrapolate from there.

There really is no substitute for a site visit to understand the condition and value of the property. The lender is probably loaning his own money and that of his family and friends, as we have seen. He isn't selling the note to some big Wall Street fund that doesn't really care about any single loan that they are buying. If he makes a bad loan with bad collateral, he is the one who stands to lose his and any other's personal money. It's a funny characteristic, but most hard money lenders that I know don't like to lose their (or anyone else's) money.

A bank, on the other hand, will rely on some disinterested appraiser who ultimately won't lose anything even if his evaluation is completely wrong. Notice that when a property doesn't bring what it was supposedly worth, the lender never calls the appraiser to make up the difference. If the appraiser isn't going to be held responsible for his evaluation, why would the hard money lender loan his hard earned money based upon this type of a "no risk" opinion?

As an aside, I have always thought that there should be some liability for a negligently prepared appraisal. It's what hurts everyone in the transaction, except the appraiser. Imagine what would happen if you told appraisers that if the property did not bring at least 90 percent of the appraised value at sale, they would have to pay the difference? It's fun to daydream: Do you think that appraised values would change? I certainly do!

> **Steve Sez:**
> Hard money lenders like site visits as the means of inspecting and valuing your collateral because an appraisal won't tell him about the houses next door, the neighborhood, the trends, and the junk car sitting on the front lawn of the house five lots down. Nor will it tell him about the gas station across the street with old underground tanks that had leaked two years ago and were "hopefully" cleaned up sufficiently.

Obviously, a site visit is much easier for a local lender than for an out of state lender. Be prepared: if you're working with a hard money lender from across the country, his or her travel expenses will be added to the amount the loan will cost you (and these expenses will be due in advance of giving you a loan commitment). After all, the lender hasn't yet had the opportunity to see and value your collateral. Other than speaking with you about your property on the phone, he or she has no way of knowing whether there is even a chance of making you a loan. All the lender has at this point are the facts you are giving him during the call. And, of course, all borrowers seeking a loan will always be completely honest and accurate with lenders at all times. What do you think?

How does your potential lender know your assurances are correct? Obviously, everyone is very proud of what they own and they value it highly. It's human nature. But, is the owner's valuation realistic when reviewed by an independent party looking at all of the factors involved in establishing a true market value? The hard money lender—who is lending his own money—is not going to take the word of anyone else when it comes to making the decision to loan or not to loan his money.

An Actual Experience

Wow! What a Piece of Dead Property!

I was once asked to visit Pittsburgh to consider making a loan on a piece of ground that the borrower assured me was prime development ground. In addition, this piece of property also contained significant acreage that could be used as expansion land for the existing business. The borrower told me he had a recent appraisal that stated that the property was worth $600,000 as it sat. So far, so good.

I then went through my standard lending procedures of finding out all I could about the property before I went on a physical inspection trip. I always did this because I didn't want to waste my time and, potentially, the borrower's money for a site inspection if the probability was that I would turn down the loan request. In this case, the borrower said the property was unique (Uh Oh—a hint of trouble!). "I would love it," he assured me.

The property was a ... cemetery!!!

He said this property was in a prime location for a cemetery, and he had already pre-sold many, many plots. The existing gravesites were from the early 1900s and late 1800s. Further, the back acreage in the cemetery was the prime development ground in his mind. (Yeah, like anyone would like to have a great view of headstones from their front porch.) But, being the committed lender that I was (yes, I should have been committed for even thinking of this one), I decided that if the value checked out, we should give this request our best shot.

When I got to Pennsylvania, the first thing the borrower showed me was the cemetery and its additional contiguous acreage. From the very first moment I saw the property, I had a sense that this was going to be a very tough loan to complete. Then he took me to a cemetery that he thought was comparable in value to his property. Picture this: My borrower's cemetery had old headstones, unpaved roads, bad signage, unkempt landscaping with tall weeds everywhere, and lots of work that needed to be done to make it presentable.

The other cemetery, about two or three miles away, had beautifully paved roads, statues throughout the grounds, fountains and private sitting areas, gardens and lots of trees. And I was thinking to myself, "And this would be comparable. Why? Where would you rather spend eternity?"

A side trip to the city planning office ultimately made the decision for me. The planner with whom I spoke told me that because the cemetery was adjoining the site of a potential housing development, the city would have a tough time approving residential building permits. The access to the development portion of the land was directly through the cemetery, or significantly back from the main road. The city didn't like it at all. All the dreams of plot sales at big prices, and residential development to add value to the "project," were for naught. Tough loan application to say yes to; don't you agree?

The borrower was exceedingly unhappy when I turned down his loan request. Upon further investigation, I also discovered that this property had been listed with a real estate broker for two previous years without so much as an offer. The one real estate broker in Pittsburgh who had any familiarity with cemeteries told me he would never even take this listing because the property wouldn't sell to anyone. It was just too costly and uncertain a project to make economic sense in any development scenario.

He further said, with no hesitation, that given its location, there would be no viable developers in the area who would have even the slightest interest in this property. No one would buy a new house right in front of a field of dead people. And the cemetery portion of the land was in such bad shape that, when compared to the fancy, newer cemetery down the road, the eternal decision was easy to make, and it was not in favor of this land.

I have had a very common reaction from borrowers who call to ask about a loan. Most calls begin the same way; I listen to the description of what they need, when and for what reason. If it sounds like something I might be able to do just from the description, I tell them about the loan, its costs, and fees, including the inspection fee.

Most of the time, I get the following reaction: "Are you crazy? Why my brother Alvin is a real estate broker. He can go to the property, take pictures and send them to you, all in the next hour. And, the best part is, that I don't have to pay for it. Why do you have to come here to look? We have appraisers and real estate brokers here, you know."

Or, how about something like this: "What if you come here and don't give me my loan? I've just wasted my money." My response to this is that if the "quick sale" value of your property is as described, then what reason would I have for not offering you a loan? My business is lending. I am not in the travel business.

If you are uncomfortable with the potential for "cost runaway," merely ask your hard money lender about the kind of costs he might request in advance of the site visit. Ask him for a list of these costs in writing and ask for a guarantee that these prices won't increase without your agreement.

What kinds of fees are we talking about? I would estimate that a "reasonable fee" for performing a site visit is in the range of $1,000— $2,000 per day, plus all out-of-pocket expenses.

Steve Sez:
Do you think that a desperate borrower would stoop to sending pictures of a better property and telling the lender who he has never met and has no allegiance to, that the property is his? Is it any wonder then that the hard money lender won't take any substitutes for a physical inspection?

Occasionally, you can negotiate with a hard money lender about his expenses. It's obvious, however, that if he says no, and doesn't come to see your property, you have no chance whatsoever of getting your loan. Each lender will have a schedule for the amount of his inspection fees. What does this mean? Be prepared to spend money to get money. Sometimes, you can, however, negotiate with the lender to try to pay him one half of his fee prior to his arrival, and the balance when he gets off of the plane.

Regardless of the inspection fee schedule, as I mentioned above, get it in writing! You should have a written agreement from your prospective lender detailing the terms of both the inspection trip and the potential loan, if he approves the application. You should also have a written travel agreement signed with your lender so that you know exactly what is expected of both you and the lender when he gets there. Ask your lender to include a conditional loan commitment within the travel agreement. It should say that if he likes the value and condition of the property, he is prepared to make you a loan on terms as are described in the travel agreement. In this way, at least the lender is representing to you that if he travels to your property and that if it is as represented, he will make you the loan. Again, get everything in writing. And, it makes sound financial sense to get someone to help you with this task. You won't save any money by skimping here.

Steve Sez:
No site inspection *no loan!* Get your lender to the property as quickly as you can or you'll end up with no $$$. And ask him to include a conditional loan commitment in his travel agreement.

Let's review: Most hard money lenders are of the opinion that they must personally visit, value, and approve the property themselves before they will commit to a loan of any amount at all. They have you in a difficult spot. Therefore, make sure the hard money lender you select is of the highest integrity. Refer to Section Three of this book to learn how to check out the ethics of your prospective lender. **This is a must!**

Normally, a hard money lender's site inspection replaces the need for a formal appraisal done by a third party. If a hard money lender tells you that both a site visit plus an independent appraisal are required, be suspicious. This may be a hard money lender who just wants a free trip somewhere and really doesn't understand or have the experience to know what they're looking at when they get there.

Most legitimate hard money lenders will not require you to complete another appraisal after they complete their site inspection. Therefore, the amount you are charged for the physical inspection and valuation should be the total amount you will pay for the hard money lender's appraisal process. If the lender still wants a formal appraisal after his inspection, you have gotten a very insecure lender who has no understanding of what a smooth and efficient hard money process actually is. He is clearly not the lender you need.

An Actual Experience
Wow, What a Bad Lender! Watch Out for This One.

I once made a loan to a fellow in New Mexico using his undeveloped acreage and undeveloped and unimproved lots as the collateral. His development plans included a championship golf course, club house, commercial office and high-end residential uses for the property. My loan was to complete the payment to the golf course developer for his design and to pay some other pre-construction costs and expenses. He had the balance of the development money ready to go or—so he said.

As luck would have it, Murphy of the Murphy's Law fame ... (Remember him?) was a member of his board of directors. Our borrower took too long for the golf course design, lost most of his presale contracts as the result, and then lost his bank financing for the infrastructure and the start of construction. He had to scramble to find replacement financing. Without contracts in place for the sale of single family homes and upscale casita's (a fancy word that lets you charge more for townhouses), no bank would loan him money to complete the development.

He found a group of hard money lenders on the east coast who told him that they were interested in helping him out of his problem. They allegedly heard the description of the property, heard the borrower's estimate of completed value ($50,000,000) and told him that it would cost him $75,000 to schedule a site visit. Yes, you heard correctly—$75,000! After all, they were planning to fly three executives of their company down to New Mexico to "inspect the property" on the company Lear Jet. After he heard that three people were coming to look at his collateral on the inspection trip, he surmised that they must really mean business and are serious about making him the loan, so he wired them the $75,000. What else did you expect?

The inspection took approximately three hours during which time the lenders reviewed the plans for the subdivision with the borrower, physically saw a good portion of the 2,000 total home sites, and then inspected the balance of the acreage.

They then promptly flew to Las Vegas for the weekend, and told him they would call him the next Monday morning. Maybe they have called you by mistake because it's about eight years now and the borrower has had no word from them yet. I'm sure that the letter just got lost in the mail or they lost his phone number. After all, what do you expect for only $75,000?

The moral of this story is: please check out your prospective lender very carefully! Don't let me be writing about you in the next edition of my book in six months.

A Cautious Reminder

In some cases, especially with loans under $50,000, many lenders will say no to the application or will accept an outside appraisal because they don't want to spend the time and energy reviewing a loan with little income potential. For example, if your loan request is actually $50,000 and you are in Spokane, Washington, and the lender is in Atlanta, Georgia, and he charges a $2,000 per day, travel fee plus expenses, it's a two-day trip plus air fare, rental car, gas, meals, hotel, and other miscellaneous costs. Overall, the trip will probably cost you around $6,000. No lender with integrity will ever suggest you spend $6,000 to borrow only $50,000.

> **Steve Sez:**
> Site visits by a good hard money lender may be a real bargain to you and your need for money fast!

Weighing Your Options

If a new appraisal is cheaper than the hard money lenders site visit—and he'll accept it—go that route. As a matter of fact, why not ask the hard money lender who he would like to use and who he will accept as an appraiser, if anyone. One drawback to consider if you and your lender agree to use a third party appraiser—in addition to the amount of time it can take to complete the appraisal process—is your lost opportunity to meet the hard money lender face-to-face, which could make future deals easier to close.

Don't forget that one of the most important aspects of using a hard money lender over time is that you can easily develop a relationship that will make future loans more quickly available. He will get to know you and your on-time payment history. He'll come to know that you are probably correct when you say that the collateral is worth a certain amount. He will get to know that you're a person with integrity who can be counted on to do what you say. This may not be important to you if this is the only time you foresee using the services of such a lender. But if you have the choice, consider it carefully before you select one option over another.

If the property is valuable, and you're looking to borrow a signifi-cant amount of money, the hard money lender's fee to travel may not be the worst thing in the world. It's all relative. There is no sense in spending $6,000 for a site inspection if the loan request is for $50,000. I deliberately made this example a bad one to make a point: You can quickly see that spending a few thousand dollars to borrow a few hundred thousand dollars or more, is within the range of possibility.

This really should cause you to evaluate the profit potential of your project. If the profit potential is such that the travel fee doesn't seem worth it, then you may want to reconsider doing the project at all unless you use a local lender.

Improving the Process

With regard to real estate that you currently own, we have discussed the use of a third party to complete an independent appraisal if your hard money lender will accept this valuation.... What about real estate that you don't own but are buying and need to close fast? This is where having a hard money lender in place can be a huge help. Once you've gone through the process of selecting the right lender for you, you'll be set to invest in other properties with all of the benefits of rapid funding from the same lender.

For property you don't own, I suggest you do your own in-depth investigation of what you are proposing to purchase (as we've said before, this is called "due diligence"). This includes a trip to the local courthouse to look at real estate records. Most clerks will help you look at books that will tell you things like current mortgages on the land, any lawsuits regarding the property, and whether or not a foreclosure or bankruptcy has ever occurred. It may also tell you what the prior owners had paid for the property over the decades and how the price has fluctuated. In many states, the appearance of a document called a "homestead deed" should tip you off that the owner may have or may be about to file for bankruptcy.

You'll want to do this due diligence and much more before making an offer on any real estate. Make sure that you have the help of an experienced real estate investor and an experienced real estate broker as you analyze the property in question for its economic viability as an investment for you. This is especially true if this is your first entry into the field of this type of property.

Chapter Summary

Whether you are dealing with a hard money lender or a bank, both will want to have a clear understanding of the value of the collateral you are pledging. Hard money lenders will most often use a site visit to arrive at their estimate of value as opposed to a recent appraisal. It doesn't pay to spend a lot of time negotiating with your hard money lender with regards to his fee for the inspection. This is one example of what is commonly referred to as the "golden rule": He with the gold, rules. And if the hard money lender is uncomfortable with the valuation of an appraiser, or doesn't see the property personally and won't accept a third party appraisal, then either way, you do yourself harm. The result is: NO LOAN FOR YOU!

1. Banks routinely require formal appraisals while hard money lenders do not.

2. If you have recently had a formal appraisal completed on your property, ask your lender for a copy.

3. Do not order a formal appraisal to be completed unless your hard money lender specifically asks for one.

4. Make sure that the person who completes an appraisal is well qualified; appraisers with MAI certification have received extensive training.

5. A site inspection trip by a hard money lender may be worth its weight in gold if you are interested in establishing a positive working relationship that can also benefit you into the future.

Next Chapter Preview

In the next chapter, we are going to review how hard money lenders determine "value" in their computation of the loan-to-value ratio used in their formulas. You will learn what is meant by the concept of "quick sale value" or "fire sale value" as the baseline for most hard money lenders with whom I've dealt over the last three decades.

CHAPTER 17

How to Calculate the Quick Sale Value of Your Real Estate

Once I began following my own instincts, sales took off and I became a millionaire. And that, I think, is a key secret to every person's success, be they male or female, banker or pornographer: Trust in your gut.
—Larry Flynt

Because honest hard money lenders will want to earn a good return on their money, they won't want change their lending business into a property ownership and management business by foreclosing on their borrower's properties unnecessarily. If lenders use a lower value in their loan-to-value computations, they can price the foreclosed properties at lower values and get them sold very, very fast. And at these values, they can recover their principal, interest, fees and expenses with ease.

Quick Sale Value: What Is It, and Why It Is Important

Quick sale value is that price at which a piece of property will sell in a relatively short period of time. For some lenders, this may mean within 30 days. For other lenders, it may mean within 60 to 90 days. Every lender will have his own view of how to define quick sale value for himself.

As we have seen, it is critical to lenders who want to remain in the lending business instead of the property ownership business. While no self respecting lender would ever knowingly make a loan to any borrower who he thought couldn't make the loan payments on time, problems do occur.

If the lender had to sell properties that he ended up owning at full fair market value in order to come out OK, it could take many months or even years to recover his loan balance. And, while he owns this property, his money that he uses to loan is tied up in a relatively illiquid piece of real estate which does him no good in his lending business.

All good hard money lenders will want to know this value so that they do not own real estate for long. Bank loan officers generally don't ask about quick sale value because from the point of view of an institution like a bank, they have so much property at any time that they own as the result of foreclosure, and so much money to lend, there is very little danger that they will be unable to make more loans before they sell their real estate owned (known as "REO" property). Banks obviously have vast sums of money from depositors to utilize in their lending business and they have no need to immediately liquidate property in the event of foreclosures.

To the extent that values are important to banks (which they certainly are), they are more interested in the fair market value of the property than in any other measure of valuation.

Fair market value is computed by determining the price at which a transaction will occur between a willing buyer and a willing seller, neither side being under any compulsion to act quickly. It is this value that most appraisers target when preparing a typical appraisal. Fair market value also assumes that the time to market the property is reasonable for the neighborhood. For example, if it takes an average of six months to sell a property in its area, then fair market value is that price at which the property will sell within that period of time.

Federal regulators do not require banks to calculate any measure of quick sale value. Their guidelines require a fair market value appraisal, and then a computation of the loan-to-value numbers from this amount. I have often wondered why regulators don't understand the quick sale concept or require banks to use some version of quick sale value. If banks were to actually use quick sale value as the relevant numbers for their loan guidelines, it is probable that all loans would be lower, and their port-folios safer. This means that the real estate market would be less prone to overvalue property because banks would be lending less money on each transaction. It would keep the lid on values in a sane way, and maybe would have even slowed or stopped the 2008 meltdown in values!

Some hard money lenders are what are known as "loan to own" lenders; they are to be avoided at all costs. We discussed these kinds of lenders back in Chapter 12. "Loan to own" lenders want to own your property at the lowest possible price. So, they make the loan terms very hard to meet.

> **Steve Sez:**
> Quick sale value is of major concern to many hard money lenders who want to keep lending and don't want to end up with a large real estate portfolio to liquidate. Because it is a critical number for your lender, by osmosis, it's important to you, the borrower. Do yourself a big favor and try to understand the quick sale value of your collateral before you call a hard money lender.

An Actual Experience

I Want to Own Your Property Cheaply,
Said the Spider to the Fly.

Sadly, this story happened to a very close friend of mine by the name of Henry. Henry was in desperate need for cash for the development of his latest patent. Some large companies had expressed an interest in his product, and he needed to produce a prototype while they were hotly pursuing him in order to make a deal. He went to a local hard money lender for a loan and ended up pledging his personal residence as collateral located in a very affluent area of Denver.

True to the life of an inventor, the project didn't go quite as he had expected and he missed a payment by a few days. The lender began a foreclosure action against the property immediately. By the time all of the costs, fees, penalties and default interest were added to the principal balance due, there was no way my friend could have paid off the loan. I am certain that the lender had my friend's house in his sights all along. My friend found a lender without scruples without even trying. Too bad for him.

The lender "bought" a very fancy house at a very low price *deliberately*. My friend had no way to redeem the foreclosure at this much higher amount.

Yet Another Actual Experience

Borrower to Appraiser: The Real Appraisal Doesn't Show Enough Value for My Property So Let's Go Shopping for Better Comps and a Higher Valuation.

I received a call from two professional football players living in Kansas City who needed a loan using their two residences as the sole collateral. They needed fast cash to get into another deal or they would lose it (football players should actually stick to playing football, I'm convinced). They had completed a formal appraisal on each house that they wanted to send to me. This appraisal showed that each house was worth $875,000 and they needed to borrow $450,000 using each house as collateral (a little over 50% loan-to-value on their fair market value—pretty sweet for a hard money lender). I arranged to fly out the next day to confirm their findings and estimates of value.

Upon arriving, I first did a walkthrough of the two properties, which showed they were two lovely and large homes. The next step in my due diligence was to look at comps that the appraiser had identified in the neighborhood in order to validate the value.

As I reviewed the appraisals on the houses, and was driving through the area attempting to locate the comps used by the "licensed" appraiser, I noticed that *all* of the comps were within one mile of the two homes that I looked at. Great! Only one problem, however: The comps were directly across an interstate highway and were up on a hill overlooking the entire area. The properties on the top of the hill were in one of the more affluent and desirable areas of the city as I was later told by a real estate broker in the area.

The real estate broker I spoke with was kind enough to pull comps for me that were within the very same subdivision (which were strangely excluded from the appraisal that I had received before the trip), and found that the last six sales put these houses in the range of $400,000 each in fair market value. The borrowers were trying to pull a fast one on an out-of-state lender, believing that I would look at the appraisal and just buy off on the values without doing any more.

A bank might just underwrite and approve the loan using these appraisals because they don't physically visit each property as they make loans. Often banks will, however, order review appraisals to verify the results of the first appraisal. I kept in touch with the broker who sent me the loan and even six months after they came to me, the football pros still hadn't gotten any money, from even one lender. Am I surprised?

Be sure to ask a potential hard money lender early in your discussions how he evaluates collateral. Does he subscribe to the principal of "quick sale value" or does he use some other measure? Does he like the "fire sale" approach of an immediate sale upon foreclosure (let's hope not)? Or have you found the proverbial needle in a haystack: a hard money lender who adheres to the concept of "fair market value"? Whatever valuation measure your lender uses in his lending practices is what you need to compute before you spend the funds to bring the lender out for a site inspection. If he uses the quick sale valuation and you need to borrow more money than this measure of value will bring to you in a loan, you should either re-evaluate your project, find more valuable collateral, or find a more accommodating hard money lender.

Steve Sez:
Try to understand the definition of "value" being used by your hard money lender with your first phone call. Does your property meet his criteria with enough value in order to make your loan amount what you need it to be?

When the lender reviews a property's formal appraisal in a weak market area, he will definitely look to see where the appraiser got his "comps" (property with comparable characteristics). Did he get them from properties that are close, with lower values, or did he have to look outside the immediate area in order to find properties that sold at higher prices. It makes a huge difference to his determination of the ultimate "value" of your property.

Site visits that are required by the majority of good hard money lenders also uncover facts about the surrounding area that even formal appraisals won't uncover. The neighborhood, main roads, schools, shopping and transportation can impact valuations substantially.

An Actual Experience

Location, Location, Location: The Added "Value"
of Being Right Next Door to the Crack Dealers
Association of America, Local 461.

I had a loan request from a Chicago borrower a number of years ago and after some discussion, I decided that it might be a good loan so I flew to Chicago for the property inspection. These properties included 10 single family houses being bought in a package to be rehabbed and flipped. They were all just south and east of Midway Airport.

I walked into the very first house in the package and noticed that the walls had been damaged by what looked like an angry husband or boyfriend. I saw holes that looked like the walls were used a punching bags. The entire house had an odor that indicated it hadn't been cleaned for many, many years. When I went outside, I noticed on the front porch stoop of the house immediately next door, there were a bunch of guys sitting and holding a meeting of what looked like a chapter of the American Association of Crack Dealers. On the other side was a house that served as graffiti artists white board. While some of the "art" on the house wasn't really all that bad, I was certain that these surroundings would really excite families searching for a good house in which to bring up their kids safely.... NOT! How would you like to have your kids right next door to these fine fellows on one side and street artists on the other? Not exactly a new family's dream house!

None of this showed up in the photos of the property nor did they disclose any of this beforehand. The rest of the story was that the other nine homes were a bit better, but not by a measurable margin. The result: significant wasted time, unhappy borrower and no loan (what a surprise).

Appraisers don't have the same interest in the property as someone whose money is riding on an accurate assessment of the collateral's true valuation. So, do *not* be offended if the hard money lender wants to physically see and review your property. You would want to do the same if it were your money on the line.

The following items always affect quick sale value and therefore, are always reviewed on each and every inspection trip:

**Twenty-Three Primary Elements
in the Calculation of "Quick Sale Value"**

1. Location;

2. Size;

3. Other properties presently on the market;

4. Properties that have sold within the last six months that are close in distance and of a similar type;

5. Condition;

6. Zoning of the subject property;

7. Zoning of the immediately surrounding area;

8. Access;

9. Utilities;

10. Encroachments;

11. Easements;

12. Potential for environmental issues;

13. Real estate brokers in the neighborhood and their success;

14. Real estate brokers' opinions about the environment surrounding this property;

15. Compatible use opportunities at this location;

16. The highest and best use of the property;

17. Deferred maintenance in and around the property;

18. The appearance and condition of properties in the immediate two or three block area;

19. The degree of pride in ownership in the neighborhood;

20. Traffic and growth patterns and their effect on property values;

21. The city's plans regarding the immediately surrounding area;

22. The employment base in the immediate area; and

23. Employment trends in the area—growing, shrinking, laying off or hiring.

Valuing New and Existing Construction Projects

I have outlined a list of questions that you may be asked by your hard money lender if you have a property either under construction presently, or to be constructed as collateral. By the way, these items are no different from what you'd see in a bank's construction loan application. They are all items that you should have for your files in any event.

Residential Construction Loan Information— Twenty-Five Necessary Items Needed with a Construction Loan Application

1. Design blueprints;

2. Projected size of the improved property;

3. Complete information on the builder, including copies of the construction contracts;

4. Complete information on the subcontractors who are going to build the building (this may be harder to get because your general contractor may not know yet who he or she will use);

5. Exterior elevation of the building;

6. Comps on similar properties under construction or completed in the immediate area;

7. Bids from each sub-contractor on the job and estimated completed construction cost of the property;

8. Floor plan(s);

9. Utility availability;

10. Survey of the property;

11. Environmental studies;

12. Soil tests;

13. Foundation plans;

14. Type of roof and anticipated warranty;

15. Warranty review for all of the mechanical and structural systems in the house;

16. The variation in use from typical properties in the area, and how this will impact the ultimate value of your property;

17. Experience factor of the borrower/builder/developer and whether they have done projects like this one before;

18. The reasonableness of the construction schedule;

19. A draw request schedule (a draw is an advance from your construction loan that covers previous periods of construction);

20. Marketing plans;

21. A list of upgrades available as additional items;

22. Estimated absorption or sales schedule for the properties;

23. If well and septic are the sources of utilities, well and leach field information will be required;

24. Permit information and pricing;

25. Tap fee information for water, electricity, sewer, and gas; ... and so on.

Commercial Construction

Here are a few other items you may be asked for when building a commercial building:

1. Vacancy statistics if you are constructing a commercial building;

2. Types of tenants that are typical in the immediate area for space like yours;

3. Zoning confirmation;

4. Access information;

5. If the property is commercial, information on traffic counts on the main street in front of the building may be important;

6. Allowable signage pursuant to the local sign codes;

7. Any pre-leasing activity;

8. Lease rates in the neighborhood;

9. Pro forma rental and expense schedules; and

10. A complete review of other unimproved land in the immediate area (here's the concern: Will a comparable property be built that will take all of the subject property's tenants leaving the building in question empty or under-leased?).

I realize that these lists may seem agonizingly long; but, they are used only for construction projects. And, believe me, when you build a property from the ground up, you'll have many more lists of required information than these items.

Loan documentation in these cases should absolutely be prepared by an experienced attorney who clearly understands the construction process from the ground up. Because a construction loan can quickly become very complex for both you and the lender, here is another area where having an experienced person to provide some consulting or mentoring services to you will be quite helpful.

The moral of the story is that if you are seeking either a new or even mid-construction loan, be prepared! You will need to have a lot of information at your fingertips in order to have any chance of getting a loan, let alone face the issue of closing quickly. Start assembling all the information you can find. You will need complete project information in any event, for your own internal development planning and activities. Why not organize it for both you and for your hard money lender.

Chapter Summary

Banks and mortgage companies are highly regulated institutions. Legislation and policies enacted by both the state and federal governments require the oversight of both banks and mortgage lending practices closely. Because of the complexity of a loan, securing a bank loan with any speed at all is now all but impossible.

A hard money lender will also pay very close attention to the loan-to-value ratio for construction loans. Because they have no regulatory oversight, they can be more creative and flexible and hence speedier, in their loan structure without fear of any consequences (but for the loss of their principal).

1. Make sure that any comps that you suggest to your lender are reasonable, accurate and current.

2. A quick sale value represents the approximate value of your property should it have to be sold relatively quickly; quick sale value is computed in order to add safety to any loan made for the lender.

3. Construction loans can be very complex. Start early in your search process, and have all of your information prepared and organized.

Next Chapter Review

In the next chapter, we'll take a look at some ways that hard money lenders can employ creativity and flexibility in their loan structures in order to make you a loan where others would not.

CHAPTER 18

Loan Qualification ... and What Could Knock You Out of the Game

If you believe in what you are doing, then let nothing
hold you up in your work. Much of the best work
of the world has been done against seeming impossibilities.
The thing is to get the work done.
—Dale Carnegie

It is certainly clear in this economy that individuals and small businesses are facing a harsh financial climate. Banks are making fewer loans based upon their tightened qualification guidelines and many hard money lenders find their cash flow and funds available for investment greatly restricted. In this chapter, we'll take a look at loan qualification as well as how a prior personal bankruptcy can affect your ability to secure both conventional and hard money loans.

Creativity and flexibility—the things we covered in Chapter 4 can be applied equally in the qualification arena. Yes, you still have to qualify even with a hard money lender as we now know.

Difference #12: Flexibility

For bank qualification, you must fit into specific income and credit models. A hard money lender will work hard to be as creative and flexible as your project requires without focusing on income and credit for qualification.

Bank Loan Qualification? Okay, I can hear you say, "Oh, yeah, qualification! Steve's gonna drop the bomb now!" No, not necessarily. But surely you don't expect a hard money lender to just pass out his cash without some assurance that it will be paid back. And if that part of the plan fails to work, then the collateral value has to be sufficient to cover the principal, interest and costs ... right?

To qualify for conventional bank financing, income and credit are paramount (remember that it's all about you in the eyes of a bank). Even with acceptable collateral, if your income and credit are not sufficient to meet the requirements of the bank, you won't qualify for a loan. Banks are interested in multiple sources of income to lower the probability of a default.

And, the qualification process is hard and seems to be getting harder every time a bank consolidates with another bank or is bought out. Recently, banks have become very conservative about lending money.

The requirements to get a bank loan are significant and complex. The paperwork is cumbersome at best and ominous at worst. Think back to our list of comparative documents in Chapter 14 required for a hard money loan versus a bank loan. Remember that every fact you represent to a banker must be verified. This means you will be supplying tax returns with great amounts of additional information potentially, which could take you well beyond the date upon which you need to close your loan.

Hard Money Loan Qualification

What does it take to qualify for a hard money loan by comparison? We have discussed the various aspects of the hard money loan and what many of the hard money lenders will typically evaluate as being relevant. Compared to the process required by banks, the hard money process is streamlined, easy and, most of all *fast*.

The hard money process, as you know, focuses on the collateral's value, not on the borrower as an individual. There is one major exception to this hard money lending rule: bankruptcy. We'll talk about how bankruptcy is viewed and your options shortly.

We've already listed some items you'll need to have handy for your hard money lender in order to make the loan process sail through successfully if the values check out to the lender's satisfaction. If you plan ahead as I suggest, you'll be ready even for the most difficult of hard money lenders.

Hard money qualification isn't overly complicated even if you are purchasing a piece of property. The information needed for your hard money lender is a fraction of what a bank will require. The information about the property is something you should have or want to have anyway *before* you go through with the purchase. After you become the owner, it's too late to do anything about defects or problems that weren't disclosed to you or that you discovered on your own after closing, except to sue the seller and his broker. That's when the money flows the wrong way ... away from you.

This is the point in the qualification process where the real estate receives a valuation from the hard money lender. You may want to revisit the last chapter about valuation and how it is determined. But keep this in mind: The figure arrived at for the worth of any property may or may not have any relationship to the price you're paying (if you're buying property).

Steve Sez:
It all boils down to value. If the value and the loan-to-value are both there, you will almost always get a hard money loan.

At the start of this chapter, I mentioned one area that could be a potential qualification battlefield for you as a borrower with either a bank or a hard money lender: bankruptcy. A past bankruptcy, whether it was voluntary or involuntary, will have an effect upon your qualifying for a loan.

Bankruptcy

Taking a personal or business bankruptcy is not the end of the world, and it absolutely does not brand you as a bad or irresponsible person in the eyes of the hard money lender. It will, however, be a mark on your credit record when you speak with your lender—perhaps one that will stop you from moving past the application or qualification stage. But you need to be honest about the bankruptcy from the beginning. It is, after all, a public record for all to see.

Steve Sez:
The obvious concern with a borrower, who has previously declared bankruptcy, is that it may be a hint of how he handles adversity. Does the borrower just throw up his hands and just quit? Or does he fight until he solves his problems? I would much prefer a hard fighting borrower any day.

I won't kid you: A hard money lender will probably see bankruptcy as a red flag, and it will be evaluated and weighed. The good news is that while the hard money lender will look at the bankruptcy, he will, also weigh it and evaluate the "why" of the bankruptcy.

There Are Three Typical Types of Bankruptcy

• Chapter 7: Full liquidation

• Chapter 11: Rehabilitation and Reorganization

• Chapter 13: Rehabilitation and Reorganization for wage earners

Chapter 7 Bankruptcy

Chapter 7 bankruptcy is usually used by individuals or entities and involves a complete liquidation of nonexempt assets (speak with a bankruptcy lawyer to get this definition). The reasons behind this kind of bankruptcy are as personal and individual as you are: unexpected medical bills, a death in the family with no life insurance, loss of a job, or maybe unfortunate business results. By the time that you are through this process, you will be relieved of almost everything that you own save for a bit of exempt property. Most of your unsecured debt will be wiped out (herein lies both the problem and the opportunity—someone has lost money with you). The secured debt remains—and must be repaid. One of the worst aspects of a Chapter 7 bankruptcy is that it is reported on all credit reports for 10 years.

Chapter 11 Bankruptcy

A Chapter 11 bankruptcy is ideal if you have a foreclosure action that has been commenced against your property or if you have either secured or unsecured debts that are overwhelming your business operations. . In these cases, an individual or company can file a Chapter 11 bankruptcy and possibly retain possession of their property.

Chapter 13 Bankruptcy

Chapter 13 bankruptcies are referred to as "wage earners' plans." This type of bankruptcy gives individuals with regular income the opportunity to propose a plan to use installment payments to meet their delinquencies. Typically, the repayment plan can't stretch beyond five years. While a debtor is in Chapter 13, no creditor can begin or continue any efforts to collect debt. One of the biggest advantages of this type of bankruptcy is that a homeowner can stop foreclosure proceedings and propose a plan to cure the delinquency over time. There are eligibility requirements, however. Corporations and partnerships are ineligible to file Chapter 13 bankruptcies.

To a lender, a bankruptcy just looks bad. It wouldn't be uncommon for the hard money lender to believe that the debtor was either financially irresponsible or had little conscience. A new lender is left to wonder if it can happen to them if they proceed to make a loan to someone who then encounters additional financial challenges. Will he simply walk away? There is one proactive choice you can make beforehand.

If you or your company's bankruptcy was the result of any special circumstances, I have found that a special, one-page document that you provide to new lenders with your loan information makes good sense. Prepare it long beforehand so that you don't have to re-remember the pain of your past experience. Actually, here is one area where I would look for a professional coach or writer to help you write this letter in a judgment-free manner that will be very effective in explaining the reasons for your bankruptcy.

My purpose here isn't to give you a lesson in bankruptcy. It's only to remind you that bankruptcy is seen by each lender differently. Most of the time, a bank will frown dramatically on a recent bankruptcy. A hard money lender may well overlook the bankruptcy if the collateral is good enough regardless of how recently the bankruptcy was filed. This is especially true if you can show a lender that you are now doing better and can actually pay him back with regular payments. The hard money lender is a better resource for loans that can't withstand the scrutiny or timing of a bank.

Steve Sez:
A hard money lender may well overlook a personal or corporate bankruptcy if the collateral is good enough.

Chapter Summary

Qualification: To some, bankruptcy is a hard word to live with—particularly if you have less than stellar credit. Although hard money lenders look at the value of collateral and not at you personally, they are still interested in how you manage your money and how you deal with adversity.

If you do have issues in your past that are reflected in your credit, be up front with your hard money lender; he will probably be a pretty understanding kind of guy. If the reasons for your financial problems were clearly beyond your control—severe illness in the family, theft or fraud—then you're in even better shape with a hard money lender. The reason for your bankruptcy in these cases has little to do with your ethics and integrity (not to mention with your fighting spirit) and everything to do with random, uncaused incidents that life just throws you from time to time.

1. Banks have specific income and credit models a potential borrower must fit into; hard money lenders do not.

2. A hard money lender will closely scrutinize a potential borrower who has declared bankruptcy.

3. There are several types of bankruptcy and each variety is used in different situations.

4. A bankruptcy will remain on your credit report for up to 10 years, depending on the type of bankruptcy you filed.

5. If you have filed bankruptcy, be upfront with your hard money lender. Its public information and he'll find out anyway; trying to hide it will only destroy your integrity.

Next Chapter Preview

The next chapter will really be of use and benefit to you directly. I'm going to describe one of the benefits of finding a creative hard money lender. It's about cross collateralization and in a few minutes, you'll have a pretty good understanding of this very creative technique that can put you across the finish line in first place in your race for funds.

CHAPTER 19

Cross Collateralization

Well, when you're trying to create things that are new,
you have to be prepared to be on the edge of risk.
—Michael Eisner

You can't imagine how powerful this technique can be when you need funds fast! In this chapter, we're going to take a look at creative cross collateralization, a powerful tool of hard money lending that banks cannot easily match; particularly when the additional collateral is in a state other than the state where you live and are doing business. Most banks and other conventional lenders are restricted to lending in their primary market areas and do not have the capability or the interest in reviewing collateral in distant locations. Many hard money lenders by contrast, have the ability, if they choose, to add this major element of flexibility that may make a deal work.

The concept of *cross collateralization* is basically pretty simple. It is the addition of sufficient other collateral, no matter what kind or where it is located, in order to provide enough additional equity to your loan package that will cause your hard money lender to approve your loan request. Cross collateralization is an excellent technique to consider when your primary collateral fails to provide enough value to make the loan work at the level needed for your transaction.

Cross collateralization works *only* in those situations where the borrower has other collateral available to him no matter who owns the additional property.

Most, if not all banks are very resistant to making loans in unfamiliar areas of their state or even worse, in other states. And heaven forbid, if the additional collateral is other than real estate. You'll never get a banker to even look at out-of-state, non-real estate collateral—and you can bank on that! It will take either a national bank with branches everywhere, or a banker with a very liberal outlook (unlike any banker whom I've ever met) who will seriously look at a loan with two or more pieces of geographically disbursed property.

Keep in mind that if your lender allows your use of additional collateral, you are likely going to be adding to the amount of time that it will take to get the loan approved and closed. Each step of the loan process including a physical inspection and valuation must be completed for each individual piece of property pledged as collateral, no matter where located. If collateral is located far away from your location, you have the problem of coordinating a site visit by your hard money lender with someone at the property who can explain the attributes and negatives of this additional collateral.

> **Steve Sez:**
> You can use anyone's property in any location to cross collateralize your loan with many hard money lenders. Think of everyone you know regardless of where they are located. Someone out there is a good candidate to put up collateral to help you.

Let's look at how the numbers add up when you elect to pledge several pieces of property. If you want to borrow $100,000 and you have an asset worth $200,000 with an existing $75,000 first mortgage already in place, there isn't enough equity left in the property to support your need for $100,000. Remember, if your lender will not exceed a 60 percent loan-to-value ratio, the most that a hard money lender can loan will be $120,000 (60 percent of $200,000) less the current first mortgage of $75,000. With this in mind, the lender will loan you a net of $45,000 in new money, which is $55,000 less than you need. Sadly, without more collateral, you will not be able to borrow the money you need, using only this property.

There is a solution, however. Remember that because of the magic of hard money cross collateralization, you will be able to add additional collateral to the loan in order to secure the lender sufficiently so that your loan can be approved and closed.

A Numerical Example

Let's assume that Uncle Norm's property in Ft. Lauderdale is worth $100,000 with no mortgage. If you (and Uncle Norm, of course) will allow the hard money lender to cross-collateralize this loan by taking a mortgage on both properties, the lender is likely to approve the request for the larger loan amount. If you assume that the lender will loan you 60 percent of this value, then you will get an additional $60,000, which, when added to the net cash disbursement to you of $45,000 on the first property, solves your problem.

How does a hard money lender go about legally securing multiple properties? If the first property is located in California, and the second property is located in Florida, mortgages may be placed on each property. The legal process of doing this, however, is something that is handled completely by your lender. As far as you are concerned, all you need to do is to have a bit of patience and you will get the funds that you need, quickly.

There are other cross collateralization issues that also need to be considered.

One Loan/Multiple Properties/Different States

Cross collateralization is a little more complex when the property is located in multiple states. The same legal principals basically still apply to the transaction from state-to-state. As you know, every state has its own laws that govern real estate transactions and mortgages (or deeds of trust).

A good hard money lender with his lawyer, however, will be able to coordinate parties, title companies, and attorneys in multiple locations and make sure that the process is highly organized and efficient. I have actually had closings involving properties in multiple states that have closed within days of the loan request. Don't let the potential complexity discourage you from going forward with your search for a loan using multi-state collateral. It's out there for the taking.

The greatest obstacle in the loan process if you have properties in different states, is finding a hard money lender willing to consider properties in various locations. I'm not going to kid you; it's difficult to find lenders who are truly national in scope and who will even entertain a loan application with collateral in more than one state. It isn't impossible though. It just isn't nearly as common as finding a hard money lender who will make loans when the collateral is located within the same state. Make sure that you study the portion of my book dealing with how to locate a good hard money lender in your particular situation. It will take some research, but it's worth it to find the right lender for you.

The total cost of your loan will obviously be higher when you have one loan that is cross-collateralized by two or more properties. However, you will not have to fly to different locations to sign the documents for each specific piece of collateral. Typically, title company closing agents are willing to overnight the documents to you for your signature and notarization. You then merely overnight the signed documents back to each title company for recording, and your loan is ready to disburse once the title company receives confirmation of the recording in each state.

In the middle of all of the logistical issues, make sure that you only sign one promissory note no matter how many pieces of property are involved. This is the document that lenders love because it is the one that you sign promising to repay the loan. In the case of multiple promissory notes that are signed by you, each such promissory note could be considered a new original, so be very watchful of what you sign or don't sign. There should only be one original promissory note in existence for your entire loan. And, this is no matter how many pieces of collateral you are using to get your loan properly secured or where they are located. This topic is so important that I deal with it a bit later on in the book.

It's important that you understand that even though you won't physically have to go to each state if you have multi-state collateral, it will be necessary for the hard money lender to feel comfortable with the values of each property. Take another look at Chapter 16 where we deal with the due diligence process that must be completed by your hard money lender. There will be extra time and extra expense incurred in order to complete the physical inspections that your lender will typically perform on each such property.

On balance, this loan structure is not anything new or novel for a good hard money lender. The ability to close quickly, however, is dependent upon your being proactive and dealing with the issues and mechanics of the loan before they become problems. Issues cost money and take time. Become an active part of the closing process and you'll insure a fast closing.

Cross collateralization is definitely more of a headache for your lenders attorney in terms of coordination of documents, their recording, the title work, and so on. Again, your hard money lender will have definite ideas about how he would like to close the loan including the choice of lawyers, title insurance companies and other mechanics (such as the timing of the disbursement of cash after the closing has been completed).

The entire concept and practice of utilizing multi state properties is to accomplish the combination of values together to make the overall loan satisfy the lenders loan-to-value requirements. It would be a great time to review the section on loan-to-value computation in order to fully understand the math involved.

Steve Sez:
Cross collateralization is absolutely worth the extra money and time if it gets you your loan within days. If it represents more work than your lender really wants to do, get another lender!

Let's focus on how and when you will get your funds after this multi-state closing occurs. Obviously, your lender will need to be an integral part of the timing. In all likelihood, your lender's attorney will arrange the disbursement after he has received confirmation that all documentation has been received by the title company in each state. In addition, the lender will not disburse unless and until he knows that he has a fully secured and fully insured loan in each of the relevant states. Each title closing officer in each state will either email, fax or call the lender's counsel to let him know that all of the paperwork and recording is complete for his property. At that point, when the last of these communications has been received, and the title insurance companies are ready, willing, and able to issue title insurance to your lender in each state, then and only then will the funds be disbursed to you.

Imagine a situation wherein you, the borrower, have properties in four or five states. Further, it takes the combined values of all of them together to get the funds that you need from a hard money lender. If you will just reread the discussion above and assume that two or three more states are added to the mix, you will see how easy it really is to cross collateralize a loan regardless of where the collateral is located. This is one of the big benefits to working with a flexible hard money lender. It can get you money very fast whereas a bank would most often turn a blind eye to this arrangement without even a thought.

Steve Sez:
Never, never sign more than one original of the promissory note in a cross-collateralized loan unless you want to risk paying off your loan more than once. (For most of my borrowers, paying the loan off once is sufficient—it should be for you as well.)

I know you want to get your funds as quickly as possible. However, all of the necessary legalities are likely to be quite a bit beyond your expertise. And, I would hope that you don't want to start to practice law at this point. My advice, therefore, is to have an experienced friend or a good real estate lawyer stand by your side to make sure that all of the mechanics are handled in their proper sequence and timing—even if the lender has his own attorneys overseeing the process.

You need someone to look out for *your* best interests. It will cost a bit more, but you will be pleased with your loan when it closes in a matter of days because of this experienced assistance. And, you'll feel as if you can sleep well at night knowing that you didn't get taken advantage of, and that there is nothing in the loan structure that you didn't realize or understand.

One Loan/Multiple Properties/Same State

When you cross collateralize your loan with multiple properties within the same state, the process should be quite easy. It will involve only one closing agent for the lender, probably only one title insurance company, and only one property insurance company. Therefore, it will not only be less expensive all the way around; it will be much faster than a multi-state closing as you will only need one closing with mortgage documents that will be recorded against each of the separate properties in their respective counties.

This is how it typically works:

Let's say that you have two parcels of real estate that you want to use as collateral. One of them is a duplex in the eastern part of the state and the other is a vacation property in the western part of the state. As both properties are in one state, in all likelihood, there will only be one closing at the title insurance company. They will coordinate the closing, recording of each of the mortgages, and the disbursement of recording expenses, all of the closing costs and other expenses. In most circumstances, you will receive your proceeds check after the recording of the mortgages has occurred. It's the only way that your lender knows for sure that he is fully and properly collateralized.

The property description in the mortgage document will either include the two pieces of property being used as collateral, or one such document may be prepared for each of the two properties.

The benefits to the latter include the fact that you won't have to wait for a sequential recording process, but rather a simultaneous process which may result in a check to you sooner.

Don't be worried about signing each of these multiple originals of the mortgage or deed of trust. They may be couriered or sent via overnight express for recording with virtually no risk to you. The mortgage document is not the evidence of the loan, so no one can collect on just that alone. Anyone would also need the original promissory note in order to claim that they are owed money, of which you are only signing one.

Once you have the mortgage recorded on two or more different pieces of property either within or outside of your state, the result is that each piece of property serves as equal collateral for your one loan. If you borrow money using multiple properties, one of the issues that you need to clarify with the lender is what happens if you would like to sell or refinance one of the properties but not all of them at one time? In this case, you need to negotiate a partial release of the mortgage on various pieces of property, as we have discussed in Chapter 4.

Steve Sez:

In the area of loans, verbal agreements do not work to your benefit! If you negotiate "partial releases" from the mortgages with your lender, be sure that they are explicitly described in the loan documents (usually in the mortgage document).

Here is a bit more on negotiating partial releases:

There are several strategies that you can pursue in order to introduce partial release language into your loan documents. The single best way to obtain a partial release for separate pieces of collateral, in my opinion, is to offer your hard money lender a disproportionately high amount of principal pay down so that with a diminished principal balance due to the lender after the pay down, the remaining collateral represents sufficient remaining value for this reduced balance.

I have always allowed my borrowers to partially pay down their loan and release parts of their collateral. This is simply part of what should be the philosophy of a good hard money lender who is oriented towards doing what is in the best interests of the borrower and not always for himself. As long as the lender's loan balance is safely collateralized, with an adequate margin of safety, the lender should be more than willing to accommodate you. You should avoid a lender who will not consider granting partial releases (if you are using multiple pieces of collateral for your loan) from the mortgage upon the payment to him of part of the principal due on the loan.

Do you remember the old mortgage burning parties in the 1950s and 60s? They happened when a borrower made his final payment to the bank and now owned his property free and clear. Getting a partial release is like that. You'll again own the property free and clear of the lien (the mortgage) recorded by your hard money lender. You may have other liens on the property but, in reality, it means that the released piece of collateral is no longer securing the loan that you obtained from your hard money lender. If there are no other loans on the property you'll have 100 percent equity. How nice does this feel?

Take extra precaution to be sure that you have the details of the partial release schedule clearly reflected in both the Promissory Note, and in the mortgage document most importantly. Again, this is where having someone on your team who understands the legalities and construction of loan documents is truly valuable.

You may have noticed that I continually suggest to you that having someone help you through this process might not be such a bad idea. I might even say it stronger like: Never even think of entering this, or any loan transaction, without the assistance of competent counsel. In this case, he should review the loan documents to make sure that the partial release language is clear and unambiguous. If you make the required payment, you want the release to be merely mechanical so that it will occur without any further discussion, discretion or decisions.

Chapter Summary

If you are "moving up the business ladder," taking on larger projects, it is likely that you will not have any single piece of property that is sufficient in value to serve as the complete collateral for larger loan amounts. While that may be a show-stopper for a bank or other commercial lender, most good hard money lenders will understand cross-collateralization. In short, you can combine two or more properties into one collateral package. Additionally, there are a number of excellent and creative hard money lenders who will work with multi-state collateral.

1. Cross collateralization is a tool that can help you get your loan approved when any single property by itself won't qualify for a hard money loan.

2. Traditional commercial lenders frequently are unwilling and unable to make you a loan that includes multi-state collateral.

3. When using properties in several states as collateral for your loan, it is likely that both the costs associated with the loan and the time necessary to approve and close your loan will go up. But, if your project is excellent, the extra cost and timing shouldn't matter even in the short run.

4. You should always try to have an experienced professional stand by your side as you negotiate the terms of your potential collateral based loan. This is especially true in the case of cross collateralized loans.

5. If you anticipate the ability to pay down all or a portion of the principal balance of the loan before its maturity date, you should negotiate a partial release of the mortgage on individual properties in advance of a loan closing.

Next Chapter Preview

Are you ready to learn about the structure of Notes and Mortgages? I think that you will be quite pleased to find out how flexible a hard money loan can be!

CHAPTER 20

How to Negotiate Your Promissory Note and Mortgage to Get the Best Possible Terms

*Always borrow money from a pessimist,
he doesn't expect to be paid back.*
—Author Unknown

At the heart of all real estate based loan documents is the promissory note, the mortgage (or deed of trust), assignment of rents, and other "standard" real estate loan agreements. In this chapter, we'll take a more detailed look at the common documents that you will be expected to sign at your loan closing. While banks and commercial lenders subscribe to a fairly rigid set of lending guidelines (and hence, loan documents), you will find much more flexibility with a hard money lender and hence the documents will not tend to be cookie cutter forms of agreements.

For anyone new to loans, the promissory note is the document that you will sign at the loan closing. Within the promissory note is your promise to repay the money that you have borrowed on specific terms. It is the single most important loan document in the closing file to both you and to the lender.

The mortgage—or deed of trust—is the document that is recorded in the appropriate city or county land records and which conveys a security interest in the property to the lender as collateral for his loan. Does this mean that you don't own your own property anymore? Do you think that you are actually signing over your property to your lender? I can't believe how many poor borrowers misunderstand what they are doing at the loan closing. They often think that when they sign their loan documents, somehow, they no longer own their own property. It definitely does *not* mean the loss of your property at the closing.

When you sign a mortgage, you are giving the lender a security interest in your property. It merely becomes collateral for his loan. He can't stage a party for his 500 closest friends in your apartment building, open his office in your house, or decide to open an ice crème store in your shopping center. He really has *no* rights to do anything with the collateral with the possible exception of physically inspecting the property to assure himself of the fact that the property is being maintained properly. He doesn't want his collateral to go down in value before the loan is repaid completely.

Granting your lender a mortgage on your property does mean, however, that he may take your property and sell it if you don't make your mortgage payments as promised. Before he could do this, though, he must comply with the state's specific foreclosure laws that prevent you from losing your property unless you are given the opportunity to cure the default. If you do not successfully resolve the issue within the time prescribed by the state statute, then this is when you should get quite nervous (unless you don't want to own your property any longer). The foreclosure process is what a lender (actually all lenders including hard money lenders) go through to ultimately recover the loan balance due. Once they own your property as the result of the foreclosure process, they realize value out of your collateral by selling it at the conclusion of this process.

Difference #13: Loan Terms

Borrowers are locked into bank's prescribed requirements when it comes to negotiating the terms of their note. Borrowers have more room for flexible loan terms with a hard money lender. You will be thrilled to see the difference that a creative lender can make!

The note is the place where having a hard money lender is like having a personal chef. Want to pay only interest for six months and then add a dash of principal? Okay. How about no payments for two months, then payments on the last day of each quarter? No sweat. Would you like to sprinkle in some principal prepayments throughout the loan and have your new payments adjusted to reflect the new principal balance? Can do! Hard money lenders can often comply with your needs, easily. And they should always listen to you regardless of what you need in your loan structure.

You'd Never Be Able to Negotiate Terms Like These with a Bank

But you can with many hard money lenders. Find a good one who is flexible and you've found the missing ingredient to your financial growth. Once they feel secure with the collateral, they should be willing to allow you some creativity in your loan structure. Have a good reason for a special structure and more often than not, a flexible hard money lender will at least listen seriously if not agree completely to your terms.

> **Steve Sez:**
> Be happy that the bank has said no! You heard me, I said happy! You'll see a big difference in loan structure with many hard money lenders that you would have never found if the bank had said yes.

Remember that I've been saying that a hard money loan is among the most creative available? The promissory note is where your hard money lender can be the most creative.

The Promissory Note

The note—sometimes known as a promissory note—is where you'll find all of the details of your loan (also known as the *loan terms*). It is the document you will sign at the loan closing wherein you promise to repay the funds with interest and costs in full to the lender. It describes all of the terms of that repayment obligation.

It describes the definition of default. It may describe partial pre-payments ... and so on and on. Read it carefully! And after you have read it carefully, reread it again. It's too important to treat lightly. Remember to have someone familiar with loan terms review the note for you as well in order to highlight anything in it that is unfavorable to you.

Promissory notes, as a general rule, are not recorded. Only one original promissory note should be signed regardless of how many properties you use as collateral for your loan. You may not realize this, but each signed original of the promissory note can be deemed a separate and enforceable promise to pay. Don't you just want to pay once? I would think that this would be enough.

A day or two before closing, you should be given copies of the documents that you'll be asked to sign at the actual closing. If no one offers them to you, call the lender and ask him for copies of what you will be asked to sign at closing. He should be very accommodating as he should want you to understand the terms and conditions of your loan.

Always review the promissory note and the settlement statement very carefully. Although it may be tempting to skip over their review, don't! Review each and every term of the note very carefully.

Review each line item on the settlement statement carefully. The settlement statement describes who pays for what in the transaction. Once you sign it, it becomes final.

By asking for the loan documents in advance of the closing, you will get a good idea of what you'll be looking at when you go into the closing room. Make sure that everything that you and your lender talked about is contained within the note and nothing more (and nothing less either). Make sure that the terms are precisely as you remember them, or don't sign any documents.

This is another area in which a side-kick would be of great value. Make sure, once again, to find someone familiar with your deal with the lender, and equally as familiar with promissory notes, and loans.

Critically Important

Remember: Ask questions early. As a matter of fact, I have always urged my borrowers to retain the services of a lawyer or other expert to review their loan documents so that there are no surprises at the closing. In this way, borrowers are aware of all of the provisions of each of the documents that they will be signing at the closing.

> **Steve Sez:**
> If the promissory note and other documents aren't exactly what you want or expect, **DO NOT SIGN THEM UNTIL YOU UNDERSTAND THEM COMPLETELY!**

Loan documents are filled with legalese (a strange foreign language only spoken and understood by lawyers which mere mortals have great difficulty in comprehending). In this regard, my biggest sadness is that it is not an endangered language.

Don't assume that everything's all right just because you've read it and it seems okay. Make sure you have someone experienced on your team to review the documents. I have consulted with many borrowers in many phases of their application process with other hard money lenders, for example, and have reviewed many, many documents and made suggestions for changes and deletions to many of them.

Lenders don't like this process, but borrowers are ultimately appreciative of not being taken advantage of by lenders. Don't forget that often, the terms that are left out are equally as important as those that are included. How would you ever know if something that would act in your favor were deleted from your loan documents? You typically don't know what is not in the documents unless you have significant experience.

Once you're in the loan closing, make sure everything you want or expect is referenced in the note. If things are missing or erroneous, find out why. If there are terms in the documents that you either don't understand, or weren't in the original understanding between you and the hard money lender, then do not sign anything until you have someone read and review the note, and give you some guidance. Believe me when I tell you that you are better off not taking a loan rather than to take a bad loan. You could regret it for a long time.

Any hard money lender worth his salt will want to make you happy and will want to find out why the note doesn't include what you had expected. Don't let the pressure of being at the closing force you to sign something you don't want or didn't expect. Take your time; make sure the terms are correct. This one suggestion might save your property from foreclosure and its subsequent loss to an unethical lender. I *always* take the borrower through the terms of the promissory note that he or she is being asked to sign. I believe that a responsible lender should always do this for you. Typically, after his easy explanations, you will understand what is being agreed upon and will feel much more comfortable signing the loan documents with a clear mind.

Once you sign each of the loan documents, you'll have to live with their terms and conditions for the full length of your loan (and maybe beyond as well). These terms govern what you are required to do, and what the penalties are for your failure to comply with these requirements.

Steve Sez:
Find an experienced friend, a lawyer with real estate lending experience, or an experienced consultant who knows the hard money formula and documents to help you through the process. You'll be glad you did.

At the closing, ask your lender to go through each paragraph slowly with a synopsis of what each says, just to make sure that you are signing a note with the terms with which you agree. If they won't do that, then dust off your reading glasses. You can't agree to something that you haven't read. And what you don't understand will come back around to bite you. Let's take a look at how you might negotiate some of the terms of your note.

Fourteen Critical Terms of Your Note That You Must Understand in Order to Negotiate Strongly

1. Payment Terms

Most commonly, I have found that borrowers overwhelmingly want to borrow money with the smallest payment due each month. If that is your situation, I would opt for a monthly payment of interest only. An amortized loan (like your parents' 30-year home loan) basically pays off the principal and interest each month with the result that at the end of the loan term, the remaining principal balance is zero. A one-year loan is so short you cannot possibly afford to pay the principal balance off completely over only twelve payments.

For example, if your loan is $200,000 and it is amortized over 12 months, your monthly payment of principal alone is $16,667.00 per month. If you add the interest on top of that, you could have a payment that is nearing $20,000 per month. I have never met a borrower to whom that was a tolerable amount.

Steve Sez:
Your best payment amount in order to preserve your cash flow is one with only the interest due on your loan each month.

2. The Loan Term

Your preference in terms of when your loan will be due is a decision that you should make with due regard to the timing of when you have funds coming to you. Always try to realistically anticipate how much time it will take for your project to work, for you to sell the property, for you to refinance, or for your other source of funds to be realized.

It never hurts to be conservative when choosing the term of a loan. If you think that you will have your property purchase refinanced within 90 days, then by all means your loan maturity should be no less than six months. And if you think your newly purchased property should sell within six months, then I would take no less than a one-year term. It is always better to under-promise and over-deliver. Your lender will be thrilled to see you performing better than agreed. Actually, in life as we know it, who does that very often? You'll definitely catch his attention in a good way.

3. Principal Reductions

A good hard money lender should always welcome principal reductions on your loan. This will allow them to utilize their funds for more loans within a year and hence earn more origination fees. Whether or not the principal reduction is required (your lender wants a principal paydown) or discretionary (you may pay the principal down if you wish), with a smaller balance against the same property, the loan gets safer with each such principal reduction.

Steve Sez:
If you agree to partial repayments of principal over the loan term, make sure you can meet the payment schedule. Otherwise you are agreeing to be foreclosed upon (not a good idea!)

In some cases, however, the lender may have his own cash flow issues and needs his cash back sooner so that he can continue to make loans. In these cases, the principal reductions could be required within the loan documents. Often, I have been completely loaned up without any cash with which to close even the most perfect of loans. In these circumstances, the recovery of cash was important, making possible the granting of more loans.

4. Prepayment Penalties

Prepayment penalties are penalties which may be charged by your lender if you make any principal payments before the due date of the loan. Prepayments may be either:

1. Partial prepayments (e.g. pay $10,000 of principal in month three of a 12-month loan for $75,000), or

2. Complete or full prepayments (pay off the entire loan balance before the due date).

This "early payment penalty" is not all that uncommon amongst hard money lenders. I know of many lenders who believe that they won't find other good loans easily. Because of this, they want to keep the good loans on their books as long as possible.

5. Fixed vs. Floating Interest Rate

Lenders, with a line of credit that is tied to a floating index as one of the sources of their capital, may want to tie the interest rate that they have on that line of credit to your loan, and to all of their loans for that matter. When their cost of funds increases, they want to pass this increase along to their borrowers. For a lender to tie all of his loans to an increasing rate is probably good planning for them, but quite bad for you. Most of the time when I have seen a floating rate note, there is always a floor below which the interest rate cannot go, but no limit on how high it can go.

> **Steve Sez:**
> The existence of a prepayment penalty in your loan documents is highly negative for you. It robs you of flexibility in how and when you utilize your property and your cash. Do not agree with this in your note until you have first thought through all of the negatives.

As an example, the interest rate for a hard money lender's loans could be priced at "prime rate plus five points, with a floor of 12 percent." What this means is that your initial loan's interest rate is going to be the prime rate of interest at that time, plus five percent (remember that one percent equals one point) and if the prime rate of interest goes up during the term of the loan, the interest rate on your loan will follow it up. If, on the other hand, the prime rate drops during the term of your loan, your loan will not drop below a 12 percent per annum floor.

6. Provisions for Extensions

If there is any possibility whatsoever, that you will not be able to repay or refinance your loan within the term of the loan, you should make sure that

> **Steve Sez:**
> A floating interest rate loan can usually only work to your disadvantage if there is a floor below which the rate will not drop. Evaluate these terms thoughtfully before you agree.

Steve Sez:
An extension of the maturity date in your loan documents will give you the advantage of knowing that if you can't pay the loan off when the initial term has been reached, you can then extend the loan for another period and you won't be in default.

your promissory note contains a provision for its extension. It's far better to be safe than sorry. Just be aware of the fact that it is likely that if the lender agrees to your request for an extension of the initial term of the loan, it is highly likely that he will charge you an extension fee for this privilege. In most cases, the longer the extension that you request, the greater the extension fee will be.

7. Provisions for Subsequent Advances

The goal of including a provision within the promissory note for subsequent advances is that if your lender agrees to advance you additional monies after the original loan is made, there will be no need to redo the entire package of loan documents. It does not, however, eliminate any origination fees that you might have to pay on each new advance.

Make sure that the existence of a subsequent advance clause within your promissory note is clearly agreed to by your lender before going on. In most circumstances, the discretion about whether to advance more money to you or not, will be in the hands of your lender. Just make sure that your payments are made on time, your collateral remains valuable, and you may well be eligible for another advance under the loan documents. Ultimately, the decision to advance more funds to you will be a function of your collateral, and its loan-to-value ratio at that time.

Note that a subsequent advance is completely different from the way that lines of credit work. A line of credit is a structure whereby you can draw funds from your line of credit and subsequently then pay it down or pay it off, over and over again. The subsequent advance clause within a promissory note merely avoids the cost and time of preparing new loan documents if you should need additional funds at any time within the loan term. The advance then becomes a part of and due in accordance with the terms for the first disbursement of loan proceeds.

8. Who Is Signing the Promissory Note?

Each individual or company that signs the promissory note is responsible for repaying all funds borrowed as they become due. The thought process of a lender is that even though the collateral will cover all amounts due with a nice margin of safety, just in case it doesn't, for any reason, the "makers" (that's what people who sign notes are called) will have to dig into their personal assets to pay the loan off. Do not take the issue of signing or guaranteeing any promissory note lightly. I once had a banker share with me that in over 85 percent of the cases when cosigners are required, it is the cosigners who ultimately pay them off.

> **Steve Sez:**
> Safety says that when you present your loan request to a lender, make sure he knows that it's only you who will be signing the note.

9. What Is a Default?

I would like to give you some pointers about what constitutes a default as you review the promissory note.

What is a default? A default constitutes the following:

- You do something you're prohibited from doing, and/or,

- You fail to do something you're required to do.

It sounds so ominous; something to be avoided at all costs. A default is simply not living up to the strict terms of your promissory note and each of your other loan obligations. For example, if your interest payment is due on the first day of the month, and you mail the payment late so that it's received by your lender on the eighth of the month, it's possible that you will be committing an act of default. The results of causing a default are that the cost of your loan will go up significantly (late fees, penalties, and default interest).

A default can also be committed as the result of missing an item of non-monetary performance—like a failure to keep the property in good repair. If you commit a default of your loan terms, the price that you'll pay will include the payment of a penalty, a late fee that may be separate from the penalty, and default interest. If there is any good news here, it is that you probably won't face a foreclosure until the default continues for a period of time. But if you push your lender's good graces and allow the default to continue for an extended period of time, it won't be long before the balance due may become so inflated by these default charges that you won't be able to bring the payments current no matter how hard you want to make the entire mess go away.

And, lest you think that all is lost if you default under the terms of your promissory note or mortgage, because a hard money loan is not a bank loan, and because there is no third party regulation of your lender's portfolio, he can certainly forgive any or all of these default charges. It always pays to ask.

Steve Sez:
If you can't cure a default in your loan requirements, seek legal counsel immediately. You must deal with this situation efficiently and effectively so that the default fees and costs don't inflate the balance due so dramatically that you can't repay the loan no matter what.

If you have unknowingly chosen to work with a bad lender, also known as a "loan to own" lender who is just waiting for you to make a mistake before swooping in and taking your property, get help immediately! Call your lawyer, call your confidant, call your consultant, call the district attorney, but call someone who can investigate these practices. Chances are that if you are having problems with your lender, others are as well.

There are two places in your loan documents that commonly describe the events that can become defaults:

1. The promissory note, and

2. The mortgage document.

Obviously, very few borrowers who apply for a loan with any lender are ever planning to default. I always recommend to my borrowers that they review all of the loan documents prior to closing with someone who is experienced with real estate loans in order to fully understand the terms of their loan. Call your lender immediately if there is anything in any of the loan documents that is confusing or that raises a question. Once you sign the documents at the closing, you have to live with their terms for the life of your loan.

As I'm sure that you will understand, very few, if any, good hard money lenders will do more business with a borrower who continually defaults. Therefore, the big benefit in finding a great hard money lender with whom you can work is nullified by not doing what you say you are going to do. True, the lender makes his default interest, which is great for him. But, most good lenders that I know will always rather avoid the aggravation of a default and work with a borrower who performs as he agrees to do in his loan documents.

10. What Is a Default Rate of Interest?

Here is a little strategy about how to approach your hard money lender with a request to lower the default rate of interest in your promissory note. After you have had the chance to review the final closing documents, I would recommend that you always ask your lender to explain the logic behind a high default rate of interest. All that such a rate really does is to make it more likely that he will end up owning your property over what could amount to a relatively minor default that causes the balance due to grow quickly.

As the amount due grows quickly, it makes it increasingly more unlikely that you will be able to repay the amount due in full to the lender. Any lender with integrity will not want to own your property, but would rather see you be successful, and he get repaid with an interest rate that reflects his cost of money and the perceived risk of making you the loan.

Then, I would ask him if he would consider lowering your default rate of interest in the spirit of making him his desired interest, and you the best chance of repayment. I would then make it clear to him that you don't default on your obligations (if that is true) and that you would appreciate it if the default interest rate could be lowered in your promissory note. Tell him that the risk of losing your property is all of the motivation that it takes for you to be timely in your payments. All the lender can say is no.

In that case, just don't default. How easy!

You may think that the default interest described in the promissory note is very high, and in truth, it usually is. The purpose for this rate of interest is to give you that subtle but usually effective suggestion to avoid a default at all costs. Make sure that you do what you agree to do in the promissory note.

It typically only takes one experience of paying default interest before most borrowers understand how seriously they should take the obligations and promises that they have agreed to perform in their promissory note and mortgage document.

Steve Sez:
Don't worry too much about the default rate of interest unless you have a chronic problem with lateness in your life. If so, paying the default interest one time could well cure you forever.

As I'm sure that you will understand, very few, if any, good hard money lenders will do more business with a borrower who continually defaults. Therefore, the big benefit in finding a great hard money lender with whom you can work is nullified by not doing what you say you are going to do. True, the lender makes his default interest, which is great for him. But, most good lenders that I know will always rather avoid the aggravation of a default and work with a borrower who performs as he agrees to do in his loan documents.

11. Recourse vs. Non-Recourse Loans

The difference between recourse and non-recourse is absolutely critical for you to fully understand. What is that difference? It has to do with you as a borrower being personally responsible for the full repayment of the loan. Recourse can also be applied to a business or a corporation.

There are many examples of individuals who have collateral that is so valuable, or who have such a long track record of doing what they say they will do that they don't sign the promissory note personally. For the most part, given the recent economic events that have actually brought large billion dollar banks to their knees, the days of borrowing money without personal recourse are mere memories until the market becomes normalized.

Expect to sign personally for your loan. Expect to be personally responsible for the payment of monthly interest (and principal when required). Expect to be personally responsible for the repayment of the total amount borrowed when the loan matures. And expect to be personally responsible when you make representations that are found in the mortgage document.

Believe it or not, some folks out there borrow money without intending to repay their loan, or who expect to get loan proceeds without signing legal documents. You are not going to be that naïve after reviewing the following material.

11(a). Recourse Loan Terms

In note parlance, the person or company "holding" the note is known as a "lender" or "holder." When you sign for the loan, you're known as the "maker" or the borrower. A recourse loan means the note holder can demand payments from you, the maker directly and individually at all times. If you don't live up to your promise, that means foreclosure and a subsequent sale of the property to recover some or all of the money loaned.

With a recourse loan, you agree to remain personally responsible for all of the payments and you do that by personally signing the note and mortgage. It is the recorded mortgage that gives the hard money lender the right to foreclose if you don't pay. And, it is the note that gives lenders rights to proceed against anyone (that would be you), who has signed it personally. Recourse loans, then, mean that the lender has recourse against you personally and directly.

Financially Important

There are many reasons to take borrowing money seriously and one of the worst is as follows. Let's say that you default on your payments and the lender is forced to foreclose on your property because you don't pay the loan as you've agreed. If your property ultimately sells for an amount that is less than the amount due under the note (including all costs, expenses, attorneys' fees, default interest, and principal), some states permit the lender to come after you personally for the difference.

What is happening quite often is that lenders are taking whatever the property sells for either in a foreclosure sale or directly to a buyer, and at the same time, agreeing to not legally move to collect the difference from the individual borrower(s). This has become known as a "short sale" and it is a phenomenon engaged in primarily by banks and large mortgage companies. Do not expect a hard money lender to engage in this practice because the money that he fails to collect is money that comes directly from his pocket. You wouldn't walk away from monies due you either.

An Actual Experience

But Steve, It's Only a Signature. What's the Issue when
My Collateral Is Worth the Money?

Let us analyze one of these fairy tales. I have many sad examples of this statement from those who have been asked to personally sign on a loan for a relative or a friend. Typically, these instances of what I affectionately call "mercy signings" occur when a borrower is attempting to find another lender to refinance his existing loan to pay off the earlier lender. Or, it could be a circumstance of your friend wanting to take advantage of an opportunity and not having the money to do so. He never intended to put his entire family or his friends in the soup, so to speak.

When the borrower goes to his friends or family members with a request to help him get a loan by personally signing on his loan (therefore, becoming a "co-signor" with him on his loan), he's all bright-eyed and bushy-tailed about how great this opportunity is and how much money he is going to make both for himself and for his co-signor. After all, he has found the perfect deal and he plans to make millions. What's more, it can't fail. Have you ever heard about the deal that is too good to be true? Well, it *always is*!

So, while he has everyone excited and convinced that this is the deal of the century, he may ask his father, sister, or friend to sign on the note with him either out of guilt (that's what families do sometimes), or in order to participate in this "no lose" deal.

But, as always happens, Murphy (of Murphy 's Law fame) rears his ugly head and causes the deal of the century to become the deal that should have died before it was born. And as if things aren't bad enough, the co-signor finds himself having lost money even after the foreclosure and subsequent sale of the "no-lose" collateral that fails to bring enough to repay the loan in full. And then, as the fairy tale goes, the big bad lender sues everyone personally and ruins the credit of all concerned. And they each live happily ever after making payments to the lender until the day that they die, and beyond.

Isn't recourse borrowing exciting? Fun story, don't you agree? Take cosigning very seriously and consider the downside before you ask anyone to do it for you.

The amount by which the sale of the collateral was short in generating enough money in order to pay off the promissory note in full is called the "deficiency." In states that permit deficiencies, the maker's of the promissory note are then legally obligated to pay the lender the amount of this deficiency. This is but one of the drawbacks to recourse loans for borrowers. The obligation to repay can continue long after the property has been liquidated. In my experience, most hard money lenders will pursue the borrower for a full recovery of this deficiency.

This is a bit of an academic discussion, as in recent times, both banks and hard money lenders will require you to sign personally on their loans. The collateral can be owned by a corporation, an LLC or a partnership, but the note must be signed by the entity and then again personally. This requirement always disappears for awhile and then reappears in down times.

Steve Sez:
Hard money lenders will usually only make full recourse loans so they can look directly to an individual to repay the loan and its deficiency.

Why do you think that the personal liability of a borrower to repay the loan is a requirement? Lenders have found that if someone signs a note personally, it gives the signer much more motivation to make sure that the payments are made when due. With only a business signing the note, there can be little enthusiasm for repayment. The individual typically will say to himself, "Why should I worry? I haven't signed anything, so I'm not in harm's way." This is one area where banks and hard money lenders agree: If a lender is putting their money on the line for a borrower, they expect the full attention of their borrowers in making the loan a success.

So, recourse is the rule, in most cases. But, what about non-recourse? Does it exist? Yes. And it has to do with collateral value and the amount required to fully repay the loan.

11(b). Non-recourse Loan Terms

Non-recourse loans bar a lender from taking legal action against the individual borrower personally if there is a default on the loan, or if the foreclosure proceeds from the sale of the collateral still result in a deficiency (the amount not repaid from the sales proceeds).

By way of example, loans to farmers from the federal government are made on a non-recourse basis quite often. Non-recourse is the best of all possible worlds for the farmer because he gets the money he needs for his crops and doesn't have to obligate himself personally to repay the loan. Who wouldn't take money under these circumstances? This is the reason that non-recourse financing is all but unavailable to almost all borrowers currently.

In the 1970s and 1980s, non-recourse loans were common. As a matter of fact, I can't count how many borrowers used to brag to me about how they were taking advantage of their bank's foolish loan practices. Shortly after that, banks started going out of business at a furious rate due in part to the fact that many borrowers had no personal stake in the outcome of their loans. They simply didn't care if the loan got repaid or not.

> **Steve Sez:**
> People repay loans ... companies don't. Without a personal signature on a loan, there is no one person who feels compelled to keep the commitments contained in the loan documents.

12. Due on Sale, Transfer or Encumbrance Clauses

One of the key items that your new lender will look for in his review is the existence of a "due on sale, transfer or encumbrance" clause in the first mortgage on your collateral, if you have an existing first mortgage. A "due on" clause as it's sometime known contains the following elements:

1. A clause or provision in your existing first (or more junior) mortgage or deed of trust;

2. Wording that prohibits you as the owner of the property from getting a loan that is secured by a mortgage;

3. Words prohibiting you, the property's owner from selling, transferring, conveying or borrowing more on your property until the first mortgage loan has been repaid in full;

4. Wording that expressly disallows junior mortgages;

5. Wording indicating that the mortgage uses the same collateral as security; and

6. The consent of the holder of the senior mortgage.

The reason for such a provision related to additional encumbrances is the thinking among lenders that the more debt there is on your property, the more payments you must make in order to keep all of the loans current. Because in total, the payments are higher, so is the probability of a default on your loan. It takes more cash to make all of the payments on a first and a second loan in a timely fashion, than it does to pay just the first mortgage loan. If you are lucky enough to get a hard money loan secured by a junior mortgage, the holder of the first mortgage with a "due on sale, transfer, conveyance or encumbrance" clause in his loan documents can, if he finds out about the new junior mortgage, simply call his entire loan due and payable immediately. This is tricky stuff and I want you to do it correctly. Always, therefore, be honest with all concerned and you can never be caught with a problem.

How would you like to leave the closing on Friday morning, having signed the documents for a new second mortgage loan with a hard money lender, only to have the holder of the first mortgage demand the immediate repayment of his entire loan because of your default on Friday afternoon? The default in question is the one caused by merely putting a second mortgage loan on your property without getting the written consent of the holder of the first mortgage loan in advance of signing the new loan documents.

The likelihood of that happening is greater than you would think. Save yourself the headache of having to come up with lots of cash when your primary lender calls the loan due. Tell your senior lender what your plans are and ask if they'll waive their "due on encumbrance" clause as the result of your taking the hard money junior mortgage loan.

If they see the junior mortgage as no problem and agree to waive this clause, *get it in writing immediately*. This document will prevent significant trauma and aggravation and the potential loss of your property as the result of a foreclosure initiated by the first mortgage holder. This is another case where an advisor will be highly useful to you. Make sure that a lawyer reviews or prepares a waiver of the default. A small slip of the pen or forgetting a crucial term may do you massive harm by raising the possibility of losing your property if the senior loan is accelerated.

An Actual Experience

Water, Water, Everywhere, but Not a Drop to Drink.

A hard money lender who is a friend of mine told me the following story about one of his potential borrowers. I must admit, however, that I have heard similar stories time and time again. It's another lesson in how important it is to get everything in writing.

He had a loan request from a borrower who owned a piece of land upon which 100 homes could be built in an area of the country suffering from a drought. The client wanted a fast loan because when he bought the land, he went to the local community for assurance that there would be sufficient water available to complete building out the total project. The day that he went to the water department, he met with an engineer who told him that water was plentiful in the city and, therefore, not to worry.

Again, Murphy (of the law) being on the board of directors of this developer, saw to it that by the time that development was about to commence, there were no water taps available for purchase. Why? Because the amount of development that was approved at that time had taken the cities total allocation of the remaining year's water taps for developers!

The bad news was also that there was no water available for his use until the following year. He needed a fast loan to enable him to hold onto the property until he could start to develop and sell houses on his piece of land. He needed to pay the taxes, insurance, interest, and all of the other holding costs related to a piece of undeveloped land. He had planned to get these needed funds from the construction loan, which, of course, never occurred because of the lack of water taps.

Therefore, in addition to all of the other items that are contained within your loan documents, make it a habit in your plans for all of your business interests, especially with your hard money lender, to ALWAYS GET IT IN WRITING! Find a good lawyer and experienced consultant and keep him/her around. Need I say more?

13. Assignment of Rents Clauses

With any commercial property that produces rental income like an office building, a retail center, a warehouse, an apartment building or even with one single family rental house, an "assignment of rents" is typically a standard provision included in most mortgages for the further protection of the lender. In some states, the lender may have to draft a completely separate document for this purpose that can be recorded in the appropriate city or county.

The existence of an assignment of rents gives each lender in the order of their priority of recording their mortgages in most states, the rights to require the tenant(s) to pay the rents directly to him in the event of a default. This means that you, the borrower, will lose the ability to receive the rent payments due to you from your tenants after a default.

These provisions are commonplace in all loans. The first mortgage holder is entitled to obtain all of the rents from the property up to the amounts due him at that time. Thereafter, if there are any leftover amounts remaining, these amounts are available for payments on junior mortgages by priority.

In all loan documents for both senior and junior lenders, there will usually be an assignment of rents included as standard operating procedure if the loan documents are prepared by a lawyer. In reality, after the holder of the first mortgage exercises his assignment of rents upon any default, there is usually nothing left for any junior lien holder to get.

14. Wraparound Mortgages

We've discussed the uncertainty that a hard money lender may feel in providing you with a loan that is not in first position. One of the big discomforts with lending in a junior position is that if the monthly payments are not made in a timely manner on the first mortgage loan, a foreclosure by the holder of this senior mortgage loan could result in all others losing their security for the loan (and maybe losing all of their money as well).

The best way around the risk of not getting the senior mortgage paid on time is called a *wraparound mortgage*. A wraparound mortgage is a mortgage that is actually recorded behind (junior to) the pre-existing first mortgage on the property, as a second mortgage most typically . But, the structure of this mortgage has a twist: you make one large monthly payment to the hard money lender who is now in second position and he then takes money out of your large payment to make the payment that is due on the underlying first mortgage. Your hard money lender then keeps the difference as his interest for the actual dollars that he has lent to you.

In this fashion, the holder of the second mortgage (your new hard money lender) knows that the payments will be made on the first mortgage because he is the one who is actually making these payments out of the one larger payment that you make to him each month.

The two large benefits to a wraparound mortgage for your hard money lender are:

Steve Sez:
Many hard money lenders themselves don't even understand wraparound mortgages. If you like this structure conceptually, ask a prospective lender if he would consider a wraparound mortgage structure for your loan and see what he says. It may even lower the overall interest rate on the hard money loan as well.

1. The fact that the payments on the underlying first mortgage are being made on time directly by him, so he has control over defaults on more senior loan(s).

2. The second large benefit that will flow through to you immediately is that the lender can still earn his target yield by lowering his effective interest rates to you. In addition,

he makes more money. Here's an example of how a wraparound mortgage works.

Numerical Example

Let's return to our property worth $250,000 that has a $100,000 mortgage on it. The current monthly payments are $750 per month. If you want to borrow another $50,000 as a second mortgage on your property, you may want to entice your hard money lender by suggesting that he structure his loan as a wraparound mortgage instead of a second mortgage.

Here's how this will work: the hard money lender will make you a $150,000 hypothetical "second" mortgage loan. In this example, because you already have a pre-existing first mortgage of $100,000, you will only receive a net cash disbursement at closing of $50,000 (less all of the normal closing costs) which is the amount in excess of your first mortgage loan balance. Within this new obligation, interest is computed on the $150,000; this is to insure your loan repayment obligation to the hard money lender.

Assume that the payments to the hard money lender are $1,500 per month on the $150,000 and, out of this payment, the lender sends the $750 payment to the holder of the first mortgage. The hard money lender keeps the difference as his interest for advancing the $50,000 to you (his net outlay of cash to you). In this example, he then retains the other $750 as his interest payment.

This is equal to $9,000 per year in interest to him, or an 18 percent yield on the net advance of $50,000 made to you by the hard money lender. If we make the assumption that the hard money lender would have charged 15 percent for the loan, you can see that this technique will allow him to earn a higher yield while feeling safer knowing the payments on the first are being made in a timely fashion.

In the creation of the $150,000 second mortgage, the owner is given "credit" for the preexisting mortgage balance of $100,000. And, therefore, the interest is computed on the full amount of this "loan."

An additional benefit to the hard money lender is his ability to ask for an origination fee (points) on the full loan amount, even though it is only an advance of $50,000 of new money.

At this time it is only important that you remember that origination fees are charged by lenders for making a loan to you. Additionally, understand that these fees due to the lender are computed as a percentage of the gross loan amount. Therefore, you are getting a net advance of $50,000 but your fee may be based on the "gross loan" of $150,000.

There is one great argument for you to make to your hard money lender in order to keep your origination fee as low as possible. You are only receiving $50,000 of cash and, therefore, you should only be charged an origination fee on this amount. Many lenders who make wraparound mortgage loans will understand your position and some may even show a bit of mercy if you just ask for a lower origination fee. In my negotiations on behalf of my clients, I always and firmly ask for an origination fee that's computed on the net amount due to a borrower at closing. There is no way that I ever let my borrowers pay a large origination fee on this "phantom gross loan amount."

Remind the lender that he is not making a real $150,000 loan, but is rather just using a technique that increases his interest rate, and keeps him safer as a junior lender by being able to make sure that the underlying first mortgage will be paid on time.

The other important thing to understand is that most typically, the interest rate on wrap loans (as they are often known) is lower than the hard money lenders normal range of interest rates. In the normal wrap-around loan, the interest rate charged by lenders is lower than those normally charged because the lender is also earning the interest rate charged on the entire $150,000 loan less the amount of the pre-existing loan at its interest rate.

Even though you may have an additional cost to bear for a wrap-around mortgage loan, the benefits to you are as follows:

- You've converted a loan turn down into a win-win situation for both of you (you get the money that you need and the hard money lender earns more interest).

- The lender gets a great yield on a mortgage that's as safe as a second mortgage loan could be.

- You are able to keep your low cost first mortgage in place so that after you have repaid the hard money loan, you haven't lost the advantage of the existing interest rates and the smaller payments that you had in place before your hard money loan was ever made.

Chapter Summary

In this chapter, we've taken a look at various loan terms that are often found in hard money loan structures. There are many potential solutions for each issue so that your loan will work expressly for you and the nature of your project.

1. You should work with your hard money lender to tailor your loan to meet your specific needs.

2. It is possible to write opportunities for loan extensions into your hard money note; but, you should expect to pay a fee for this service.

3. There are very few hard money lenders who will be comfortable placing themselves in a junior position when making a loan.

4. Be aware of any due-on-encumbrance provisions in your note or mortgage.

5. You may wish to consider a wrap around mortgage if you want to preserve the low interest rates.

Next Chapter Preview

I have been asked so many times that I couldn't even estimate the number: do we make second mortgage loans? Let us investigate what is involved with a "junior" mortgage loan, and why it just might work well for you.

CHAPTER 21

Junior Mortgages and How They Can Make Life Easier for You

*If you lend someone $20, and never see
that person again, it was probably worth it.*
—Author Unknown

What is commonly referred to as a "second mortgage" is what others call a junior mortgage. A junior mortgage loan will often be just what the doctor ordered for your situation. As we have seen, a junior mortgage is generally considered to be any mortgage (2nd, 3rd, 4th, and so on) behind the first mortgage position.

The vast majority of potential borrowers apply for a loan with a pre-existing mortgage loan on their property. If you need additional funds, it becomes very important to know how to approach a hard money lender with a request for a "junior" mortgage loan. And, yes, it's different from seeking a first mortgage loan in some important respects.

A hard money lender who puts a junior lien on your property will not want to risk having to pay off the first if there's a problem. Why? Because the amount of cash that this can take may be substantially more than most hard money lenders have immediately available with which to pay off large, first mortgage balances. This equals significant risk to any hard money lender.

Because no lender wants to be put into such a squeeze play, all hard money lenders will review the existing first mortgage loan documents and your payment history very carefully.

In the last chapter, we described what are known commonly as "due on sale, transfer, or encumbrance" clauses that could trigger an acceleration of the loan balance on that loan. After telling you that hard money isn't about you as a borrower, this is one circumstance where a hard money lender might want to review your credit report and credit score to see if you have a history of late payments. In addition, obviously your cash flow will be of specific interest to a hard money lender who wants to make sure that you can make all of your payments on the senior loans on the property completely on time. This means that in the case of junior mortgages, verification of income may become very important. Therefore, don't be surprised if your hard money lender asks for this information if you're applying for a junior mortgage loan.

Let's Wrap Our Arms Around Wrap-Around Mortgages; They Can Make All the Difference

Junior Mortgage Loan

We have only spoken thus far about first mortgages, also known as senior mortgages. If a loan is made thereafter, the recorded mortgage will be junior to the senior mortgage. Your hard money lender will want to be in first position so that he'll be the first one repaid in the case of a default. But here is where hard money lenders shine. There are many of them that offer junior mortgages. Let's look at these types of loans now.

A first mortgage is often called the primary or senior mortgage. If any mortgage is recorded after the first mortgage has been filed, it is called a "junior" mortgage.

Hard money lenders make junior loans in many circumstances. For example, what if you have a very nice, low cost, long-term first mortgage in place on your property and you don't want to replace that loan with a higher cost, shorter term hard money loan? The type of loan that you will be seeking is a second mortgage loan, or a junior mortgage. Remember that it's called a junior mortgage because it is second in place to the primary or senior loan.

Being junior to the primary or first mortgage causes significant additional risk to all lenders. In the event of a foreclosure sale, the sales proceeds must pay the first mortgage in full. Only if and when there is anything left over after the repayment of the first loan, will the more junior mortgages get paid in their numerical order. If there is a drop in collateral values, there are fewer dollars left with which to repay all of the loans in total, regardless of position. Reduced sales proceeds results in greater risk to all of the loans secured by a piece of collateral.

Pretty easy so far, isn't it? It's not so easy for the holder of a junior mortgage. It is, however, pretty easy and safe for the senior lender. That senior lien holder has the prime position and really calls all the shots in the event of a default. Additionally, if sufficient proceeds are not achieved through the sale of collateral with which to repay all of the mortgage loans on the collateral, the junior mortgage holders are the ones at risk.

If your lender is in a junior position on your property, and there is a default on the first mortgage, he must keep the first mortgage paid monthly or risk losing his security position in your real estate. Most lenders view a junior mortgage as being very risky and most are not overly excited to make junior mortgage loans.

> **Steve Sez:**
> Most lenders don't like to be in a junior position with respect to any collateral. One day they can be receiving checks from their borrowers, and the next day they can experience the pain of having to keep the first mortgage current if the loan goes into default. This is why it is hard to get anyone to make second or third mortgage loans.

Are there actually any lenders out there who will consider making junior mortgage loans? Most borrowers are eager to keep their low interest rate, first mortgages in place. The answer is most certainly yes, there are some hard money lenders who will consider junior mortgages. The problem is they will charge more than they would if they were in the first position on your collateral. The risk factor of being in a junior position is greater. That is what justifies higher loan costs and interest.

Junior mortgages don't just stop at second mortgages. What if you needed a third or even a fourth mortgage? The days of finding easy junior mortgages have come and gone. The market over the last decade has been slowly shifting towards lenders making loans only if they are in first position. Still, given sufficient equity left in your property, you will find a hard money lender who will consider making you a loan if you just keep looking. Don't give up easily.

Over the years, I have gotten many, many requests for junior mortgage loans. My position has always been that if the first mortgage balance is low in relation to the collateral's value and the amount that our borrower needs keeps the loan to value ratio very conservative, I would always consider making such a loan.

Additionally, there will certainly be an analysis of the payment history to your existing first mortgage lender. In addition, your new hard money lender will carefully review the terms of your existing first mortgage to make sure that the risk that is inherent in that loan is not too great to undertake in a worst case scenario.

> **Steve Sez:**
> Hard money lenders will always prefer to be in first position. It's a much safer position for them. Remembering this may be the key to getting your loan.

Alternatively, you may want to consider allowing the hard money lender to completely refinance all of your loans in order to avoid this less than familiar technique. In addition, if you ask a hard money lender to make a first mortgage loan to you, your chances of a favorable response to your loan application will be increased greatly.

Financially Important

A word of warning: if you end up combining your junior loan with your primary loan, you'll have a higher interest rate as well as a larger origination fee to pay, simply because it is a larger loan. Make sure the reason for the loan in the first place is profitable enough to justify this.

In the process of completing your due diligence on various lenders, make sure to ask them if they ever consider doing junior mortgage loans or even more exotic types of loans. Most will say no. That is why you have to start early so that you aren't caught at the last minute needing something that can't easily be done by most lenders.

> **Steve Sez:**
> Loan structure is critical to your success. Don't just go down the path towards a "wrap-around" blindly. Understand the pros and cons.

The two large benefits to a wraparound mortgage for your hard money lender are:

1. The fact that the payments on the underlying first mortgage are being made on time directly by your lender so he has control over defaults on more senior loans; and

2. The lender makes more money.

Remind the lender that he is not making a real $150,000 loan, but rather, is just using a technique that increases his interest rate, and keeps him safer as a junior lender by being able to make sure that the underlying first mortgage will be paid on time.

It pays to always ask your hard money lender if he makes wraparound loans. He may not be aware

> **Steve Sez:**
> Make sure your lender only charges you an origination fee on the "net" amount of the cash advanced to you when you get a wraparound mortgage loan.

of this technique, and it could help convert a loan turndown into a loan approval.

The additional legal fees necessary to complete this type of a mortgage may be slightly higher because the loan documents are more complicated than for a normal vanilla, second mortgage loan of $50,000.

Therefore, no matter what the structure of your loan, your lender will not compromise the safety of his loan.

Even though you may have additional costs and expenses to bear for a wraparound mortgage loan, the benefits to you are as follows:

- You've converted a loan turn down into a win-win situation for both of you (you get the money that you need and the hard money lender earns more interest).

- The lender gets a great yield on a mortgage that's as safe as a second mortgage loan could be.

- You are able to keep your low cost first mortgage in place so that when you have repaid the hard money loan, you haven't lost the advantage of the existing interest rates and smaller payments that you had in place before your hard money loan was ever made.

Steve Sez:

Whether the loan is a basic mortgage loan or a wraparound mortgage loan, the "loan-to-value" ratio will need to be in the same safe range or you will have a very hard time getting a loan from any hard money lender.

As an aside, make sure that if you get the lender to employ this technique on your behalf, explain to your title insurance company that this note is a wraparound note and includes the underlying and preexisting note, and not a new advance of $150,000. The difference is that the title insurance company should only charge its premium on the $50,000 increase and not on the full "new loan" of $150,000.

Wraparound mortgages work in any position. If the borrower already has a first mortgage and a second mortgage, and doesn't want to pay either of them off, he can request that his lender consider making a third mortgage loan which is structured as a wraparound mortgage, including leaving the preexisting first and second mortgages in place. In this fashion, the lender is earning the interest rate differential on the first and second mortgage interest rates and loan balances, as well as assuring that these two payments will be made on time assuming, of course, that you make your payment to him on time.

Chapter Summary

In this chapter, we've taken a look at various loan documents that are common to both a hard money loan as well as a commercial loan. The hard money lender has tremendous flexibility with respect to tailoring the loan terms to fit your needs. But, as always, make certain you get the professional advice of an attorney experienced in real estate transactions and hard money lending, or a trusted individual to advise you, should you have any questions or concerns.

1. Lenders do not want to risk changing a loan that is producing positive cash flow in the form of monthly payments into a loan that causes them negative cash flow because they must keep the senior loan current.

2. Hard money lenders will only consider making junior loans as long as the combined loan-to-value ratio is in the acceptable range.

3. Ask your hard money lender if he makes junior loans, or wraparound loans. It never costs anything to ask, and the answer might work to your significant benefit.

Next Chapter Preview

Let us analyze what happens and what is important to observe at the loan closing. Turn to the next chapter to find out the details.

CHAPTER 22

The Loan Closing—
the Day You've Been Waiting For

It frees you from doing things you dislike.
Since I dislike doing nearly everything, money is handy.
—Groucho Marx

At the loan closing, all of the documents that must be filed are completed, the promissory note is read, discussed and signed, and fees and other costs are itemized, discussed and agreed to, and you ultimately get your money. In this chapter, we'll take a closer look at this process of closing your loan.

Difference #14: Closing Costs

Hard money loan closings that involve real estate as collateral will look like a traditional loan closing with the same documents, except that there will be far less paperwork than at a bank or mortgage company closing. The lender will always have his lawyer prepare the loan documents for the loan closing. Because of this, you would be wise to have your own lawyer or consultant review these agreements, the promissory note, mortgage and any other loan documents you will be executing at closing.

Give your consultant your written notes of the representations made by your lender about the terms and conditions of your loan.

The representations made and the final loan documents have to match or there has to be a good reason and a pre-agreement of both you, the borrower, and the lender for the difference. If not, then you may be dealing with a dishonest lender.

Steve Sez:
Most borrowers are so happy to be at a closing table that they will let excitement take over and not review their documents before signing. Don't be blinded by success. Success can turn into failure in one instant if you don't know what you are doing and/or signing.

If you use a lawyer to help with your closing, make sure that he has some closing and real estate experience. You should rely on him to guide you through your review of each of the loan documents. When you sign each loan document, you will want to do so with a full understanding of what the terms are, what performance is expected of you, and what penalties you'll face in case of a default.

While the loan documents prepared by the lender's counsel for your signature aren't significantly different from those of a conventional lender's loan documents (except for the promissory note), it's still quite important that you have someone review the actual closing documents as a check on their proper preparation. The transaction is too important to rush into with a chance of losing your property on the line.

It's not that most honest lenders will be trying to do anything to change the terms of the loan at this late date in the process. It's just that the documents were prepared by a human being, and people do make mistakes. After you've signed the loan documents and the closing is completed, there's no going back. You must live with the terms of the loan that you've just signed up for.

If a lawyer isn't performing the closing, make sure that the documents you have previously reviewed are identical to the ones you're signing at closing. The settlement or closing agent who is conducting your closing is just there to make sure that each document is signed properly. This person will obviously not have any interest in this closing beyond that. Each loan closer has literally hundreds of loans to close per week, and your closing is just a number in the larger picture. Actually, no closing agent will have anyone's interest at stake; except to earn the fee. And she is not a lawyer, so how could she give you any helpful advice in any event?

Infrequently but occasionally, a loan closing agent will assist you in comparing the documents that you will be signing at the closing table with the ones you've already reviewed. Bring your advance copies of the closing docs that you've already reviewed in order to compare with the closing documents presented to you at closing.

No closing agent can give you legal advice or give you an opinion as to legal sufficiency. At the risk of being tirelessly insistent on this point, you should always hire an attorney or other experienced person to help you with the closing issues.

If you compare this closing to others for the purchase of a piece of property, your closing was probably divided into the purchase portion for the buyer, the sale of the property for the seller, and then the balance of the closing was about the buyer signing the loan documents. Remember the volume of paperwork you had to execute in order to obtain the loan? This closing will be much the same, except that the paperwork is far less voluminous.

So far we've discussed some of the documents you are likely to see at closing, but it's worth repeating:

Settlement Statement

The settlement statement itemizes all of the costs and expenses of your loan as well as the amount of money you'll actually net after those expenses have been deducted from the gross loan proceeds. When you review the settlement statement, pay particular attention to the deductions from your gross loan proceeds and make sure you understand and consent to each one of them. Review the common mistakes, check for overcharging and how to identify those charges, fees and costs that shouldn't be there at all.

New Title Insurance

Title insurance is critically important in every loan closing involving real estate. How else could your lender know for sure that he is in first (or another) position on the collateral? In all of my lending experience, I've actually had title insurance companies pay a few claims when problems arose, and I'd never (and never will) close a loan without having title insurance insuring the mortgages on our collateral.

The Promissory Note

Go through the promissory note with a fine tooth comb and make sure that everything you asked about and everything that the lender has agreed to are contained within this document. If there is one "most important document" that you will sign at the closing, this is certainly it. This is your actual promise to repay the loan. It is this document that can be easily enforced by a court if there is a default under its terms. Read it carefully. Make sure your lawyer or other experienced party reviews its terms and discusses it with you.

Steve Sez:
Don't sign anything you don't understand and haven't read completely! This goes for all the loan documents, but especially the promissory note!

The promissory note is rarely a standard document (no matter what anyone tells you). The only standard notes I have ever seen are one-page notes that come preprinted from a legal form company. While the note will certainly be tough in terms of its penalties, default interest, default provisions and so on, it should only contain that to which you've agreed.

It is important—no, make that critical that you see and have the opportunity to review the promissory note *before* you execute it.

The Mortgage or Deed of Trust

Some states require the use of mortgages; others require the use of deeds of trust. The major difference between the two is that a mortgage appoints the lender as the "constructive owner" of the property until the loan is repaid. A deed of trust uses the same basic format but in this case, title to the property is conditionally transferred to a public trustee or to a title insurance company in some states. When the loan is paid off, the title is transferred back to the borrower by this "constructive owner."

This distinction is one of semantics and state law. Regardless of which document is used in your state, you're giving the lender your property as the collateral for your loan. Both types of agreements contain provisions that allow the lender to foreclose and sell your property in the event of default. Both will contain other provisions such as the assignment of rents being generated by any tenants in your building. You will also be directed to maintain the property, to pay insurance and taxes, to keep the property in good repair, and other property and payment provisions.

This is the document that may contain a due-on-transfer, sale or conveyance provision that can accelerate the entire loan balance if you put a junior mortgage on your collateral as well.

An Actual Experience

As a Concession to the Shortness of Life,
Can You Please Read Faster?

I once attended a closing with a borrower who had obviously heard my suggestions somewhere about reviewing each and every loan document, many years ago. I got to the closing on what was a pretty simple loan. There were absolutely no unusual issues; payments were interest only, monthly; one year term with no renewals; first deed of trust on his commercial property; and no prepayment penalties (we really never have resorted to using this technique).

At the loan closing, this borrower sat down in the title insurance company's office and asked for all of the loan closing documents. When the closing agent handed him the rather voluminous paperwork, he proceeded to start to read the first document, which happened to be the deed of trust. Then, he read the promissory note. Then, he moved on to the assignment of rents, and from there to the settlement statement. As a grand finale, he wanted to read the title insurance commitment and the policy.

Needless to say, the closer and I who were sitting there with him were ready to get up and leave, with instructions to the borrower to turn out the lights when he left. The closing started in the morning at 10 a.m. Finally, at 4:30 p.m., he had finished reading and asking questions and started signing. I finally got out of the title insurance company office at 5:30 p.m. After that, I swore I would never let anyone go to a closing that hadn't had the opportunity to read the documents *before* the closing.

I donated one full day of my life to this point. Make sure that you don't let me down: Insist that you get your loan documents to review before your closing.

These documents can be complicated and, preferably, should be reviewed by your lawyer or your trusted advisor (who understands loan documents), before the closing. The mere length of the documents dictates against reviewing them while at the closing. The loan documents are typically multiple pages with terms, conditions, warranties, representations, and so on. Once again, it is important that you know what you are signing as these documents grant the security interest to the lender and dictate the costs and the process that takes place in the event of a default.

You are certain to make everyone at the closing quite angry at you if you sit there all day reading loan documents. If you haven't gotten the loan documents at least a day or two before the closing, then by all means call your lender and tell him that you need them to review before you go into the closing. He should accommodate you with enthusiasm, or something is wrong.

It's probably a good idea for either you or your lawyer to list all of the representations you are making in the security document as a refresher for your responsibilities and for what you have promised to do by signing your loan documents. You don't want to create a default merely because you're unaware of what you are supposed to be doing under the terms of the mortgage document. In this area, an ounce of prevention is the best idea. And ignorance of your responsibilities is not a valid legal excuse after you have signed the documents.

Here are some other documents you might see:

Broker Fee Agreement or Invoice

If you use a broker, this person should have sent an invoice to you billing you for his or her services in securing the lender for your loan. Typically, the broker's fee will be shown on the settlement statement so everyone knows what he has earned. In most cases, the payment of the fee will be made directly to the broker by the settlement agent. The amount of the fee will be shown as a deduction from the gross loan amount. Make sure it's computed correctly. It comes right out of your pocket.

If the lender makes a payment to the broker outside of the closing, this should also be disclosed to you. It has directly impacted the origination fee that you have paid. After all, he had to build the fee that he was paying to the broker into his origination fee. So you got charged twice for the broker's fee.

> **Steve Sez:**
> Dishonest brokers will try to earn money by requesting that the lender build in for him a few points at closing as well as the direct fee that you pay to him. So you pay TWICE! Let's watch Karma get this bad guy!

Doesn't that make you angry? It infuriates me because at the time that you find out, you are in the most vulnerable position possible: You are sitting there with closing documents in front of you, and have just been told that you have paid the broker more than the deal that you struck with him about his fees. And, of all of the betrayals, what if you find out after the loan has closed? I would encourage you to go to your lawyer with these facts. The circumstances will dictate what can be done. But if you have paid thousands of dollars twice, quite possibly you have a claim against someone. Go for it!

Environmental Indemnity

At the closing, you will probably be asked to execute an environmental indemnity document assuring the lender that the real estate is free of hazardous materials and that you are unaware of any previous use that may have caused contamination on the site.

If you are purchasing new property, your lawyer should require the seller to indemnify you against any environmental contamination on that property. If you suspect, or if there is any possibility of contamination on the property, you should require the seller at his cost, to order and pay for a Phase I Environmental Report that will give you some idea of what types of contamination might be present. In addition, your lender will probably require such a report if the property location and property type suggests a possible problem.

Environmental concerns are extremely important in the world of lending and, therefore, they should be important to you as well. The existence of a hazardous substance on your property will make your loan almost impossible to refinance and equally as hard to sell as well. Even if the person selling you the property failed to properly disclose the existence of environmental issues, once you know about them, you have the affirmative obligation to make a buyer aware of such issues. Otherwise you face the consequences (and none of them are good for you).

Environmental issues can also arise during the term of the loan. For example, if, after you close the loan, you start to contaminate the property, the ramifications for you, the lender, subsequent purchasers and any new lender will be extreme. There must be a cleanup of this contamination before any other transactions can occur ... and you'll have to pay for it. This indemnification will make you personally liable for any such cleanup. Do you see why this area of the law is so critical? The costs for a cleanup can be substantial at a time when you don't have the funds.

Because environmental contamination can be overwhelmingly expensive to clean up and, currently, there is no viable way of estimating total cleanup costs, everyone associated with a commercial loan will be concerned and watchful for these issues. If you are going to use the property to house a business that uses contaminants, you should do all that is possible to eliminate the possibility of problems.

Steve Sez:
The environmental condition of your property is of critical importance to your hard money lender as well as to any subsequent buyer or lender. For this reason and more, you should be highly sensitive to this issue.

Business Purpose Affidavit

At closing, you'll also be required to sign an affidavit which certifies to your lender that the loan proceeds are not being used for a household, agricultural or consumer purpose. A hard money lender is a commercial lender. After the wave of predatory lending laws pertaining to owner-occupied residences that have been implemented in every state's statutes recently (refer to the usury and licensing laws that we discussed earlier), hard money lenders now only make commercial loans. It is by making only commercial loans that hard money lenders can earn their rates with few state or federal legal issues.

Because of these new laws, at the closing, you will be required to execute a letter that confirms that you are not obtaining this loan to consolidate your debts, pay for Johnny's orthodontia, to take the family on the cruise of a lifetime, or any other consumer or household purpose. Hard money loans are only made for income generating or investment projects. By having an affidavit in the file, the lender has evidence that the loan is not within the regulated consumer or owner-occupied loan category.

Other Title Insurance-Related Documentation

You may also be asked by the title insurance company to execute a mechanic's lien affidavit which declares that no work has been done on the property that hasn't been paid for in full, on or before that date. If anything is left unpaid, the title company will require you to reimburse them in the event that they pay any unpaid contractor for labor or any supplier of materials.

Mechanic's liens can be senior in priority to recorded mortgages by state statute. Title insurance companies always want to limit their exposure to these claims as fully as possible which is totally understandable. By executing a letter to the title insurance company that there are no outstanding unpaid invoices for work done or materials supplied to the property as of the date of closing, they will agree to insure the lender against the existence of any of these potential mechanic's liens.

Miscellaneous Documents

There may be other documents that a lender or a title insurance company will ask you to sign in order to give the lender greater legal protection on a case-by-case basis. Some of these may include:

- Assignments of leases;

- Assignments of contracts;

- Assignments of surveys; and

- Other special purpose documents that may apply to your loan.

Again, I can't stress strongly enough how important it is to get copies of each of these loan documents in advance of the closing. You and your lawyer or other expert need to be able to review each of them before you are asked to sign them at closing. What you sign at closing will have a dramatic effect on the way the loan gets enforced by the lender. It can make the loan easy or difficult for you to live with after closing. Hang on to all of the closing paperwork. The fees and costs may be deductible for tax purposes, and therefore, it's important to save copies of all closing documents for your accountant when he prepares your tax returns.

There are obvious differences between a closing for a hard money loan and a bank loan closing. Hard money loans are constructed primarily to meet the needs of the lender. Bank loans are constructed entirely to meet the needs of the state and federal regulators of banks. In a nutshell, this is why you have no flexibility with banks as you attempt to negotiate your loan terms. At the closing, make sure that you are given a complete set of copies of each document that either you or your lender signed. And, make sure that you get all of your questions answered before you sign any documents. You don't want to be saddled with indecision at the closing table. At that moment, everyone there is ready to close. If you overlook your concerns, you'll get a check, which is your primary goal. But then the problems will start because you were too emotionally involved and excited at the prospect of getting the money that you need. You won't get to negotiate at the closing table so make sure that you've had the maximum time possible to review the documents and to ask questions of your lender while there's still time to correct any mistakes in the terms or in the documents.

Steve Sez:
Obtain competent assistance to help you review the loan paperwork. Otherwise, you are betting that the lender is a good person, and that there are no human errors in your loan documents. Once the loan documents are signed, there is nothing that you can change even if you find errors or misstatements in any of the documents.

Chapter Summary

1. It is always a good idea to retain the professional services of an attorney familiar with hard money lending, closings and the legal language of real estate when you borrow money from such a lender.

2. Remember that closing agents cannot provide you with legal counsel or advice.

Next Chapter Preview

It is commonly thought that real estate is the only thing upon which hard money lenders loan their money. In the following chapter, we turn our attention to some of the most viable and common non-real estate collateral that I encounter.

SECTION THREE

Use of Non-Real Estate as Collateral

CHAPTER 23

Collateral to the Left of Me; Collateral to the Right of Me

Itaxication: Euphoria at getting a refund from the IRS, which lasts until you realize it was your money to start with.
—From a *Washington Post* word contest

As a new lender, I realized that the world didn't revolve around real estate only. Early in my lending career, I had borrowers come to me with so many different forms of non-real estate collateral that in order to be of the greatest benefit to the most people and to build my business intelligently, I had to look at more than just real estate as acceptable collateral. In the process of reviewing literally thousands of non-real estate loan applications, I came to understand that almost anything of verifiable value can qualify as acceptable collateral. In this chapter, we're going to discuss the benefits and drawbacks of using something other than real estate as collateral.

You should understand at the outset: Most lenders—including hard money lenders—consider real property to be the safest form of collateral. As a result, finding a true hard money lender willing to consider alternative forms of collateral can be a challenge. Expect to spend time and energy locating a lender who will be interested in other potential, non-real estate collateral.

What other forms of collateral, besides real estate, have been used to secure hard money loans? There are stock and bond portfolios, equipment, inventory, accounts receivable, and even special collateral such as car collections, artwork, antiques, or even oil and gas reserves. And, let us not forget promissory notes that are due to you from another business transaction. Virtually anything with value could qualify as collateral with the right lender.

Stock and Bond Portfolios

Stock and bond portfolios can be every bit as safe as real estate but most lenders will not consider them because of their historical volatility. These securities are uniquely risky because their value fluctuates moment by moment. Every time a security is traded, its price will either move up or down. Conservative hard money lenders see this potential fluctuation in value and don't understand how to protect themselves adequately. Logically, one can understand the difficulty in dealing with intangible assets that are absolutely certain to change in a minute or in an hour.

Fluctuations in interest rates, inflation rates, unemployment rates, trade deficit levels—just about anything economic throughout the world—adds even more uncertainty to the valuation of securities. For example, as general market rates of interest go up, businesses become less profitable because the cost of their borrowing becomes more expensive. Because of the resultant overall declining profits, the value of stock may decrease. Here's an example to illustrate how a rate change can either be good or bad depending upon the industry:

> Robin is a potential borrower wanting to use the shares that she owns in a public home building company as collateral for her loan. In the home building industry, if interest rates go *up*, fewer people will qualify for mortgages. The construction business will obviously slow down as the result, with no easy way to determine when rates will return to their lower levels. A lower profit forecast will inevitably drive down the value of her stock which is the collateral that she plans to use for her loan.

If, on the other hand, interest rates are going *down*, Robin recognizes that this is good for the company's business. When more people can qualify for residential mortgages, home sales rise and the builder's profits go up. Therefore, her stock should actually become a more valuable asset over time.

Both stock and bonds are speculative for these and many more reasons. The price of stock can fluctuate wildly depending upon economic conditions over which no person has control. It is because of this that shares of publicly trading stock (and bonds as well) are so hard to use as collateral unless the companies are large, very well-established, strong and relatively immune to economic movement. There will be a track record of performance that a savvy hard money lender may recognize.

If you have stock to offer as collateral, there are lenders out there who will react favorably. Any hard money lender willing to evaluate a portfolio of securities will take a hard look at the worth of the underlying companies as he determines how much he can loan on the collateral. And, in keeping with the hard money lender's practice, the stock portfolio is reviewed in the same fashion as is real estate. Loan decisions on stock and bond portfolios aren't about you at all. It is the underlying quality and value of the stock that makes all the difference.

What can you do to make a hard money lender feel safe and secure that your collateral will hold its value and that his capital won't just disappear? I have suggestions that may help in this situation drawn primarily from how I've structured loans in these circumstances. Suggest one or more of these to your lender before he suggests them to you and he'll be impressed with your understanding and knowledge of how to make him more secure:

Steve Sez:
The safer your lender feels with your collateral, no matter what the type, the better are your odds of getting a loan from him.

1. You can suggest that you are willing to segregate your collateral in a separate account or location for his protection;

2. You can attempt to find a buyer who will sign a conditional contract to purchase either the promissory note or the collateral itself for enough money to make your lender whole in the case of your default. These situations can become complex quite quickly. Make sure that you have an experienced lawyer helping you with the documents necessary to accomplish this goal.

3. You can offer to cross collateralize your loan with other items, making the loan-to-value ratio much more conservative for your lender; or

4. You can prepare a detailed and specific plan for your lender that describes what will happen to keep him safe in the event that the value of your collateral decreases while the loan is outstanding.

Pledging your non-real estate assets as collateral will eliminate your ability to sell or convey any of these items while your loan is outstanding. You need to understand and be comfortable with these ramifications to your business.

Loan-to-Value Ratio
for Non-Real Estate Collateral

A smart lender will always want to maintain an acceptable ratio of the loan amount to the value of the collateral, regardless of what it actually is. If you will remember, we discussed how important this one ratio is to all hard money lenders and how it applies to all categories of collateral.

Numerical Example

Let's say your original loan was $50,000, and the value of your beautiful purple micro-widgets on the day the loan closed was $100,000. Do you remember how to calculate "loan-to-value?" If you said the loan-to-value ratio was 50 percent, you're on the road to becoming a lender yourself; good job.

What happens if tomorrow, your purple micro-widgets are worth less, say $92,500? This is because a new variety of green micro-widget that is faster, smaller and cheaper hits the market? What just happened to the lender's loan-to-value ratio?

You can see that the loan-to-value ratio of your loan just went from 50 to 54 percent, making the loan riskier for the lender (there is less of a cushion for the loan as the value of the widgets goes down). What happens if within two weeks of the new, green micro-widget hitting the market, a newer, faster and smaller orange micro, micro widget hits the market at one half the price of your widgets? What if the market value of your old, large and slow purple micro widgets drops to $55,000? Now the loan-to-value ratio of your loan is approximately 90 percent. What started as a very safe loan has turned into a very risky loan literally overnight. Why? If the value of micro widgets goes down the slightest bit and then a lot more, the $50,000 loan could ultimately be backed up by less than $50,000 of collateral.

What should you expect the lender to do to protect himself? There are really only a few things that he can do, and each of them requires monitoring the value of widgets in the marketplace. This loan suddenly becomes very management-intensive and is one of the primary reasons most hard money lenders don't consider these types of items as collateral. The lender must have a way to check the values of your collateral each day (week or month) if he is going to stay diligent about the safety of his loan. He needs to compute new loan-to-value ratio values based upon the changing values of the collateral.

A good lender will build into his formula, a loan-to-value ratio that cannot be exceeded before obligations to pay the loan down or pledge more collateral are triggered. And, typically, borrowers don't have the necessary cash to solve the problem, so they routinely give the lender the right to sell some of their collateral in order to lower the loan amount.

What other sorts of collateral can be used? Let's take a look at equipment.

Equipment as Collateral

Equipment is a category of collateral that many hard money lenders find exceptionally difficult to accept. There are so many types of equipment made by so many different manufacturers, in so many different industries, with so many specifications, that very few people (including lenders) are able to determine the functional and monetary value of any given piece of equipment.

Equipment in particular is very difficult to evaluate because equipment values can vary dramatically based upon the difference in just a few years of technological age, a few hours more on the engine, or a different maintenance schedule. With older equipment, a newer model may have additional features that render this older equipment significantly less valuable, perhaps even obsolete.

Consider how the evaluation procedures are completely different for printing equipment, farm and ranch equipment, and pizza making equipment. One lender cannot possibly have the extensive knowledge that is needed to understand all categories of equipment.

Imagine how geography can influence values as well. An example of this is what would a businessman in Nashville pay for large commercial fishing nets? Probably, the value in Nashville is absolutely zero. If that same net were in southern Louisiana, however, it will have a different value to prospective purchasers in those areas. The same goes for different types of restaurant equipment, construction equipment, oil drilling equipment, and so on. Your challenge is to make this complexity and uncertainty as easy as possible for your lender to understand.

An Actual Experience

This Was One Cold and Fishy Loan!

At one point early in my lending business, I made a loan secured by refrigerated fish cases—the type you will commonly find in a grocery store deli area. They had compressors to keep the food cold, the slanted glass in the front for better viewing, and were brand-shiny new and beautiful (Can a refrigerated fish case actually be beautiful?? The borrower evidently thought so).

The fish market was well located and had the elements of success written all over it, so I did my due diligence and found resale values for cases of this type at approximately 40 cents on-the-dollar. Because of the inevitable and significant decline in value even on new equipment, I decided to loan 20 cents per dollar of purchase price of the fish cases, just to provide myself with that margin of error.

Of course, as I have known for decades, Murphy is on the board of directors of every company ever formed and always bringing Murphy's Law with him. You guessed it: almost immediately, the fish market started to have cash flow problems. Ultimately, what happened wasn't good for me or for the borrower. The loan went into default when the owner of the fish market had a heart attack and ended up in the hospital. Because I felt badly for him, I attempted to help him liquidate the store in a friendly fashion without resorting to any legal proceedings.

When I went back to the used equipment dealers who had originally quoted me 40 cents on the dollar as the value of used equipment of this type, they now told me that within the last few months, many markets with these types of cases had gone out of business and as the result they were in no position to pay me anything (that's exactly like zero) for these "like new" refrigerated cases at this time. The demand for refrigerated cases was absolutely gone. I mean the quote wasn't 40 cents on the dollar; it was literally *zero* cents on-the-dollar. This was absolute "Oye Vay!" What's a lender to do in this circumstance?

I called around and quickly found that every used equipment dealer was having the same issues. The best I could negotiate on behalf of our borrower was that one (and only one) dealer said he would come and *pick them up* and not charge anything for the transportation. All of the others wanted to charge for the pickup of these barely used refrigerated cases that originally cost new over $75,000 within the last six months.

Because of situations just like this, the number of lenders who will consider equipment as collateral is extremely small. The only lenders who will consider this collateral type are those with experience in one of the variations of equipment, such as ex-farmers who understand farm and ranch equipment or ex-restaurant owners who understand used restaurant equipment.

Equipment typically depreciates deeply and quickly. Technology, size, capacity, speed, or any of hundreds of other factors can render your equipment valueless and there is—sadly—absolutely nothing that you can do about it. Because of this, loan amounts on equipment will usually be very small in order to maintain a good margin of safety (whatever that means to an equipment lender) between the loan amount and the equipment's liquidation value.

A Rock and a Hard Place

Be prepared to physically hand over the possession of your equipment to your hard money lender until the loan is repaid in full. This is because the condition of equipment can deteriorate quickly if it's not maintained properly. Taking control literally requires taking physical possession of the equipment and placing it into a secured, bonded and insured warehouse or lot until the loan has been fully repaid!

As you contemplate obtaining a loan secured by your equipment, think about how your business would operate without the use of this equipment each day that you are open. From the lender's standpoint, if there's no control over your equipment (his collateral), how can he be sure that the equipment will be properly maintained and thereby keep its value while the loan is outstanding?

Remember the basic premise of all hard money lenders: collateral is everything. If the value of the collateral is risky, you probably won't get a loan without great luck. Smart hard money lenders will go over applicants' cash flow statements with a "fine tooth comb." Of course, this violates the basic premise of hard money lending; that it is all about the borrower's collateral and not the borrower himself.

The issue is that any equipment-heavy company must keep that equipment highly utilized and generating revenue in order to cover the company overhead. But remember that the equipment will be stored by your lender until you repay your loan. You will not, therefore, have the use of this collateral for months and months. How does this smaller equipment pool impact your cash flow? You guessed it. Less cash flow means a far riskier loan. No lender will voluntarily step in and make a loan that he knows will go into default almost immediately after the loan is closed.

> **Steve Sez:**
> **You should be prepared to over-collateralize your equipment loan by a significant amount, and even then, the prospects of getting a loan are dicey at best.**

Here's An Alternative to Hard Money Equipment Lending

No, hard money is not the ideal solution in all cases, and I'm not afraid to let you know when this is true. In this case, you can see that equipment is a difficult alternative to real estate as collateral for a hard money lender. The best place to go with equipment if you need a loan is back to the dealer who sold it to you. He'll probably know a specialty lender who understands your equipment and who is in that market continually.

Alternatively, there are equipment leasing companies. And, as an alternative to traditional equipment leasing, some companies have been known to enter into what are known as "sale/leaseback" transactions. In this circumstance, you will receive the "sales proceeds" from selling your equipment with the ability to exclusively lease it back from its purchaser. In this way, you can maintain full control over your equipment. Most of these sale and leaseback transactions contain the option that will allow you to repurchase the equipment at the end of the lease term for a fixed price. Therefore, if you still want your equipment at that time, you can actually repurchase it from the person who bought it from you, so you aren't actually giving up your equipment completely and forever.

If you thought equipment was a tough category, let's take a look at inventory.

Inventory as Collateral for a Hard Money Loan

Inventory is about as difficult a non-real estate collateral category as there is for lenders. Think about what happens to inventory in the ordinary course of business—it's sold to customers each and every day. If you're the lender, this means your collateral is being sold every day.

Borrowers in business need to sell their inventory in order to develop the cash with which to purchase more inventory and to run their businesses. By selling your collateral, you are converting your inventory, which is the security for the loan, into cash and then using that cash for operating expenses. The lender's collateral is therefore being converted into cash with each sale, and the cash may be spent on items that are not included in a pay down of a loan.

Steve Sez:

I would suggest that if you need a loan on your inventory, you will need to become very creative. Inventory hard money lenders play hard to get, and are equally hard to find.

One of the only ways that your lender can protect himself in an inventory-based loan is to review and check on the collateral often. This is to assure himself that his loan is still secured by your collateral, collateral that he believes is still there. By making continual inventory checks as a normal part of a loan, the lender is doing all he can to insure himself that you are staying honest with him and that his loan is still safe.

Only a few categories of inventory are considered to be "easy" forms of potential collateral. They include inventory that is small in number of units, large in value and easy to monitor by serial number, or some other tracking method.

Automobiles are just such a category. Because tracking this inventory is easy (cars are few in number and large in value on most dealers lots), many banks make auto inventory loans available to their dealer customers regularly (called "floor plan loans" in the auto business). Banks regularly send out their auditors, however, to count cars and to verify the titles held against cars in inventory in order to keep their loan safe. This type of loan, while fraught with other risks, is, at the very least, easy to verify if you have a VIN (vehicle identification number) for every piece of collateral with which to check and verify on each inspection trip.

An Actual Experience

Ski Equipment Has Its Ups and Downs.

I was once approached by a ski shop in beautiful Aspen, Colorado, with the following request: They had advance notice of a ski store in Baltimore, (—yes, Baltimore, the center of the skiing universe) Maryland, that was contemplating filing for bankruptcy. My potential borrower found out there was a liquidator who was selling the inventory to try to raise quick funds to save the business (at which they ultimately failed). My borrower wanted to purchase this inventory before anyone else had gotten word of this bargain sale at a significant discount to cost. When I was called by the potential borrower, I was quite fearful of this class of inventory as collateral for each of the reasons that I have already mentioned to you.

I came up with the following solution to the problem of using inventory as collateral in this particular case, however. I structured the loan as follows: If my borrower would allow me to physically put the inventory into a bonded warehouse in Denver, I could work out a "partial release" schedule that would give the Aspen ski shop a list of what the loan principal pay down was for each item of inventory being held as collateral. The resale value of each of those items was quite easy to understand. My proximity to prime ski areas in Colorado gave me the contacts to get comparable sales figures for the liquidation of many, many varieties of ski equipment.

Because the value was clearly there, I structured the loan to account for all of the perceived risks that I faced with this type of collateral. In this case, it was a win-win because the ski retailer in Aspen had no place to store the inventory of skis and other related equipment. They could drive down to Denver at any time with their truck and give me a list of the inventory they wanted released, and a cashier's check for the same. In this way, they could take possession of their inventory only as it was needed in their store.

I felt comfortable because I had physical possession of the collateral. They got the advantage of purchasing new inventory for their continued operations at a significant discount. I got paid as the inventory was drawn down. The point? It takes the creativity and flexibility of all parties to make an inventory loan work well.

Conversely, with inventory that is smaller and of a lesser unit value, the problems of managing this kind of loan can become magnified.

Want a simple example of this theory? Let's say you have put up the inventory in your hardware store as the collateral for your loan. Because your inventory consists of thousands of items, your lender will need to have some idea of its daily or weekly sales and purchases by item. How could a lender reasonably achieve that measure of comfort without it costing you a fortune in oversight?

Counting nails, nuts, and bolts every week (or more frequently) is an impossible situation for any lender, don't you think? Ultimately, this becomes a pretty expensive situation for you, the borrower, as well. Who is going to pay for these inspection issues? Yes, I'm afraid it's always going to be you.

What this means is that inventory loans are very difficult to get unless you have a way in which to address these issues. If this is what you have to offer as collateral, however, see if you can develop a system that will allow you to operate without the full complement of inventory on hand at all times. And, it's always better and easier to administer if you have serial numbers for each item of inventory. Don't forget that it's you who are going to pay for the lenders' inspectors to verify everything at all times.

Therefore, the same advice that I gave you regarding equipment applies here as well. Start early researching your lender base. Always call an expert in your area to see if they have any suggestions about sources of inventory financing. With items of inventory that are numerous and small in price, you will really need to begin the process of searching as early as you can. You may have such an administrative nightmare with small, low value items, that you will be kissing lots of frogs before you find your ideal lender.

Loans on Collectibles

This is an item of collateral that is typically overlooked by all. Throughout this country, there are literally millions of people who collect things. I mean everything from cars, to old typewriters, to antique cameras, matchbooks, art, first edition books, coins and stamps, sterling silver commemorative spoons, classic rock albums, and so on.

I have been fortunate over the years to have been presented with some of the most interesting collateral proposals of almost any other lender whom I have known. Among those proposals, I have had loan requests secured by collections of the most unusual items (gun collections, rare letter collections, jewelry collections, antique perfume bottle collections and so on). As a number of the members of my loan committees over the years have had significant collections of unusual items, I am proud to be one of the hard money lenders who put together many of these otherwise undoable loans.

Basically, even though most lenders would shrug at the thought of lending on collectibles, the same principles we have been discussing up to this point all apply to these items as well. Just remember that if you have a collection of something with substantial value, you

Steve Sez:
Collectibles can be very valuable as collateral. The same principals apply to this category of collateral as they do for real estate. It's ultimately all about value of your collection.

potentially have acceptable collateral for a loan. The trick will be to find the right lender who appreciates and understands the value of collectibles, which will require a thorough nation-wide search started well in advance of any idea you might need a loan. You need to find the right lender who understands your type of collateral. Once you find the right fit you will be able to get a loan in a flash at any time in the future!

How to Value Your Collectibles for a Hard Money Lender

Your potential lender will be interested in the "quick sale value" of your collection before any loan can be seriously considered. Consider these five suggestions regarding where to look for values:

1. Acquire and keep auction records for at least the last five years of items similar to yours that have sold.

2. Subscribe to all of the trade magazines and other periodicals related to your area of collectibles and keep them as far back as you can.

3. Talk to other collectors about what you have, and see if you can find evidence of significant and unreported sales that have occurred recently which will establish value.

4. Keep all catalogues of sales of similar items for as far back as you can find.

5. Go to every trade show that focuses on your area of collectible and pick up anything you can that will prove the value of your items.

When you have a need for capital, you must prove to your hard money lender that your collection has a fair market value that is defensible with written proof.

Make up your mind early in this process that you will have to temporarily give up the physical possession of your collection in order to get your loan. Always insist that the lender put all of your valuable items in a secured and fully insured storage facility until the loan is repaid. It is important to request that no one be allowed access to the collection until the loan is completely repaid.

Make sure you keep full insurance in force for loss, theft, damage, and destruction (with a listing of each item and its current market value). I would suggest that you itemize and photograph each item in your collection as you put the items into storage. Make sure to have the custodian who receives the pieces sign a receipt for each item individually. I would also insist that your hard money lender also sign a receipt for each item at the closing as well. In addition, make sure the storage facility is also fully bonded insured against all risks. Actually see and review their policy if you can.

Steve Sez:
There is almost no effective way to get a loan on your collectibles without your lender taking physical possession of all of the items within your collection. Carefully think through how this possessory interest will be handled so that your collection is safe.

As a hint, make sure that your collectibles loan contains a partial release schedule that requires the lender to release portions of collateral from his lien as you pay the principal down. It is critical that you are represented by a lawyer in these cases as these transactions have many moving parts that all have to be completed correctly. Do not try to save money here!

Chapter Summary

There are many, many forms of collateral other than real estate. Look carefully at your business and non-business assets for collectibles or other valuable personal property which can be used as possible collateral for a hard money loan. While not every hard money lender will consider making a loan secured by collateral other than real-estate, there are many that will.

1. A significant number of hard money lenders will consider accepting stock and other securities as collateral—provided they are able to protect themselves adequately from falling investment prices.

2. You may be able to secure an agreement with your lender that allows you to sell collateralized stock if its value suddenly rises or falls dramatically.

3. The LTV (or loan-to-value ratio) is particularly important when using non-real estate as your collateral.

4. Pledging equipment as collateral for hard money lenders requires that you substantiate its value and liquidity to your new lender.

Next Chapter Preview

In the next chapter, we will investigate an intriguing area of non-real estate collateral called "accounts receivable factoring or financing." It's so prevalent that there are many specialists called accounts receivable factors throughout the country.

CHAPTER 24

Accounts Receivable Financing & Factoring

I'm living so far beyond my income
that we may almost be said to be living apart.
—e e cummings

To set the stage for understanding this type of hard money financing, let's first define what constitutes a valid account receivable in the eyes of a lender. An account receivable is money that is owed to you without any conditions, for goods or services that your customer has received as ordered and fully accepted, on credit. Said simply, when someone (your customer) has received and accepted what they have ordered from you, they then legally owe you money and on your books, it's an account receivable. These legal accounts receivable constitute collateral that you can then use to obtain a loan.

What Are Good and Valid Accounts Receivable?

Accounts receivable, in order to be acceptable to a lender, must be due as the result of a *completed* transaction. The money actually has to be due and payable to you, the borrower. What a simple concept, but one that is lost on so many borrowers. They believe that if they have signed a contract to provide a service or a product to one of

---

Steve Sez:

An "account receivable" becomes real when it is due to you NOW. You've done all that it takes to raise a legal obligation on behalf of your customer to pay you in full for the item or service. A purchase order is not collateral to a hard money lender. It is merely an order to purchase your goods and it does not give rise to your right to receive any funds whatsoever yet.

---

their customers, the mere existence of this contract makes the unpaid amount an account receivable to them. But they haven't even started work, so how is any money due yet? I've never figured this one out, but borrowers are insistent. Sadly, there is no legal basis for their argument and, therefore, there are no lenders who will take them seriously.

Can you see why a signed contract doesn't become an account receivable at the moment of signing an order? If the service or product hasn't yet been provided, the purchaser is under no obligation to pay for what they haven't received. With no obligation to pay, how is there anything that would remotely resemble an account receivable? With no valid and legal receivable, there is no potential collateral. And, of course, if there is no collateral, there will be no loan.

An Actual Experience

Dealing with Royalty and Fame.

I was sitting in my office one beautiful November day when the phone rang. The voice on the other end had a thick accent; he inquired about an accounts receivable factoring arrangement. He said that he anticipated receivables from a very large and very credit worthy company, and wanted to come to our office to discuss the situation. I agreed of course, and on the appointed day a large, stately gentleman entered my office to discuss the factoring of his accounts receivable. He introduced himself with a very familiar last name and about three minutes into the discussion, I asked about his family. He admitted his father was a very high official of a South American country and that his family was frequently in the news. What a great twist to an interesting transaction. Dealing with royalty!

As we spoke about his situation, he explained that he purchased food products from growers in the late fall and early winter months. These months are, however, summer in South America. The products were then put on a boat bound for Los Angeles where they would be offered to buyers who came from all of the major grocery chains and restaurant chains to inspect and purchase these items for their markets and restaurants. Upon their sale, an account receivable arose from the largest grocery companies in the country, all of whom are financially very strong.

The poor farmers from whom he had purchased these items needed to be paid almost immediately. They had no ability to wait until the grocery stores paid the bill to him before they got their funds. Our potential borrower couldn't pay the farmers before he got paid as he didn't have the funds independently of this transaction. So, he had to have a way to bridge this gap (remember the term "bridge financing") to protect his suppliers. He knew that he would get paid, but he just didn't know when.

Large companies who owe money take advantage of the fact that they are large and that everyone wants to do business with them. They pay when their accounting process is completed and the invoice is ready to pay; and not one minute sooner. Sadly, there is nothing that you can do about it in any event.

What an incredible opportunity and highly unique customer! I think that it was our broad and creative approach to non-traditional finance that took us to the threshold of a very high level transaction. Ultimately, the capital needs for this loan were so large, however, that we couldn't handle the amount of cash needed by our borrower.

Some hard money lenders will understand these transactions and actively seek out accounts receivable loans. These lenders usually specialize in account receivable factoring. And, they are easy to find—lucky for you.

There is a very large difference between *"financing"* and *"factoring"* your accounts receivables. *Factoring* is the age old practice of "selling" your accounts receivable for a price equal to something less than 100% of the balance due to you. At the time of the sale, the purchaser gives you the right to buy the receivable back from him at a specific price that reflects the amount of time that it took you to exercise the repurchase option. The longer you take, the more it costs you to buy it back from him. The higher price reflects your "cost" of the transaction. Read on to understand this process better.

Accounts receivable *financing*, on the other hand, is turning the account receivable into collateral for an actual loan. There are no sale and subsequent repurchase terms in this type of transaction. It is like any other collateral based loan made by a lender. Note that in this case, the collateral is completely intangible and yet you can still get a loan.

Factoring

Factoring is basically the "sale" by a business of one or more of its accounts receivables at a discount, to a purchaser known as a "factor." The "seller" of the account receivable (being the borrower) receives fast cash which is his goal.

By factoring your accounts receivable, you will get cash quickly instead of having to wait for your customers to pay their bills. As you can see, this hard money technique is yet another way for you to gain access to fast funds for other projects.

I have seen too many small businesses agree to act as the bank for their customers. Rather than get paid immediately when they sell their product or service, these businesses are essentially loaning their customers money when they agree to not get paid until some later date. By making loans to their customers instead of getting paid at that time, they have no cash with which to pay their own suppliers or to grow their businesses.

In just a few days, a good factor can purchase the account(s) of yours that are credit worthy, taking you completely out of the involuntary banking business. Factoring can be used for one account, a group of accounts, on a one time basis, or on a continuous basis.

A *factor* (as these *lenders* are known) will want to analyze the past payment history and check the credit rating of each account that you want to sell. He will want to know the age of the account (is it new or did the transaction occur 60 days ago,which may or may not be a danger sign). This due diligence will help him decide to buy your accounts on a recourse basis (you are personally responsible for late payments or even for accounts that fail to pay entirely), or on a non-recourse basis (the factor buys the account and bears all of the risk, with the exception of fraud).

Steve Sez:
Don't be a bank for your customers. Each loan to a customer is money out of your pocket that you could have used for inventory, working capital, advertising or payroll. You are not an ATM machine for your customers.

Accounts receivable factoring companies can provide many benefits to your company and provide them very quickly. Factoring results in a dramatic increase in the speed of your cash inflows. This in turn gives you the following benefits:

Five Benefits of Accounts Receivable Factoring

1. It increases your operating flexibility as you will always have cash on hand from the sales of your receivables.

2. It allows you to purchase additional inventory or raw material immediately (often at a discount).

3. It allows you to increase your production volume, and therefore, to service your customers in a timely fashion and on a larger level.

4. It ultimately increases your sales and profitability.

5. By allowing the factoring company to handle the credit analysis, the billing and collection service, you eliminate a significant amount of overhead.

Factoring is far different from accounts receivable financing (pledging your account receivable as collateral for a loan). The emphasis in both factoring and accounts receivable financing, however, is on the value of your receivables and not your company's creditworthiness. To understand this transaction, you need to understand the players. There are three parties in accounts receivable factoring (and only two in accounts receivable financing).

The three parties in factoring are:

• The company who sells the receivable (that would be you—the business owner);

• The company or person who is responsible for paying the account to you (your customer); and,

• The factor who is the purchaser of this account receivable from you.

When the factor buys the account receivable from you, you will be asked to sign the equivalent of a "deed" which transfers ownership of all of the rights and risks of the receivable to the purchaser (the factor). This transfer of ownership includes the right to receive payments that are made by the debtor on this account and it also includes the risk of loss if the debtor doesn't pay his account (unless caused by fraud).

When the transaction is put into place, the debtor (your customer) is notified of the sale and is instructed to pay the factor directly. Additionally, your debtor is also asked to sign a representation that it has received your goods or services and that there are no disputes or offsets to the payment of the invoice in question. The debtor is directed to pay his bill to a lockbox instead of you so the factor can receive the cash directly. After all, that is what he has purchased; the right to collect the cash from your customer.

The biggest impediment to factoring is that if your customers find out that you are factoring their account, it is a sign of financial weakness and they may pay late, or worse yet, not pay you at all. And, what if they stop ordering from you because they are afraid that you will be out of business shortly? This fear is real and needs to be dealt with in the structure of your arrangement. Here is another circumstance where you should have an experienced person stand by your side in the completion of this financing in order to help you structure it properly.

In a factoring arrangement, you will receive the difference between the amounts collected by the factor less the "interest" which applies to this transaction. If you have a very small profit margin built into your products or services, be very wary of using factoring due to its high cost. If that describes your circumstance, I would recommend using factoring for your accounts only after you have met your break-even volume.

Steve Sez:
When either factoring or financing of your accounts receivable, there is likely to be some communication with your customers by your lender or purchaser. Treat this with extra care so as not to worry your customer base.

With a small profit margin, I would counsel you to consider accounts receivable financing instead. It's much less expensive typically.

It is critical to your cash flow to discuss with the factor how much he is going to charge you when you repurchase your accounts. The "advance rate" is how much he will pay you for each dollar of account receivable balance. After all, you are entering into this transaction to increase your cash flow. If you have a $50,000 account receivable, and the factor gives you $25,000 for it (a 50 percent advance rate), has this really helped you? This is a complicated issue and will vary greatly depending upon the facts of your particular business.

Another critical point to negotiate is how you and the factor deal with your accounts that become uncollectible. There are many ways to deal with this problem including the following three techniques:

- The factor bought the account so he absorbs the loss (of course, he will charge you a great deal for this);

- You can agree to buy those accounts back that haven't paid within 45 or 60 days, the idea being that if the customers aren't paying, there must have been some problem with your goods or services and the factor doesn't want to get in the middle of the dispute; or

- You can agree to substitute another account receivable for the bad one.

Most factoring purchase agreements contain provisions that describe how to deal with an account that is becoming excessively delinquent. The choices include sanctions or penalties to you, or a trigger that requires you to repurchase the account receivable from the factor including the premium that the factor would have received at the date of repayment as if the transaction had occurred without any problems. There is typically a 60 to 90 day time period before these sanctions or repurchase requirements are triggered.

If a debtor or rather "your customer" hasn't paid the account owed to you by some predetermined date, many things could be happening:

- Your customer could have bad cash flow;

- Your customer could have a problem with the product or service he purchased from you;

- It could just be an innocent oversight;

- It could be an internal policy to withhold payments to vendors just to keep their cash intact as long as possible.

Regardless of the particular circumstance, the factor doesn't want to be in the middle of a dispute between the debtor and the vendor (you).

The profit motive for the factor is in the ability to earn the difference between his purchase price for your accounts, plus an amount which we will call "interest." Additionally, factors often charge a monthly service charge for the administrative expenses of keeping track of a multitude of invoices, payments, collection activities, and so on.

Drawbacks to Factoring

Because this source of fast capital is more complex than the loans we've been discussing before, it's not without its issues. The first of which is that factoring may send the message to your customers that your business is in trouble. And if your business were so good, why would you need capital so badly? This is the last message you want to convey to your customers upon whom you depend to keep your business strong and viable.

> **Steve Sez:**
> Factoring can be very complex and expensive. Seek the advice of someone experienced in factoring to guide you through this minefield. It's exciting when it works well, as you will be able to maximize the velocity of your money; you are not waiting for two or three months to be paid.

Potentially, if your customers sense that you are having financial problems, they will simply go to another supplier. The mere perception of financial problems could cause your customers to make their payments slower, or even to call you and request big discounts for less than full payment on their account because they think you are desperate.

Another drawback to factoring your accounts receivable is its high cost when compared to obtaining a bridge loan using your real estate as the collateral. How expensive is it? Factoring can cost anywhere from two to five percent each month (that's 24 to 60 percent on an annual basis) to even more in many circumstances.

As if this weren't enough, factors often charge the five percent for the whole month even if only half a month is used. This means that if you get paid by your customer in 32 days and your factoring agreement is set at 4.5 percent per each 30-day period *or any portion thereof*, the cost for the factoring arrangement is 9 percent because the payment was received a few days after the new month began. If you compute what this rate is annually, you will come up with a shocking number. Nine percent for 32 days is equivalent to 102.60 percent per annum. Not a bad rate of return, especially if you are the one earning this rate as opposed to the one paying it.

Steve Sez:
BEWARE: It can be a matter of business life and death that your customers don't think anything is wrong internally. If it gets out, it could easily become a self-fulfilling prophecy.

Factoring is not for the faint of heart and should only be used if you have no other reasonable alternatives. In spite of it all, many industries were started and financed almost exclusively by factoring.

The apparel industry as we know it today would never have grown as big or as fast if it weren't for factoring. Imagine that clothing is manufactured months before the season is actually upon us. Winter clothing is seen by retail buyers and purchased in early to mid-summer of each year. The clothes may be shipped as early as mid-fall, and the selling may not begin until Labor Day or even early October. The retailer can't be expected to pay for his order until the merchandise is selling on his floor, which means that the poor manufacturer would order fabric in spring, manufacture the goods in summer, send the goods in September or October, and not get paid for the shipment until November or even December. It's a manufacturer's worst cash flow nightmare!

Some hard money lenders also factor accounts receivable but it's more typical to find a factoring company that specializes in this category of financing only. Don't overlook this variety of collateral as a means of obtaining the financing that you're seeking, but be exceedingly careful as you jump into this arena.

Shop Carefully for Your Accounts Receivable Factor

The pricing for accounts receivable factoring varies greatly. Make sure that you shop around for rates and terms. I can't emphasize this enough, so I'll say it once again. The cost to you of dealing with an accounts receivable factor can be different (but always expensive), depending upon the particular factor. Each will probably have a formula that is not completely comparable with other factors, so the comparison will be that much more difficult.

My advice: Prepare a spreadsheet that compares the cost of the factoring arrangements depending upon when the payments are received from each receivable. Formulas vary significantly and each little difference can affect your cost of funds greatly. To compare costs with any confidence, place the costs of each factoring arrangement side by side. Make sure to include all of the set up charges, attorney's fees, collection expenses, and all other costs of the factoring arrangement.

This area is complicated and without an organized method of comparison, it can quickly become overwhelming.

> **Steve Sez:**
> Compare the true cost of each factoring proposal on an annual basis so that you are comparing kiwis to kiwis. No matter how you cut it, it will be expensive. Don't fall out of your chair when you compute its rates.

Account Receivable Financing (This Is Not Factoring)

As we have seen, factoring is quite complicated. For those with a fear of the great unknown, there is good old commercial lending, using your accounts receivable as the collateral. Here, when the dust settles, you still own your assets, you have the control over your clients, and you can probably sleep better. It is easy to understand as long as you keep in mind that the hard money lender is always interested in the value of your collateral. Do you notice how this primary concern is the same in all types of hard money loans.

When you go to a bank, the loan officer will evaluate you as a borrower with all of the paper requirements and timing drawbacks of a real estate loan. He may never even get to the evaluation of the receivable before they turn you down. Their loan approval process is about you as the borrower and not the quality of the collateral. Refresh your memory about how frustrating and aggravating it is to do business with a bank in these circumstances; how time consuming it is; and, how much the bank's decision is driven by your credit, your cash flow, your business history, and so on; and, how likely they are to say no.

The terms of an accounts receivable loan are quite different from those of a factoring arrangement. The loan may be payable over a number of months, and interest may be payable only as you receive income. Or it could be a revolving line of credit that must truly revolve (be fully paid off and then drawn upon again, paid off in full and then be drawn again, and so on). The promissory note for the loan will contain all of the standard clauses that we've already analyzed.

In the case of a loan transaction, your hard money lender will need to file the requisite security documents with the county or the state recorder's office. Your account receivable will then be secured until the loan is fully repaid in this manner.

This is a perfect place for a hard money lender to shine. The speed of review and closing can be exceedingly fast. The longest part of the process is to get your customers to sign the needed documents regarding their account payable to you (it's an account receivable on your books, and an account payable on their books).

Steve Sez:
There are many ways fraud can occur in an accounts receivable factoring arrangement. Both borrower and lender should be mindful of this fact, and use experienced people to put this arrangement together.

The only possible issue here could be the financial strength and creditworthiness of your customer. Your account receivable is only as strong as your customer. In the case of both factoring and financing, the lender (or factor) could reasonably ask for a credit report and a financial statement from your customer. If your customer is weak, the receivable may not be eligible for financing or factoring. Maybe you should have thought about this before you sold the company any of your goods or services.

Chapter Summary

Putting your accounts receivable to work for you is one option that is increasingly popular with small and mid-size businesses. It has been a staple of large corporate operations for decades. Before you pledge your receivables as collateral, however, you should seek the advice of attorneys and others well-versed in the practice.

1. You should not have to be a bank for your customers.

2. At its base, factoring is the sale of your accounts receivable—at a discount—to a purchaser known as a "factor" who will then collect the full amount owed and remit to you any amounts over his "interest" charge.

3. There are drawbacks to factoring; one of which is the message it sends to your customers—make sure you communicate the benefits of this process to your customers when you implement the process.

4. There is a real difference between factoring and accounts receivable financing.

5. Using accounts receivable to collateralize a hard money loan will require the hard money lender to have legal work completed to document the terms of the transaction that will add to the cost of your loan.

Next Chapter Preview

We have discussed securities, equipment, inventory, collectibles and accounts receivable factoring and financing. There are multitudes of other forms of unusual collateral about which to be aware.

CHAPTER 25

And Yet More Forms of Collateral

I have enough money to last me the rest of my life,
unless I buy something.
—Jackie Mason

If you have read the last few chapters, I'm hopeful that you have the message that by getting creative with your choice of collateral, you don't have to own even a single piece of real estate in order to get a loan for your business opportunity. Your friends and family will actually wonder in amazement at how you get loans without having any real estate. You will surely be the envy of everyone. This chapter will enlighten you even more with thoughts of more non-real estate as collateral.

Are you saying to yourself by now, "But Steve, I still want some more direction about how to go forward with my 'un-real estate.' It is clear that I need additional funds, so please continue to give me more direction and understanding."

Here are more suggestions about what we have been offered as collateral in the past. Notice the variety:

1. Livestock;

2. Oil and gas reserves;

3. Intellectual property (like copyrights and trademarks);

4. Automobile and motorcycle titles;

5. Airplanes and sailboat titles;

6. Gold in both refined and unrefined states;

7. Purchase contracts;

8. A 212 carat ruby;

9. Elvis memorabilia;

10. Rare letters;

11. Standby performance guarantees;

12. Certificates of deposits;

13. Secured promissory notes; and

14. Air development rights over a piece of downtown commercial property.

It often takes work to find these lenders, but it will pay big dividends if the day comes when you need funds quickly, and you don't have any real estate that will meet a hard money lenders requirements.

Steve Sez:
Almost anything with any value, no matter how unusual, may constitute sufficient collateral for a creative loan. Be wise and review all of your assets before the need appears.

The most progressive of hard money lenders understand that there is value everywhere. And, broadly speaking, collateral is really just about making sure that your lender feels comfort in knowing that the collateral will pay him back if you don't.

A creative hard money lender just might take a look at a loan secured by your collection of old Citroen 2CV automobiles for example, because of their rarity and easily determinable value. I actually know of a fellow who owns such a collection and will have a very easy time finding a lender to make him a loan using these unusual cars as collateral. If you can find value in your items, and you can verify this value for a lender, you may well find someone who would advance you funds using the item(s) as collateral.

An Actual Experience

Can the Rain Forest Itself Become Collateral for a Loan?

I once received a loan request using slightly less than 200,000 acres of prime virgin rain forest on the border of Venezuela and Brazil as the proposed collateral. As the individual told me, his need for funds was to "harvest" (his word, not mine), all of the valuable rare and exotic rainforest trees for milling and then subsequent sales to custom builders and lumber dealers in the United States for high-end homes and stores.

Little did the fellow know but the preservation of the rain-forest is one of my primary passions in life and the thought of cutting down these rare and beautiful natural trees and disturbing or eliminating habitat for both endangered species and other animals was completely unacceptable to me regardless of profit.

I did listen politely to his story, however. He said that they would fly me to Caracas, Venezuela, from Denver where I would be picked up by a helicopter and flown over the land for my inspection. Can you see any possible problems with this approach? I saw problems everywhere. For example, how do you go about coming up with a value for this property? A large problem is how could I know what was growing on this large piece of land in order to assess the quantity and quality of potential lumber to be "harvested?" How could I actually see what was down there with just a fly over? How do you know that they owned what they represented that they did? What about the existence of a survey? They had none, as it turned out. In that case, how do you know where the boundaries of the property were? And so on, and so on.

As a funny aside to this story, as I told some of my friends about this loan, they noted that there were many kidnappings occurring in Venezuela at that time where foreigners were taken and held hostage in some far off place until a sobbing relative agreed to fork over significant dollars for their release. And sometimes after the ransom payment, they got released, and sometimes ... they didn't. So I asked around and was unable to find anyone who would pay $1 million for my safe return. For this and my love of the rain forest, I chose not to go. I think that this was a great choice in hindsight.

I have personally reviewed loan applications for each of the categories of collateral listed above as well as oil wells, to art collections, to a triple crown quarter horse, to motion picture scripts to an extensive collection of Chinese antique furniture, to an original El Greco painting, to a cruise ship, a corporate jet aircraft, and much more, as potential collateral.

In every case, a prudent lender will consult with experts to provide estimates of value and marketability of the collateral. The focus then shifts to how to make sure the collateral will be there if and when the lender needs to look to it for the recovery of their unpaid loan balance. And finally, lenders and their lawyers are always aware of how to perfect their security interest in each variety of collateral so they are legally protected should the worst happen.

In the case of many of these unusual asset categories, it would not be out of the question for lenders to want physical possession of the asset itself in order to make a loan. Just to refresh your memory, lenders want physical possession of some types of collateral so it doesn't disappear or diminish in value due to carelessness, desperation, or just neglect. How to find movable collateral is always a challenge that is cured with possession.

By keeping the collateral in his possession (not really, but in a bonded and insured warehouse with restricted access), the lender will know that the assets are safe from deterioration, damage, and loss or theft. You should plan to physically turn over your collection, your automobile, even part of your inventory to your lender if that's what is required for your loan.

It's All in the Presentation

As I have said, finding the lender who will consider these wonderful types of collateral requires preplanning. Remember my friend with the collection of Citroen 2CV automobiles? He absolutely will get the loan that he wants, but he has to begin looking for the right lender so he will not be under stress when his day of need arrives. The boy scouts always say to "be prepared" and nowhere is this statement more appropriate than in this area.

> **Steve Sez:**
> Money belongs to the creative in the world of hard money lending. Don't live life in a box with rules that will restrict your growth and success. Use hard money lenders for what they do best; be creative!

So, you might consider starting your search now. By the time you're in need, it'll be too late to start looking from scratch. There are too many variables to understand in short order for you to be effective at finding a great lender or account receivable factor, in a short time period. The search for financing could take you weeks or months that you might not have when you are in need of financing. As you begin the process of finding the best lender for your situation, focus your presentation on how the lender will sell the collateral in order to recoup his loan balance then due. Focus on how to best determine values and plan on educating your lender about the methods that one could use. If you have any written evidence of values, by all means make sure that your lender gets copies of it all. Do not be shy here! Do you want money or not?

Obviously, no borrower takes a loan planning to lose his collateral— that is, unless he's planning to take the money and run (this is also known as a crime, so try to avoid this behavior at all costs). Therefore, by guiding your lender in how to liquidate your collateral, he can see that you have his best interests at heart. You don't want him to lose money by doing business with you. You are attempting to provide him with an insurance policy against the loss of any money. You want him to do well. Business transactions work the best in the long term if they are win/win for each of the parties. You can best show him that you want his loan to be a win/win for each of you by putting together a great presentation for his review.

How to Prepare a Winning Loan Proposal Using Unusual Collateral

1. Compile a complete listing of each and every individual piece in your collection if you have multiple items.

2. Compile a complete and detailed list of all of the other collateral that you're offering the lender (Remember cross collateralization?).

3. Prepare your estimate of the value of each individual item of the proposed collateral.

4. Prepare your estimate of the combined value of all of the pieces of collateral as a group.

5. Add a discussion of how you came to the values for your collateral that you did. What is your basis for your valuation?

6. Assemble and take pictures of each individual item within the group.

7. Prepare a listing of all of the logical places to go in order to sell the pieces in the collection with a complete description of each place. The information you provide should include names, addresses and phone numbers as well. It won't hurt to add a little comment next to each place about why you believe they are included in your list.

8. Also, provide a complete listing of all trade and hobby groups involved in this hobby or business for more substantiation.

9. Prepare a full and complete listing of assets that have sold recently that are just like yours. Include the location of the sale; when it was held; a complete description of what was sold; a complete listing of the prices that each individual item brought at the sale; a complete description of the differences between the item that sold and yours including comparative photographs if possible.

10. If you have the data, and can prepare historical information about the trend of values over the years, all lenders will appreciate this data. In this fashion, the lender can tell if the trends are up, down or sideways, and the depth of the market as well.

11. Take a close look at online and other auction sites. It's possible that there are items just like yours that have sold and will therefore represent excellent comparable sales figures. Print and save these examples as further proof of value.

12. Search all other auction records that may show proceeds realized by sellers (after the auctioneers fees and expenses) and a description of each item sold. This will be quite helpful to a lender.

13. Request a letter of valuation from someone who is recognized as an expert in your type of collateral.

14. If you can possibly get a letter of interest regarding the purchase of this asset in the event that your lender owns it someday, from an independent and unrelated party, this will give your lender a safer feeling about your collateral. You cannot overlook someone who is arms length with the seller who wants to purchase the

collateral. It will be important to a lender. You might think of letting your lender call this person to further discuss your collateral and his offer.

15. Compile three or four years of sales notices of comparable assets in newspapers, journals, magazines, and especially from vendors and auction houses regularly involved in this business.

16. If you have the records, your lender may be comforted by understanding the details of how you purchased these items, from whom, when, and for how much.

Why have I suggested that you take all of these steps? Is it because I love torturing you? No, my motives are completely pure. I want your loan request to be accepted. Not rejected!

One step that might just carry the day in the case of unusual collateral is to include a third party testimonial about the safety of this asset class, and of our borrower's items in particular. Often a third party statement can add credibility to your presentation to all potential lenders. Compiling the important materials listed above is geared towards making the strongest case possible for the valuation of your collateral.

Here are the three items that you'll want to present to a potential lender in the most complete and professional way possible:

1. That your assets have an easily determinable quick sale value;

2. That the lender can easily find a place to sell your assets in a worst case scenario; and

3. That the market is relatively liquid with sales that occur frequently.

These suggested materials, when presented to a lender, should make a compelling case for loan approval. Of course, the lender will want to complete his own due diligence to confirm the information that you've provided. If you've been truthful (it is historically wise to shoot straight with everyone and at all times) it's only a matter of time before a lender somewhere reviews your presentation and puts your loan together.

What you're doing is educating your lender. It'll be worth it because without it, you won't get your loan. Take the time to put a good presentation together, and sell it to your lender. The rewards will include a good loan that can be repeated over and over again with the same lender.

Terms of a Non-Real Estate Loan

When you locate a lender with an interest in considering your non-traditional collateral, he will perceive the loan to be riskier than a real estate-based, collateralized loan. When there is a perception of higher risk, the pricing for the loan will reflect this added level of risk. This is so whether the added risk is real or merely perceived. As the result, interest rates and origination fees will be a little higher in order to reflect this increased level of perceived risk. What does this mean to you?

Because the loan costs are higher, it means that the reason that you're seeking funding should be even a bit more profitable. Said in another way, it means that if the probability of success of your project is low, you should probably not be borrowing on this type of collateral at higher rates for your venture.

Proving Your Title to Your Assets

If you are using non-real estate as your potential collateral for a hard money loan, you will always have to prove that you have good title to your assets before you'll find any lender anywhere who is willing to loan you money. No lender I've ever known will take collateral that has a questionable origin, or questionable ownership.

Before you offer any of your non-real estate assets to a lender, you should assemble the evidence of how, when, where and for how much you purchased these assets. It would be ideal if you still have invoices, and copies of cancelled checks to prove how you acquired the property and at what price.

You obviously don't need the same information if you are using titled assets like autos, boats, airplanes, and the like. There will always be a public record of dates, amount paid (in many states), and from whom you purchased the asset making your job much simpler.

In the case of untitled assets, it is always harder to prove ownership because there is no public record of the transfer of ownership, nor the price paid. The lender will always be concerned in the back of his mind about whether your assets have been stolen, otherwise not fully paid for, belong to someone else, or are involved in litigation. He doesn't want to become involved in title disputes, possession disputes, or any other disputes for that matter. There's only one more step in our hard money journey. Have you learned a lot so far? I hope you'll continue to learn more about hard money and how it is a wonderful alternative to a bank loan or a small private loan. One of the most important things that I keep repeating is that I highly recommend that you either hire a lawyer of your very own, or a consultant to help you with the complexities of the loan structure.

Hard money lending can become complicated quite quickly and you will need someone to stand by your side to guide you through the process. You'll thank me many times over when you obtain such a person.

Chapter Summary

If you plan to offer an unusual form of collateral to secure your loan with a hard money lender—banks won't even consider this type of collateral—be prepared to verify ownership, value and future value. Additionally, you should be prepared to relinquish physical possession of the object, in many cases, to the lender until the loan is completely repaid.

1. You should always consider unusual assets as collateral if you need access to cash and do not have real estate to pledge as collateral.

2. The loan request presentation you make to potential hard money lenders is crucial when offering non-traditional collateral.

3. You should have a clear sense of the value of your collateral and know why you have such a sense, before approaching any lender.

4. Anything you can do to reduce the amount of risk a hard money lender perceives is worth the time required to develop that assurance.

Next Chapter Preview

Let's move forward to Section Four, where we answer many of the questions that all of you might have, discuss whether a hard money loan is for you, and give you some thoughts about your exit strategy options from a hard money loan.

SECTION FOUR

Exit Strategies
and
Frequently Asked Questions

CHAPTER 26

Finally, It's Your Chance to Ask Questions

*Money won't buy happiness, but it will pay the salaries
of a large research staff to study the problem.*
—Bill Vaughan

I hope that by now, you have a pretty good understanding of how hard money borrowing works. And, I am also hopeful that you can now see why I'm so enthusiastic about its use in the proper circumstances and how you can benefit from having a source of fast capital available to you immediately. Over the three decades of making hard money loans and speaking to literally thousands of potential borrowers, I want you to hear the answers to some of the most important questions that I have been continually asked.

Here are questions and answers that contain important information in your quest to become the most informed borrower that you can become:

How long should a good hard money lender take to close my loan?

Unless there's something unusual with your property or project, you should be closed and on your way with funds within one to two weeks. Sometimes it'll be faster than that but, just like each borrower is different, each loan is different. Don't forget that the speed of the application process is, to some extent, up to you. Most hard money lenders will require a site visit in order to verify the "quick sale" value of your collateral, as well as the area and condition of your property.

It also depends upon the advance work that you do before you absolutely need to have funds fast. You now know that you have two jobs to complete. The first is finding the correct lender for your loan structure and your collateral. And the second job is to get your lender whatever he needs to evaluate the entire situation and to determine the quick sale value of your proposed collateral.

The faster you are at getting the lender what he needs in order to evaluate your property, the faster your answer will be. And, if that answer is positive, you will be pleased with yourself for completing all of the work that you did in advance of actually needing funds.

The lender may even want to inspect the proposed collateral in the case of equipment, inventory, automobiles, and many other types of personal property. This will obviously have an impact on how quickly your loan request will be acted upon.

It's a difficult process to find the right lender and if you begin your search early, you'll be ready for a fast closing when the need arises.

If it's so great, why doesn't everyone use hard money lenders?

Not everyone uses hard money lenders because few people know about it as thoroughly as you do now. Additionally, very few people know how to access this type of fast funding as they have no idea how to find these "private bankers."

Hard money lending has been around for centuries in one form or another. It hasn't been well-known or well-used except for those in the know who like the speed and the ease with which a hard money loan can be closed.

But, that's why I've put this book together so that everyone can use the information to their best advantage. This book can and will open up an entirely new world of funding for your projects. If you use the book correctly, it will greatly increase your access to opportunities and the profits that go with them.

Habit and a lack of awareness of the alternatives guide most of us to banks first when we need a loan instead of looking for alternative sources of money. Hard money lenders can be difficult to locate and it certainly takes a bit of creativity and perseverance to find just the right lender for you.

In addition, the perception is that all non-traditional lenders are loan sharks ready to pounce on you if you miss one payment by one minute. The truth is that hard money lenders are merely alternative sources of capital to be used in the appropriate circumstances. These lenders are only people like you and me who happen to have money to lend. They are not, as a group, anything like the back alley knee breakers that symbolize loan sharks. This is a legitimate source of fast and easy money for you, so use it!

What if I'm almost out of time? Who do I call?

Hint: not Ghostbusters. It becomes a very difficult situation if you have allowed yourself to get down to the wire in your need for money. Luckily, there are a number of possible solutions to your problem. First, call a hard money broker. They're easy to find. They are all over the Internet when you search for hard money. Hopefully, you'll get someone with integrity. *Never, never give any of them money before they have shown any performance that assists you.*

As you are struggling to find just the right hard money lender for your situation, the second place to look for fast capital is with a partner, a relative, or with a friend, who can provide what you need to get out of your problem fast.

And, the third place to look for fast capital is with those people that you know who have ever dealt with or heard of a good hard money lender. A reference in this area is worth a great deal. There are many bad lenders out there, and I don't want you to lose your collateral because you are desperate.

What can I do if I have marginal credit, and/or no regular income?

Remember, hard money loans are premised upon the *quick sale value* of the collateral offered for the loan that you are seeking. Your credit, income and employment are only critical to traditional lenders. The focus on your collateral is what allows hard money lenders to react so quickly.

If you run into a "hard money lender" who tells you that he is expecting minimum credit scores of a certain number, debt coverage ratios of a certain number, and a steady five-year job, you have really found a banker in disguise. True hard money is only about the collateral.

Wouldn't I be better off getting a partner rather than a hard money loan?

What a great question. It's one that I am continually asked and one that is really important to understand.

One of the biggest advantages of a hard money lender over a partner is that you can pay off a hard money loan and be done with the lender. How easy do you think it is to pay off a partner and just be done with him? Getting rid of a bad partner can cost you tens of thousands of dollars and years of your life in litigation. And this is not to mention sleepless nights, anxiety, and the overall stress in your life.

Yes, it is true that you might be paying more in monthly cash expenditures (primarily interest) to a hard money lender than you would pay to your partner. But if there is a dispute over business goals and philosophy with your partner that can't be resolved, you'll wish you could just write a check to get rid of the problem, and that would be that. Once you start with lawyers, lawsuits and business interruption, you will drown in negativity for the next year or two of your life.

The answer to the question of whether it's smarter to get a partner for your project or a hard money lender is unequivocal: choose the lender every time! Get a hard money lender with knowledge, experience, and speed. *Given the choice, run from a partner.*

Just a word of advice from the lawyer in me: If you form a partnership with someone to complete a project or purchase a business or piece of real estate, always get your agreement in writing. That would be *always*! I can't stress this point enough.

Too many people think just because they are friends with their partner that it will always work out well. If that were so, there would never be divorces. Who is more in love than a newly married couple? And yet, we know that over 50 percent of marriages end in divorce. I'm sure that this statistic is even higher for partners in a business venture.

Make sure that you either have a lawyer prepare the partnership agreement for you or review the agreement that is drafted by your partner or his lawyer. These agreements need to be done correctly for your safety. OK, now I'm off my bandwagon.

How can hard money lenders act so quickly when a bank takes 45 days to close a loan?

A hard money lender looks primarily to the "quick sale value" of your real estate or your non-real estate collateral. They don't order appraisals, typically, but instead do their own valuations much more quickly.

A good hard money lender will ask for the relevant information (which you will now have at your fingertips as the result of following the suggestions in this book), schedule an inspection trip quickly, make a fast decision, and order closing documents to be prepared ASAP. This is all very "unbank-like" and will give you celebrity status among your friends because you got your money fast. You took advantage of an opportunity and made a handsome profit.

What is the best use for the proceeds of my hard money loan?

Few borrowers ever ask this question. So, I'm asking and answering this question as it illustrates how to utilize higher cost funds appropriately.

The best use of your loan proceeds is to invest in a venture that is a high profit business or in a potentially high return investment. Interest rates for hard money loans are higher than bank rates, always. It is important to earn more than you spend (pretty basic, isn't it?) Therefore, the difference in the cost of funds may have a potential impact on the level of profitability that can be achieved by any particular project.

Make sure that what you are doing with the money has enough profit built into the transaction such that the cost of your loan will be eclipsed by the profit from the project. By going through an evaluation of whether or not the cost of the hard money loan is worth the experience, it forces you to evaluate the profit potential of your project. This exercise alone is worth the price of admission.

The other primary use of a hard money loan is when you must solve a problem quickly. It may be a foreclosure, a loan being called due, unpaid taxes, a creditor who needs to be paid now, an investor who needs to be paid off quickly, or any of a number of other circumstances. In this case, it's not about a profitable transaction versus the cost of funds. It's all about speed. You need money *now* to solve a problem.

Why can't banks make this type of financing readily available?

The short answer is that Federal banking regulations prevent these types of loans from being made. Banks are geared to making loans that are blessed by federal regulators. After historical banking problems (including those recent banking issues involving large scale defaults and foreclosures) federal banking regulators want to make sure that banks are strong financial institutions making only wise and conservative loans. They do this by imposing strict requirements on the loans made by each regulated bank. The cash flow requirements and debt-to-income ratios have recently become much stricter. Credit requirements have increased. All of this is not even to mention the fact that the paperwork required by a bank from borrowers is voluminous.

Hard money loans do not have much in the way of document requirements. Actually, each particular lender will have document requirements. He reports to no one, which gives him total freedom over how he makes his own loans. Much of this federally regulated and required paperwork is mandatory if you apply to the bank for funds. Hard money lenders have no such requirements.

I now feel informed about borrowing hard money, where to look, how to structure it, and its danger areas. How can I find out more about hard money lending (the other side of the transaction)?

To date, the only comprehensive guide that has been written on the subject of borrowing hard money is this book. How to become a hard money lender is the subject of my next book. Please email me at Sreplin8@yahoo.com to put your name on the pre-publication order list, and I'll send you a notice when it is "hot off the press."

Where do I find hard money lenders?

To find the best hard money lender for you, start your search early. By definition, hard money lending ("yesterday" money) is the choice you'll make when time is the issue, or credit or income is the issue. Don't wait until you need it to start interviewing potential lenders to find out who would be the best for you. Every hard money lender is different, and it's wise to start early.

Steve Sez:
We are currently preparing materials that will make you a more savvy borrower/ investor and if you'll send us your email address, (send to: sreplin8@yahoo.com), we'll be happy to add you to the mailing list and let you know when the materials are ready.

Ten Excellent Methods for Locating a Good Hard Money Lender

1. Talk to others who have used hard money lenders. Get referrals to good, honest lenders who do what they say they can within a certain time frame.

2. Talk to people in the real estate investment business. They are probably more experienced with hard money than other groups.

3. Call a mortgage broker. Either a commercial or residential mortgage broker may have some experience with a hard money lender, or may have heard about one that is good to work with.

4. Call a commercial or residential real estate broker who is active in your area and understands the type of property that you are going to be offering as collateral for a loan. They often know of hard money lenders because their goal is to close a loan in any way possible. Otherwise they don't earn a commission. They may know of, or even have used the services of, a hard money lender to help them get a property bought or sold.

5. Sometimes a banker will know of a good hard money lender in the area. They are sometimes solicited by hard money lenders to get the bank's declined loan applications. The theory of these hard money lenders is that if the bank has reviewed the package and has turned down a loan application because of a failure to comply with the required ratios, in many cases these potential borrowers have great collateral to offer (the dream of all hard money lenders). The most important thing to watch out for is that the banker could just as easily and innocently refer you to a broker instead of a lender.

6. Ask your CPA or tax preparer. These professionals know each of the financial positions of their clients and as the result, they will know who got loans, who is paying interest, and quite possibly even know from whom they borrowed the money.

7. Call your attorney for a referral. Very often, hard money lenders are known by attorneys because clients are always in need of fast cash. As the result, these clients

will confide in their own attorneys about how they are going about finding these funds.

8. Call real estate lawyers in your community. They always hear about hard money lenders because many, many real estate investors, developers, and speculators have an insatiable appetite for hard money. The speed of closing loans becomes addictive to real estate professionals and as such, real estate lawyers hear about every aspect of their clients' transactions.

9. Call people in the foreclosure business because they will definitely know who is active in the buying and selling of foreclosures. Almost to a person, those who dabble in foreclosures have hard money contacts. It's really the only way to purchase foreclosed properties unless you have a pocket full of cash. Don't overlook any potential source.

10. Always search the internet for hard money lenders who are in your city. If there are none that come up in the search results, then try a search for hard money brokers in your city.

How do I distinguish good and honest hard money brokers from the bad guys in the business?

If you decide to use a broker in order to shorten your search for a hard money lender, choose one with many hard money lenders as resources. Brokers can filter out the good from the bad very quickly and get you to a lender who is appropriate for you. How do you identify a good broker from the rest of the pack is the trick. This is always the challenge but once again, an early start will solve your timing problem.

There are many ways to identify brokers from direct lenders in the world of hard money. First of all, don't discount the use of the Internet during your down time. Begin your search for "hard money lenders." Make sure to carefully review the website of each listing for the first ten or fifteen pages. Remember that some hard money lenders are older and don't place as much reliance upon the internet as do younger lenders. This being the case, older lenders won't engage in search engine optimization often and will probably do little to get their website ranked highly. If you continue your search beyond the first few pages, you will be in the land of the less visited lenders. Take advantage of your position to find a lender that others don't readily discover.

Do be aware of the differences between brokers and direct lenders. As a direct lender, I have continually had to explain the differences to my borrowers and to brokers.

Dealing directly with the funding source increases the efficiency of the loan process and reduces the costs to you significantly. This is the primary reason that every potential borrower wants to find the holy grail of hard money lending: the actual lender with the funds and the power to make a decision as soon as possible.

> **Steve Sez:**
> There is a world of difference between brokers and direct lenders. As you talk to each, you'll soon be able to sense the differences. Always gravitate towards direct lenders and away from brokers by keeping your ears open to the signs of each.

Along the way to finding a good lender, there are many obstacles in your way. One of the worst obstacles is to find someone who acts and looks like a direct lender but is actually a broker in lender's clothing. You'll spend a lot of precious time dealing with someone like this only to find that they can't actually write you a check. They are merely fast talking brokers. If you are using hard money as the alternative to a bank loan because of timing, using a broker can be an economic train wreck for you.

I believe that locating brokers versus lenders and how to identify each by their internet presence, is such an important topic that I want to provide you with some of the best ways to quickly identify a broker.

1. Be aware of the language that you find on any website that indicates that there is *"unlimited capital"* available for your loan. These are most definitely brokers. In the real world, no one has unlimited capital. Common sense would suggest that this person is merely trying to entice anyone and everyone into his web.

2. Be aware of people or companies who require payment of *advance commitment fees* or some other loan fee before they give you a loan commitment. While a few lenders use this practice, it is much more common for a broker who earns his money off of front money instead of from loan closings.

    A loan broker must take on many, many loan applicants just to have one actually close. His theory may be to throw a lot of business against a wall and hope that one sticks. To do this, he must make his living some way besides from receiving loan closing fees; hence the requirement for up-front funds. Don't be deluded into thinking these brokers have your best interest at heart. It's all about the money to them.

3. Be especially wary of dealing with people or companies who advertise the ability to make a loan *anywhere* in the world. There are no hard money lenders I have ever heard of in 30 years of lending who can or would want to make loans anywhere in the world. This is the obvious advertising pitch of someone desperate for business.

    The theory of brokers who advertise this way is the same as those described above. They will accept all loan requests in the hopes of finding some one, some day, some place out there who will consider making any of their loan applications. It really makes no difference to them, however, because they have already charged you an upfront fee. They have already made their money, and in almost all cases actually have no real place to send your loan.

Again, be wary of most people in this business because in my experience, perhaps 99 percent of the ads on the internet are really brokers. Having the actual money in the bank is a rarity. People with money in the bank typically don't have to advertise its availability. Regardless of loan demand and economic activity in general, there is always more loan demand than there is money with which to fund the loans.

What is the real story with advance fees?

While I am absolutely against brokers and even lenders who charge fees up-front, some fees are reasonable prior to receiving an actual loan commitment. The most important of these are the fees necessary to perform due diligence activities on the value and condition of your property by a lender. Because you cannot get a loan in most cases without such due diligence, it is not uncommon to have a lender charge these types of fees in advance of giving their loan approval.

When a hard money lender has this requirement, a reasonable fee would be the plane fare, lodging for a night, a rental car, meals and other incidentals, as well as a per diem fee for the time that they are taking to focus only on your property. Make sure that the per diem fee is reasonable. In my mind, I would suggest that a fee of $1,000 to $2,000 per day plus the costs of the actual trip is reasonable. No hard money lender will make a trip to look at your property without getting the expenses and a fee for their time paid in advance. You wouldn't either.

An Actual Experience

A Fool and His Money Are Soon Parted.

I was once involved in a loan application on an office building that was much too large for me to do internally, so I contacted a hedge fund president in New York City to make the loan.

My borrower was the purchaser of a rather large office/parking complex in downtown Albuquerque, New Mexico, who needed fast money to close the transaction. He was told no at the last minute by his bank (now that's a surprise), and he really needed to act quickly in order to save his non-refundable earnest money deposit.

The hedge fund president was intrigued by the loan request and wanted to know more about the property. In an attempt to help him analyze the building, I gathered all of the information from the borrower on the office building, the land, and the attached parking garage owned by the borrower and sent it to New York for evaluation.

The building was located in downtown Albuquerque, New Mexico, and the borrower had said that it purportedly had a "value" of $11 million (of course, I know from actual life experience that borrowers never lie or overestimate the value of their collateral). The borrower needed a loan for $6.5 million in order to complete the purchase.

Because the lender is located in New York, and I am located in Denver (a mere 500 miles from Albuquerque), I volunteered to take a quick flight to Albuquerque to analyze the building and its "quick sale value" (remember this concept?) for him. The lender in New York said he didn't need me to do that for him in spite of my years of experience evaluating property. He elected to send someone from one of the major commercial real estate companies in Albuquerque to look at the property and then to give him the "value" as seen by that real estate broker. In his mind, he was being shrewd as he saved the cost of a trip to Albuquerque by someone with his best interests at heart. I'm sure that the trip would have cost less than $2,000 by the time it was done.

The broker came back with a statement like, "Well, in my opinion, you ought to get $10 to $12 million for this building pretty quickly." No facts, no figures, no lease information, no vacancy rate, no information on parking, no information on competitive office buildings, no analysis of the terms and pricing of the leases, nor any information on the creditworthiness of the tenants, and so on. All the lender got was just an impression formed by a "drive by" look at the building.

Of course, you can guess the next part of the story: he actually made the loan with the flimsy information that he had gotten from that "broker valuation." After all, he was a big fancy New York hedge fund president with gross assets of over $1 billion, so why should he listen to anyone? He "knew" that real estate brokers are smart and would find out all that is wrong with this property.

And anyway, why should he really care when this particular loan was such a small part of his overall investment portfolio? He pretty much knew it all. And can I tell you how jealous I still am. I wish that I knew everything ... oh well, maybe in the next lifetime.

What do you suppose happened next? Well, Mr. Hedge Fund president hadn't analyzed the operating expenses correctly. Unbeknownst to him, many of the existing tenants had given notice to the prior building owner/manager that they were vacating the building on the last day of the month. The drive-by property evaluation done by the real estate broker had naturally failed to uncover this fact. When the new owner had to start paying taxes, insurance, maintenance, utilities, fix up expenses and return lease deposits on all of this vacated space after he had just closed on his purchase, he simply didn't have enough cash to make all of these payments, and have any working capital left for operations and upgrades.

Mr. Hi IQ Hedge Fund President was quite unhappy when his borrower missed his very first payment. When he called me to tell me the news of this default, he was absolutely beside himself that the very first payment was late.

I must have suggested at least three times quite emphatically that he either go to see the property himself, or send someone with experience to evaluate not only the building and parking structure, but its tenants and the rental market and level of economic activity in downtown Albuquerque. And now, because he had relied upon a commercial realtor who he didn't even know to just drive by the building, he was in big trouble.

The rest of the story is that Mr. Hedge Fund President started foreclosure on the office building and parking lot and the borrower responded with some counter claims against the lender. There for a while, the legal fees were really flowing. As the result of this story and hundreds of others, I can tell you that I would never consider making a loan to anyone in any amount without physically seeing and valuing the proposed collateral. Therefore, if you ever hear that your prospective lender wants a due diligence fee, it may well be legitimate.

Hard money lenders who rely on appraisers are few and far between for exactly the same reasons. As the collateral is the single most important item upon which a true hard money lender makes a decision, the inspection and valuation are integral parts of the approval process.

Look out for the "lender" (Or is he really a broker?) who wants to make the inspection trip and hence charge you the fees before he has gotten detailed information on your property. My philosophy is always to get as much information as possible from my borrowers before I make the decision to spend my time and the borrower's money traveling. A good lender can always tell a great deal from the paperwork before he decides to inspect your property. If the lender doesn't ask for information about your property before he asks for travel and expense money, say to yourself quickly, "Feet, don't fail me now!"

Steve Sez:
Note to self (that would be you): Never pay up-front fees to a broker to inspect your property or for any other reason whatsoever.

If you've been lucky enough to find a local hard money lender, be especially suspicious if he is requiring advance fees of any kind or for any reason. If the lender doesn't have to travel far (I would say less than one hour) to view and value your property, leave this guy like yesterday's news if he's asking for any fee at all for the inspection.

There also is no excuse for charging any fees whatsoever that are unrelated to the inspection process before a loan commitment is given. And, the loan commitment to which I am referring is a reasonably firm conditional commitment with few ways out for the lender. The loan commitment shouldn't be conditioned on anything except the drafting of acceptable loan documents, and the receipt of a title insurance commitment stating that they are willing to issue a policy insuring the lender's mortgage in first (or second, or third) position. In no circumstances other than the issuance of a loan commitment would I suggest that you ever pay an advance loan commitment fee.

Why can't you take the travel fees out of the loan closing proceeds?

This is another great question that I'll bet you can now guess the answer to. The solution is obvious. You are the one who is telling the hard money lender the value of your collateral. How does the lender know if it's reasonable in advance of inspecting the property? If the value is not satisfactory to the lender after an onsite inspection, then who will pay for the plane trip, the expenses, and for the time involved in the inspection trip? Obviously, if the results of the trip are a turndown of the loan, the borrower will be disappointed and will undoubtedly not reimburse the lender for the funds that he has spent. Therefore, do not expect to be able to negotiate a deferral of the travel and due diligence expenses.

You just need to consider these travel fees as another cost of the loan. And no, an appraisal won't do. I have seen examples of appraisals that are so clearly wrong that it's almost a crime for which an appraiser should be held liable. (I apologize to all of you good appraisers out there). Paying any lender an inspection fee in advance of a loan commitment is one of the best ways to show confidence in your estimate of the value of your collateral.

Of course, as the borrower you must be concerned that you will send funds to a stranger who says he is a lender and then never even shows up for the inspection. What a nightmare! You need money fast, you have some confidence in the lender that you've selected, and he lets you down. What do you do in this case?

All lenders who want to come to inspect your property should issue you some type of an agreement covering the proposed trip. You should promptly get that agreement to your lawyer who will add the requisite language that covers you in the event of a no-show. I would also cover other possibilities as well. I would cover the issue of when the inspection trip will occur (remember that you need money fast) and what happens after the inspection trip has been completed. Do you get a report from the inspector? When does all of this occur? If they give you a loan approval, within how many days can they close?

And then if he doesn't show up after your advance of funds, at least you have a legal claim in writing to pursue against them. Not much solace, but it's probably the best you can do. And, of course, you always have the ability to contact your state's attorney general, Better Business Bureau, and the district attorney who could prosecute the case criminally. But, let's think good thoughts and assume that he will show up.

The inspection trip needs to be overseen by you and preferably someone you trust. It's always a roll of the dice when you have never met the person on the other end of the phone, but you can get a feeling about the person just by listening to the answers to your questions. Let your common sense be your guide. Do not be blinded by a sense of desperation needing to get your money fast! This feeling will come through to your lender loud and clearly, and you won't get the loan for just that reason. In addition, it will cause you to make bad decisions that will ultimately cost you a lot of money.

Steve Sez:
Never let desperation interfere with sound decision making. Don't overlook obvious signals you get from your prospective lender that identifies him as a bad person. Try your best to have a trusted advisor or friend with you to add an objective set of eyeballs to your thoughts and feelings.

Where do you find non-real estate hard money lenders?

If you find out the answer to this question, you'll have accomplished quite a task for yourself. Remember we identified several areas of potential collateral, none of which are real estate.

Accounts Receivable

If I was looking for a lender in the area of accounts receivable financing, I would searching for receivables "factors." Factoring is the term used when discussing accounts receivable. These folks are quite easy to locate. While there are many cities with no factors, there is no geographical preference among most factoring companies. Receivables arise where ever business is done, so factoring works everywhere.

Try to find factors in large cities like Los Angeles, Chicago, New York, Houston, or Miami (or whatever large city is near you). I would suggest that you shop around and call as many factoring companies as you can. Prices, terms and conditions vary greatly. You will get a different quote from each of them. Make sure you discuss the mechanics of how they do business as well. Following are some questions for potential factoring companies:

Eighteen Important Questions to Ask an Accounts Receivable Factor before You Decide Which Company Is the Best Fit for You

1. Do they offer non-recourse (you aren't personally liable) factoring?

2. If so, what is the premium for non-recourse over recourse pricing?

3. Can they set up an arrangement so that your customers do not know you are factoring their accounts?

4. What is their pricing and timing schedule (e.g. do they charge interest for the full period even if the payment is received early in the period—this could potentially raise your cost significantly)?

5. Are there any upfront fees for a set up?

6. Are there any account maintenance or other fees that must be paid over and above the repurchase premium for the factoring arrangement?

7. What are the credit criteria for accounts receivable before they will purchase it from you?

8. Is there a responsibility for you to repurchase a receivable that goes beyond a certain period?

9. Do they actually call your customer if the payments are late?

10. Do they send late notices to your customers if the payments are late?

11. Can you collect the payments and remit the funds to the factor after their collection?

12. Do you have to factor all of your accounts at one time?

13. Can you just factor certain accounts?

14. Are there savings if you factor all of your accounts on an ongoing basis?

15. Is there a termination fee if you decide to bring your collection efforts in-house?

16. What is the "advance rate"? How much will they pay as a percentage of the face amount of the account receivable in order to purchase each account?

17. Do you get the difference of the amount collected, minus the repurchase cost immediately after the funds are received by the factoring company?

18. How long does it take them to process a request for an advance on a package of receivables?

Collectibles

If your potential collateral consists of a collection of something valuable (old model railroad train cars, fountain pens, fire engines, etc.), I suggest the following possible resources in order to locate a potential hard money lender who will consider this type of collateral.

Seven Ways of Locating a Collectibles Lender Easily

1. Review all trade publications that specialize in your area of collecting. Often, you may find someone offering loans on this type of collateral because it's what they know best.

2. Call a dealer who buys and sells material such as that in your collection. For example, if you are a stamp collector and you have a large and valuable stamp collection, you have probably made contact with a variety of excellent and knowledgeable stamp dealers. Those people may know of someone who would be willing to make you a loan because they know what the collateral is worth, and they know how to evaluate it quickly.

3. Call auction houses that offer material similar to that in your collection. They are always on the lookout for financing resources so that if any of their bidders want to purchase something from an auction, they can direct these buyers to a ready source of funds.

4. Call museums that have collections of material similar to your collection. The curators of these institutions may

have knowledge of someone who does hard money collectable financing.

5. Try to locate other collectors. These people may have had a problem similar to yours in the past. This type of referral can be invaluable to you.

6. Put an ad in the trade paper. For example, in the model train magazine(s), consider putting a block ad in the paper advertising your collection generically and requesting a lender who will consider your collateral for a loan. By the way, I would suggest that you not put your name, address or phone number in the ad because if the wrong people know what type of collection you have, you may have uninvited evening visitors. In addition to which, you don't want other collectors or dealers to know that you are in need of money. Use a post office box for all of your responses in order to keep your identity safe.

7. Go to a trade convention for material of your kind and make sure that you make the rounds of dealers, collectors, speakers, suppliers, sellers, auctioneers and all others at the convention. It is highly possible that someone will know someone else who is in the business of making loans on your type of collateral.

Intellectual Property

Intellectual property consists of trademarks, copyrights, patents, royalties, and trade secrets. By its nature, it is not tangible in the sense that real estate is tangible. That's why using any such intangible property is especially difficult.

The most difficult part of finding a lender who will consider lending on this type of collateral is in its valuation. For example, if I owned the rights to the trademark of the Nike™ swoosh, or the trademark Apple Computer™, everyone would agree these trademarks have substantial value. But if I asked a panel of experts to give me the value of these marks, their numbers would be all over the board. With such difficulty in the valuation process, a hard money loan would be very difficult to make. By this time you know that the loan from a hard money lender is all about the value of the collateral and not the creditworthiness of the borrower.

Where to Find a Hard Money Lender Willing to Consider a Valuable Copyright, Patent, Trademark, or Trade Secret as Collateral for a Loan

1. **Attorney:** One of the best places to search within the area of intellectual property is with a lawyer who specializes in this area of the law. They are often familiar with people who are developing intellectual property for their personal or business use, and hence they are always in the middle of the financing process. In almost every case, the holder of a patent has to go somewhere to finance prototypes and the production of their patented item. The patent holder's lawyer will usually be the one to prepare or at least always to review the paperwork that secures an interest in the patent for the source of funds. Because of this, they will be aware of companies and individuals willing to finance intellectual property. This could be the same for owners of other types of intellectual property as well.

2. **Certified Public Accountants (CPA):** I would also go to CPAs in the case of royalty streams and other types of intellectual property that are generating cash flow each month or quarter. These items can be valued. A good CPA will recognize value to the cash flow even if he doesn't understand the underlying intellectual property. Actually, you could say that the value of intellectual property is in its ability to generate cash flow.

3. **Investors:** For copyrights in literary work that could be made into motion pictures, I would go to investors who dabble in motion picture finance. They may look at the loan as a way to acquire a good literary property at a discounted value if you, the borrower, fail to make your payments (but remember that I do not want you to get into the clutches of a "loan to own" lender—so be very careful).

4. **Publishing Houses:** In the case of copyrights in literary work that will be published in written form with no hint of a motion picture in the future, I would go to a small independent publishing house that publishes this type of work. They could easily give you an estimate of value as they know it. Their estimate of value will be based upon their experience with publishing works of early stage authors.

5. **Recognized Authorities:** In the case of trade secrets, you will have a challenge because you need to *not disclose* your trade secret so that you protect its proprietary nature. You may get lucky and find someone who happens to know something about the area in which the trade secret is relevant. Push that person for people to go to who would know values as well. Make sure you always get a confidentiality/non-disclosure agreement signed first. As always, make sure you go to see your lawyer *first* so that you are in compliance with your state's trade secret laws.

Mineral Rights, Oil and Gas Rights, Mining Property: Both oil and gas and mining properties with productive potential as indicated by a reserve report from a reputable engineer will represent good collateral for many hard money lenders. Lenders who consider these loans are people in the hard rock mining business, the oil and gas business and many brokers and land men in these areas of business. These people can recognize the value of the asset very quickly.

It should be obvious that each variety of non-real estate collateral requires its own version of creativity. It is here that a consultant could be of tremendous value to you. Your ability to think of how to locate potential lenders, and then to contact them and describe your collateral can be taxing. With someone by your side, it might add the momentum you need to get going and work hard and fast. And, the requisite amount of creativity may only occur with you and your consultant or friend sitting around having a glass of wine or beer, and throwing out possible places to go for money.

I think that the key to finding a good hard money lender fast is to use all your efforts, all your common sense, all your good investigative energy, all your work, all your creativity, and all your contacts. That is all the more reason to look for a great lender who will understand your collateral well before a need arises. Then, if an opportunity presents itself next week, you'll be well ahead of the curve in locating your funding source.

Steve Sez:
Persistence wins the day when it comes to searching for an appropriate hard money lender. Keep at it! You'll find success when its least expected! So don't give up; don't give up; don't give up!

Are all hard money situations time sensitive?

Hard money loans are as time sensitive as your needs are. This is the premise of our book. *Where to go When the Bank Says No!* implies that you have been to the bank and your loan request has been denied. Timing quickly becomes your most critical issue when you've tried other resources and they've failed. Life in the hard money business is all about making sure that the lenders needs are satisfied. Hard money lenders provide financing when the collateral is acceptable in a prompt and reasonable fashion in order to stay in business. You and the lender want the same exact outcome.

Due to the nature of what hard money is, borrowers don't tend to contact a lender unless and until their needs are really pressing. I see borrowers when they risk losing a great opportunity, or risk the consequences of not paying an obligation when it's due. Time sensitivity is everything in hard money borrowing and lending.

If I am fixing up a property to resell (commonly known as fix and flip loans), why can't the hard money lender consider the value of the property after it has been improved?

There are many reasons for this. Over the years this has been one of the most common questions I have been asked. "ARV"—what is the ARV? It means "after repaired value" in the fix and flip business. After all you have just learned, give it a go at why hard money lenders wouldn't lend on ARV. Might a great reason be that ARV is a problem because of the AR (as repaired) part?

"After repaired" isn't NOW. And the key to a hard money loan is its quick sale value right now, or at the time lenders actually close the loan. If we look at the NOW value, it is BRV that is critical (Before Repaired Value).

I always tell borrowers to consider what would happen if they walked outside after the closing and got hit by the proverbial bus. Their answer is always, "Well, you could come in and fix up the house and sell it." The problem is that the house was inevitably located in Pine Bluff, Arkansas, some 1,000 miles away, and I am a lender and not a rehab contractor.

This was really a roundabout way of trying to get 100 percent financing for a purchase and rehab loan. From the lender's perspective, the borrower has no money in the deal, and nothing to lose (except that he signed the promissory note personally).

And, from the lender's viewpoint, in order to get his money back, he (or she) may have to go in and fix up the property, not what the lender ever wants to do.

Why can't a hard money lender just accept the appraisal I just paid for and had completed within the last few months? All hard money lenders are very conservative. Because of this, most would be afraid that you would have called up a friendly appraiser beforehand and told him what value you needed the property to appraise for. Or, if an appraiser uses comparable properties from an inappropriate area, the hard money lender wouldn't be able to tell from afar unless he visits your property physically.

Without the lender's eyes on the property, wherever it's located, the approval process is significantly hindered. This will become counter-productive to the reasons that you wanted to get a loan fast anyway.

Chapter Summary

Earlier, I referred to hard money lending as a component of a thriving underground economy. What I hope that I have accomplished with this book is to introduce you to the risks and rules of tapping into this large pool of capital.

While there are many questions, you now know the answers to some of the most common ones. You are well on your way to becoming an informed borrower, able to access these funds when your need is greatest.

Be creative in your search, and have someone more objective about the process be your mentor as you are looking and finding different alternatives for funding. With no rules, no industry groups, and no communication between hard money lenders, they are all different in their approaches and preferences.

1. Hard money loans are designed to close quickly—even if you have marginal credit and erratic income. Remember, it's all about the collateral.

2. Take the time *before you need the funds* to locate the best hard money lender for you and your project. Talk to others in the community who are likely familiar with hard money lenders for recommendations.

3. If you are planning on using property other than real property to secure the hard money loan, be prepared to spend more time locating just the right lender—one who shares an interest and expertise in the type of collateral you are offering.

Next Chapter Preview

In the next chapter we'll take a final look at whether or not a hard money loan makes sense for you and your project.

CHAPTER 27

Is a Hard Money Loan Right for You?

All you have to do is know where you're going.
The answers will come to you of their own accord.
—Earl Nightingale

This chapter is about how to determine if the opportunity is appropriate for a hard money loan. If your project is still profitable after some additional costs, you will be able to make better decisions to either go for it or not. This is where your new found knowledge will be put to use ... so, get excited to see how you can profit with hard money!!

You are now a very knowledgeable borrower in the world of hard money loans. Few of my borrowers over thirty years have as much education and understanding of hard money loans as you do now. Our exploration of the many topics surrounding hard money loans has made you aware of the risks and benefits of accepting a loan from such a lender.

By now you understand why hard money loans are more costly. You also have a sense of how and when to benefit from hard money as opposed to bringing in a partner on your projects or dropping the opportunity completely. There are no absolute rules, but the guidelines I will share with you can certainly help to point you in the right direction. Remember, hard money is not the right tool to use in all situations. The question is: which situations are the right ones?

Let us assume that you have a project that appears to be very profitable and that you have gone to a bank to borrow the $300,000 necessary to purchase the property. Now let us further assume that the bank has said no for a variety of reasons (I know that this never happens in real life, but stay with me for a moment). In this case, you are in luck. The seller is willing to withhold the opportunity from the market for a short time for you to get your financing secured. He is even willing to help by carrying back a second mortgage in case you can't get all of the funds you need. What a perfect scenario for you.

Numerical Example #1

Now, let's simplify this example so you can apply it to any situation and not just a real estate project. Don't forget that your collateral is the primary focus of a hard money lender and not the project into which the loan proceeds are going. It is up to you to focus on your own project and its profitability under different circumstances.

If a bank made you the loan for which you applied, assume that it would have charged you eight percent annual interest for your loan amount. If the loan that you were seeking in the amount of $300,000 was outstanding for one full year, the interest charged to you for the entire year would have been $300,000 (the gross loan amount) times 0.08 (eight percent) or $24,000.

At the original loan closing with the bank, they might charge an origination fee of 1.5 points (1.5 percent of the gross loan amount of $300,000). To refresh your memory, it's not whether or not you get charged an origination fee by a bank. It's only a matter of how much of an origination fee they will charge you. Let's get back then to the numbers: One and one half points as an origination fee on this loan will cost you $4,500 at the time of closing. Let us also assume that the bank will charge you $1,000 in miscellaneous closing fees and title insurance premiums at the closing.

If you add the interest paid over a year ($24,000) to the origination fee of $4,500 plus the miscellaneous closing fees of $1,000, you would have paid a total of $29,500 for having the use of $300,000 for one year.

Now assume that because the bank has said no to your loan application, you have followed the advice that I've been giving you about finding a hard money loan instead. If you had found a good hard money lender and taken a $300,000 hard money loan to fund your opportunity, assume that the annual interest rate would have been in the range of 12.5 percent interest, and the origination fee would have been 3.5 points of the gross loan amount. The closing fees in the case of a hard money loan will typically include your lender's legal fees, title insurance, and other miscellaneous closing fees.

In addition to the above, don't forget that if your lender is out of state, you may have had to pay for inspection fees as well. Let's not forget to include them in our example as they are a "cost" of the loan as well. Your total costs of a hard money loan will, therefore, be as follows:

1. Interest for a year in the amount of 12.5 percent per annum is $37,500.

2. The origination fee of 3.5 percent of the gross loan amount of $300,000 is $10,500.

3. Closing fees are yours to pay as well. Let us assume that the total amount of these costs are $2,000 (versus

$1,000 for a bank as there are more of the lender's costs to be paid by borrowers).

4. And, last but not least, the travel and inspection/due diligence fee might have cost you $3,000.

Steve Sez:
A hard money loan only seems expensive because of its total rate and fees. I want you to consider only the marginal cost of a hard money loan over that of a bank loan as you analyze the strength of your opportunity.

Therefore, the cost of your hard money loan with these assumptions is the total of these fees and costs, or $53,000.

The difference between the cost of a bank loan ($29,500) which you couldn't have gotten regardless of your great collateral, and the cost of a hard money loan ($53,000) which you probably could have gotten, is $23,500. This is the marginal cost of a hard money loan over the cost of a bank loan (which you couldn't have gotten).

Numerical Example #2

Let's go back to our marginal cost analysis but shift our evaluation process to the project at hand which is why you needed extra funds in the first place.

In this example, assume that you are purchasing a three unit multi-family building and your plan is to remodel each of the units and to sell them individually as condominiums. Next, let us assume that the fix-up costs and expenses which are necessary to remodel these three units could be in the range of $75,000 to $100,000 in total.

Let us say that you have the funds in your own account to fully pay for the fixup expenses. Let us also say that the borrowed money gets you the building. Your total cost of the building is comprised of the following elements (using a hard money lender):

Cost of the building:	$300,000
Remodel expenses:	$100,000
Interest and points—hard money:	$ 53,000
Total Building Costs:	**$453,000**

Let's also assume that the bank loan (that they *never* offered you, by the way) would have allowed you to purchase the project for the following costs and expenses:

Cost of the building:	$300,000
Remodel expenses:	$100,000
Interest and points—bank loan:	$ 29,500
Total Building Costs	**$429,500**

In order to calculate the benefits and detriments of selecting a hard money loan to purchase your property, we have to make some assumptions about what the sales price of each unit will be. What if the total proposed net sales price of the three condo units is $600,000? By borrowing the needed funds from a hard money lender instead of from a bank, your costs increased for the total project by approximately $23,500 in order to actually get the deal done.

Remember that this transaction would NOT have happened without the hard money lender because the bank had already turned you down.

Say we had no commissions to pay, nor any other sales expenses, just to keep an easy example easy. In the case of financing the transaction with a bank loan, you could have expected to make something in the range of $170,500; and, by financing with a hard money lender, you would have made around $147,000. Clearly the higher cost of the hard money loan resulted in lower profit potential. The question that you should be asking yourself is whether or not the transaction is still profitable even at a higher total cost? Is the extra cost of a hard money loan worth it? Is it fair to say that the extra loan costs of $23,500 were worth spending in order to get the deal done (resulting in $23,400 less in profits on this project)? How much net profit did you end up making even with a hard money loan? By our calculations, you made $147,000 profit even by paying the extra costs of a hard money loan. I and most of my friends would say, "Not bad!"

Steve Sez:

Do not look at how much your hard money lender is going to make on your loan. Only focus on your anticipated income in order to determine whether or not it is prudent to take the loan. Assume that you may have lost the deal entirely unless you could have reacted as quickly as you did. Without hard money you would have missed a great opportunity. Therefore, is the profit worth the extra cost?

My conclusion to this example is that the deal produced a very nice profit even with the use of more expensive money. In that case then, if I were the borrower, I would have proceeded to complete the closing by taking the hard money loan. The profit was clearly large enough to justify the added expense and just knowing this, a borrower could better gauge what the added costs were doing to his bottom line.

Chapter Summary

I suggest that one of the lessons to be learned from this Chapter is that merely plunging head first into a new project without planning will most certainly raise the risk of failure dramatically. This advice extends to agreeing to a hard money loan without considering all of its ramifications to you, your project, and your collateral.

In this chapter, I have provided you with a structure that you can use to reach a snapshot understanding of the costs and benefits of a hard money loan. And, as always, the attorney in me reminds you that whenever you are uncertain about any aspect of your hard money loan or the process of obtaining one, always consult with experts in the field. It's much easier to keep you out of trouble than to get you out of trouble.

Next Chapter Preview

Hard money loans are rarely, if ever, long-term solutions to your need for capital. As you now know, the interest rates, costs and fees associated with hard money loans are greater than those of a commercial lending institution. The next chapter discusses what steps you should take as your exit strategies from a hard money loan.

CHAPTER 28

Exit Strategies

*Whatever your mind can conceive and
can believe, it can achieve.*
—Napoleon Hill

Exit strategies are generally a good thing to have in life. Getting into things, deals and situations is quite easy. Usually it's just a matter of saying yes and then you become involved in things about which you may have no idea.

An exit strategy is the business equivalent of knowing where the emergency doors are in an airplane. For a hard money loan, this translates into having an idea of what you'll do when the term of the hard money loan ends and you have to pay it all back. The choices that you make will require a significant amount of thought. You don't want to reach the end of the loan term with absolutely no idea of what to do then. That's why it is essential that you've given thought to the question of how you'll pay back the principal and interest *before* you go out looking for a hard money loan. Anything else would be an example of Ready, FIRE, Aim and I don't want any of my readers to become victims of this popular approach to business.

Don't expect your lender to ask you about your intended exit strategy. However, if he does, you need to have a logical and intelligent answer. There are many, many cold hard money lenders out there who are able, willing and even anxious to take your property at the first sign of trouble. They are the "loan to own" lenders about which we have spoken. You most certainly don't want to get into their clutches—particularly if you don't have a good plan for the repayment of your loan.

Let's look at some options for exiting your hard money loan. As you know, hard money loans are always short term. This usually means six months, a year, but rarely more than two years. Short term loans are often called "bullet loans" because like a bullet, the maturity date comes at you fast. The time to think about how to pay off a hard money loan is *before* you close the loan.

Here are some options for your consideration:

Exit Strategy 1: Refinancing with a Bank Loan

This is almost always a pipe dream. If you could have qualified for a commercial bank loan initially, you would have gone that route. That said, I recognize that there are always special circumstances. For instance, you could need a bridge loan from your hard money lender to acquire a property. And, after you acquire it, you raise rents and the building increases in value. Following this increase in value, you can then go to the bank and potentially borrow enough to completely pay off the hard money loan.

In theory, this can work. What jeopardizes this strategy in most cases is the short duration of your hard money loan. Can you really acquire property, make the improvements necessary to raise rates while retaining tenants, and then get the property reappraised at a higher value in just six months or one year? That's a lot to accomplish. Most people can't work that fast. Let's hope you are successful; but, plan for the worst.

I have only focused on real estate in the above discussion. Any asset has the same potential for refinancing, however. If not a bank, there are always some lenders who are willing to make longer term loans at more "market rates of interest" with whom you can refinance. Make sure that you are always improving the value of your collateral, keeping it safe, keeping up with sales trends, and remaining knowledgeable about the market for its resale and where.

Exit Strategy 2: Sell Your Property

The sale of your newly acquired property is always an option. If you got a great deal when you purchased it, this is one way to make a fast profit. If this is your strategy, however, then you should put the For Sale sign on the property very shortly after you purchase it. The amount of time that it takes to get serious interest from a buyer, receive a contract, negotiate the terms to your liking, have the buyer complete his due diligence successfully, get a bank or mortgage company to say yes to his loan request, and to get to a closing can be months and months, especially in a slow market.

If you have borrowed from a "loan to own" hard money lender, he is probably just waiting in the wings for you to default, allowing him to acquire ownership of your property at a wholesale price. So, think long and hard about putting other options in motion as soon as you can after the loan closing, just in case the property doesn't sell by the time the loan matures.

Exit Strategy 3: Refinancing with Your Hard Money Lender

Refinancing with your existing lender may or may not be possible. If this is your strategy from the beginning, you would be well advised to discuss the possibility with your hard money lender before you close. If he says that he would do it under certain conditions, then include these conditions in the loan documents. In that way, there is no question about what he is then obligated to do for you at the maturity of your loan.

If you come to the lender when your loan is due and ask for a renewal without having discussed it in advance of closing on your loan (and without putting a renewal provision in your loan documents), he knows that he's got you in a corner at that time and can charge you anything he wants. Or, he could easily just say no and then you are in real trouble.

Here's a thought: If the original lender won't give you an option to extend the loan when it's due, you might want to look for another hard money lender to pay the existing loan off. I'm not suggesting that a reputable hard money lender wouldn't want to refinance your loan, especially if your payments are timely. But, rather than to leave it to chance, deal with the situation *before* it reaches this critical juncture.

Exit Strategy 4: Pay the Entire Loan Off Before It's Due

This is an ambitious goal. If you have sufficient cash flow to pay interest and principal off completely before the loan is due, you are an exceptional borrower. To have your hard money loan fully repaid in one year requires a great deal of planning and a great deal of cash flow being allocated to this plan.

I can promise you that most people in business will give you a great deal of respect if you can pay off the entire loan balance before its due date. If this is your exit strategy, when you negotiate the terms of the loan make sure that there is no prepayment penalty associated with the repayment of the loan early. This will provide you with the option of paying anything you want, whenever you want, over and above the interest payments which are probably due monthly.

You are now a well-educated borrower and should do very well for yourself with hard money sources. You have just learned about a "magical source of capital" if used correctly—something few business people know anything at all about. This will give you a major competitive advantage in your offers to purchase properties as well as in your ability to close transactions quickly, often trumping any competition. Please send me a letter or an email describing your success with hard money loans, your failures (why the investment didn't work out or what other problems you may have had), as well as any questions or additions that would be helpful to include in the next edition of this book. I wish all of you much success!

I hope that what you have learned about this area of "underground" finance will benefit you for years to come. For those of you who already own property or are interested in investing in real estate or other business opportunities, hard money lending is truly what makes the marketplace a liquid place in which to invest. Money to close a purchase quickly and efficiently, make an investment fast, or buy distressed property immediately all contribute to making real estate and other investment opportunities a source of liquidity for its owners and investors.

Because it is such an "on demand" source of money, it attracts brokers and lenders who prey on people who have great need. Many of them are in business just to seize the opportunity to take money from borrowers up front by promising them loans, quick closings, low rates, easy approvals, and so on. But you're now an informed consumer of these services. I hope that you've learned the right questions to ask as well as the right way to evaluate the services of a potential hard money lender. I want you to be prepared to react quickly, wisely and cautiously so that if the occasion arises, you'll be prepared with all of the right information to locate the useful parties for your situation.

Best of luck, and have fun. I hope you've enjoyed learning about hard money lending as much as I've enjoyed talking with you about it. Now, go forth and profit from this instant source of money. If you connect with a good and reputable hard money lender, you've acquired the key to all of the growth you can handle. Prosper and keep learning!

Best regards,

Stephen D. Replin

Steve Sez:
Please feel free to contact me as follows:

If by email: sreplin8@yahoo.com

If by mail: Barber's Chair Press; Attention Stephen Replin; PO Box 6572, Denver, Colorado 80206

If you would like to order copies of this book, please go to: www.hardmoneybooks.com.

If you would like to download free hard money reports, please go to: www.hardmoneybooks.com.

I am always very appreciative of emails, letters and other communication letting Barber's Chair Press, LLC., know how much you enjoyed this book, and how it has helped you in your business endeavors. Suggest areas of the book that need further explanation, or give us suggestions about areas that you feel are not covered adequately. Please include your name, address, email address and phone number so that I can send you a special thank you gift.

Glossary

accounts receivable: a debt that your customer owes to you in which all of the events have occurred that solidify their legal obligation to pay you.

accounts receivable factoring: selling your accounts receivable to a third party (called a "factor") who will buy them at a discount and charge you a fee based upon how long it takes your customers to pay.

accounts receivable financing: borrowing funds using your accounts receivable (money owed to you by your customers) as the collateral.

amortized loan: a loan that is fully repaid over its term with level periodic (usually monthly) payments that include both principal and interest.

appraisal: a document that gives an estimate of the value of an asset by utilizing different valuation techniques.

assignment of rents: a clause in your loan documents (typically the mortgage or deed of trust) that gives your lender the legal right to collect rents directly from the tenant if the borrower defaults in his obligations under the note and mortgage.

balloon payment: the balance due on a promissory note that remains unpaid at the maturity of the loan.

bridge lending: a short term loan that is meant to get a borrower over a hard time until he can refinance at lower rates and better overall terms (or sell the property).

business plan: a document typically prepared by management that describes all of the factors that impact the direction and growth of an existing (or start-up) business.

closing costs: all of the costs that must be paid by either party when a transaction is completed and closed.

collateral: what you are pledging to your lender in order to assure him that you will pay the loan back or risk losing your property.

combined loan-to-value ratio: if there is more than one debt on a piece of property, the combined loan to value ratio is a ratio of the combined amount of the debts against the property as compared to the "value" of the collateral (often referred to as "CLTV").

comps: (also known as comparables) real or personal property that has been bought or sold, or is for sale by a third party that can be used to estimate the value of a particular piece of property.

co-signor: an additional party who signs the promissory note and thereby assumes personal liability for the repayment of a loan.

credit rating: the numerical rating of how well you have historically paid your bills.

cross collateralization: a group of properties that all serve as the collateral for one debt; it is the use of more than one piece of property in order to "qualify" for one loan.

debt-to-income ratio: what percentage of your income goes out in debt payments each month/quarter/year; it's a ratio of how much extra "unrestricted" income you have to repay a new loan.

debtor in possession: this refers to a debtor who is allowed to operate a business by the court, after a bankruptcy petition has been filed.

deed of trust: the document that artificially "conveys title" to a public trustee to commence foreclosure if there is a default in the repayment of any amounts.

default: a promise made to perform both monetary items (make a payment on the 8th day of each month) as well as a non-monetary item (keep the property in a neat and presentable condition); and the failure to perform as you have agreed to or to cure the problem within a specific amount of time.

default interest: an increased interest rate that is applied to a loan balance if payments due or other items of performance are not completed in time.

deferred interest: the agreement of a lender to waive the requirement to pay interest on a continuous basis; interest still accrues during this time and must be paid at some time in the future by agreement of the parties.

deficiency judgment: a judgment against a borrower in the event that the collateral fails to bring enough proceeds to completely repay a lender.

direct lender: one with the actual funds to make loan decisions and fund them internally.

due on sale or transfer clause: a provision in the mortgage that states that the entire balance must be repaid if the collateral is sold or transferred at any time before the loan is due.

equipment leasing: a strategy to use personal or real property for a defined period of time, paying rent to the owner, often with a right to purchase the personal or real property at the maturity date of the lease term (rental period), and often at a discounted price.

equity participations: a participation in the business equity of a borrower by a lender as additional compensation to the lender for taking the risk of making the loan (this can take many forms).

escrowed interest: the retention of funds in a separate account from which a lender can draw the interest due each month if not paid directly by the borrower.

fair market value: the price at which an informed buyer would purchase from an informed seller with no pressures being applied on either side whatsoever.

floating interest rate loan: a loan on which the interest rate can change based upon an index (typically tied to the prime rate).

foreclosure: the legal process that a lender will need to go through in order to obtain title to your property (each state's foreclosure laws are different).

gap loan: a loan that is typically short term that assists a borrower during that time between the purchase of a piece of property and the refinance or sale of the property.

hard money: a format of lending using collateral as the primary factor.

hard money broker: an agent that attempts to locates a provider of hard money loans working for a commission in the event that a lender is actually found and a loan closed.

interest: the charge for the use of money over time.

junior mortgage: a security document that is subject to and behind the first mortgage.

lien release: the release of a lien against a particular piece of collateral.

line of credit: an arrangement made by a lender that allows a borrower to borrow money when he needs it and to pay it down or off completely, and then to start all over again without new loan documents.

loan extensions: the addition of extra time in which to repay a loan beyond the original due date.

loan ratios: comparisons of various monetary items expressed as a percentage; ratios compare two numbers at one time.

loan sharks: bad dudes who charge illegal rates of interest and often cause a borrower physical injury or worse if the loan is not repaid with all charges, when agreed; call the police NOW if you run into one of these!!!

loan term: the time period during which you are allowed to keep your loan unpaid.

loan-to-own lenders: bad lenders who make loans at significant discounts to the true fair market value of property with very stringent terms, hoping to "purchase" the property at a fire sale value, or below, when their terms cause a default.

loan-to-value ratio: the percentage of the "value" of a piece of property that is represented by a debt.

MAI appraiser: an appraiser with a certification from the Appraisal Institute, which is the highest certification that an appraiser can obtain.

mortgage: a security document used to pledge your property to a lender, who has the power to legally foreclose and own your property if you don't repay as agreed (same as deed of trust for all practical purposes).

non-recourse loan: a loan that is collateralized by the property only; there is typically no residual personal liability to any borrower.

opportunity cost: the cost in lost profits of not taking advantage of, or the foregoing of an opportunity (e.g. "It cost me $100,000 in lost profits not to have taken advantage of that opportunity").

occasional lender: a lender who is not in the full time business of making loans but is presented with an opportunity to lend funds and takes it.

origination fee: a fee charged to the borrower at the closing of a loan in exchange for getting the loan from the lender.

partial release: a clause in a mortgage document that allows some portion of the pledged collateral to be released from this lien upon the happening of certain events (like paying down some of the loan principal).

penalty interest: higher than usual interest charged to the borrower by the lender (and described in the loan documents) when payments are not made when due.

permanent loan: a long term loan that is typically fully paid down to zero in equal payments over the full term of the loan.

personal loan: a loan made to a borrower for a consumer purpose (not for the generation of income, or for an investment purpose).

points: a point is equal to one percent of another number (for example, 3 points of $100,000 is really like saying 3% of $100,000, or $3,000).

prepayment penalty: a fee payable to a lender in the event that all or a portion of the amount due under the note is repaid before it is due.

prime rate of interest: the interest rate that major banks charge to their best customers.

promissory note: the document that is signed by the borrower that contains his promise to repay the debt to the lender, and describing the terms of repayment specifically.

quick sale value: the price at which a piece of property (either real or personal) will sell within a very short period of time.

ratios: a comparison of one number to another, expressed as a percentage.

ready-fire-aim: a shorthand way of describing action without first thinking through the ramifications.

recourse loan: a loan made to an individual or company that keeps the signor on the loan directly liable to the lender in the event that the collateral fails to fully repay the loan balance.

REO properties: properties that have been foreclosed upon and that are owned by a lender as the result of this process (typically a bank).

secured line of credit: an arrangement made by a lender that allows a borrower to utilize money when he needs it up to a definite maximum over a specific period of time, and then to pay it down or off, and start all over again without new loan documents.

seller carry-back: the amount of the purchase price that a buyer can't come up with in cash, that the seller is willing to take in payments over time.

site inspection: a physical inspection of real or personal property by a lender or someone who inspects this proposed collateral on his behalf.

subsequent advances: additional disbursement(s) to a borrower after the original loan is closed, which are contemplated under the original promissory note and, as the result, do not require new loan documents to be executed.

title insurance: an insurance policy paid for by the borrower insuring his lender that his mortgage position in 1st, 2nd or whatever the agreement is between the parties.

title to assets: ownership of assets.

unsecured line of credit: an arrangement made by a lender that allows a borrower to utilize money when he needs it up to the full line of credit balance, and to pay if down or off, and start all over again without new loan documents; this line of credit is not secured by any collateral.

usury: the violation of a state's maximum legal rate of interest by a lender.

wrap around mortgage: a mortgage which is a junior mortgage and which is responsible for the payment of all senior mortgage obligations; the borrower makes one payment per month that include all underlying mortgages to the holder of a wrap around loan.

Bibliography

Island Options. "History of Money (2001)." Retrieved November 10, 2004, from the following web site: *http://money.zezenetwork.com/history.htm.*

Island Options. "History of Money (2001)." Retrieved November 10, 2004, from the following web site: *http://money.zezenetwork.com/articles/origins_of_bankng.htm.*

Island Options. "History of Money (2001)." Retrieved November 10, 2004, from the following web site: *http://money.zezenetwork.com/articles/origins_of_bankng.htm.*

Island Options. "History of Money (2001)." Retrieved November 10, 2004, from the following web site: *http://money.zezenetwork.com/articles/commercial_bankng.htm.*

Black's Law Dictionary. Fifth Edition. (St. Paul: West Publishing Company, 1979).

Disclaimer

This book is not a substitute in any way for obtaining competent legal counsel in your state who can help you with your own specific legal issues. The information contained in this book is intended to provide general information and does not constitute specific legal advice. The content is not guaranteed to be correct, complete, or up-to-date. This book is not intended to create an attorney-client relationship between you and Stephen Replin. An attorney-client relationship can only be created with Stephen Replin by executing a written engagement agreement signed by Mr. Replin and yourself. You should not act or rely on any information in this book without seeking the advice of an attorney in your area.

The information in this book is provided "as is" and as such, there are no express or implied representations or warranties regarding this information. Your use of this information is at your own risk. You assume the full responsibility for all risk of loss resulting from the use of this information. We will not be liable for any direct, special, indirect, incidental, consequential or punitive damages whether in an action based upon a statute, contract, tort (including without limitation negligence) or otherwise relating to the use of this information. In no event may the damages or other awards to any third parties (including the reader of this book) be greater than the price paid for this book. In no event will Barbers Chair Press, LLC. nor Stephen Replin be liable for the legal fees of others. Stephen Replin has offered to be contacted by email. However, if you communicate with him electronically or otherwise in connection with a matter for which he does not already represent you, your communication may not be treated as privileged or confidential. Purchase of this book does not include consultation or legal advice from Stephen Replin.

Bring Steve Replin
to Your Organization

Steve Replin is available to present
Where to Go When the Bank Says NO!
workshops and speeches as well as private consulting.

Barber's Chair Press, LLC.
222 Milwaukee St.
Suite 304
Denver, Colorado 80206
(303) 322-1754

To subscribe to my free eNewsletter,
Where to Go When the Bank Says NO!,
or my monthly podcasts, go to:

www.HardMoneyBooks.com

Books by Steve Replin

Where to Go When the Bank Says NO!	$24.95
Pocket Guide to Hard Money Lenders—Prepublication	$19.95
Pocket Guide to Understanding Real Loan to Value Ratios Prepublication	$19.95
Pocket Guide to Using Intellectual Property and Collectibles as Collateral for A Loan—Prepublication	$19.95
Fixer Flippers: Where to Go for Fast Money—Prepublication	$27.95
Intellectual Property & Collectibles: Where to Go for Funding When the Bank says No!—Prepublication	$24.95
Realtors®: Where to Go When the Bank Says NO!—Prepublication	$24.95

ORDER FORM:

Quantity　　　**Title**

_____　　　　_____　　$_____

_____　　　　_____　　$_____

_____　　　　_____　　$_____

　　　　　　　　　　　　　　　Total Cost　　$_____

　　　　　　　　　　　　　　　+ Shipping*　　$_____

*$ 4.95 for one book; $7.50 for two books; $9.00 for three books
$10.50 for four books; five or more books, shipping is free
**Colorado Residents please add 7.8% sales tax:　　$_____

　　　　　　　　　　　　　Total Enclosed　　$_____

Please make checks payable to: Barber's Chair Press, LLC. (mail to: PO Box 6572, Denver, Colorado 80206) and please include complete shipping information.

(NOTE: For prepublication titles, you will be notified upon the receipt of your order of the estimated date of publication.)

Note: Order books for special groups in bulk and receive a substantial discount.

For larger orders, custom orders or private label orders, please call Barber's Chair Press, LLC. at 303-322-1754.

I would like to receive newsletters and/or special offers of new material: ___ yes ___ no: Email address: _____